The Complete Pattern Book of

Soft Dolls

One to Ten and down again

The Silvertop fairies

The Camel and the Car

Tiki and Taj the tiger twins

Captain Kipper's gold

Polo the bear cub

Rumples and Tumbles go to the country

Top and Toby

The Complete Pattern Book of

Soft Dolls

Valerie Janitch

David & Charles

ACKNOWLEDGEMENTS

My thanks to my editor – and very good friend – Vivienne Wells, for all her support, suggestions, encouragement and guidance. Plus her wonderful talent for always turning the tallest mountains into tiny molehills.

To Tessa Chopping, Jay Harrison (Editor of *Galatea*, the magazine for doll lovers) and Hilarie Berzins (and Amy) for their enthusiastic advice and ideas.

To the Dollmakers' Circle, Membership Secretary; Valerie Hawkins, 28 Edward Road, Farnham, Surrey GU9 8NP (0252 725798)

To Roger Cooper of Offray, for his interest and help, in addition to all the beautiful ribbons and velvet tubing used in the book. CM Offray and Son Ltd, Fir Tree Place, Church Road, Ashford, Middlesex TW15 2PH (07842 47281/2/3) and 261 Madison Avenue, New York, NY 10016 ([212] 682-8010

To Sheila Sanders of Hallmark, for gift-wrap papers. Hallmark Limited, Hallmark House, Station Road, Henley-on-Thames, Oxon RG9 1LQ (0491 578383)

To Pamela Harper, and Brenda (BMF), of Twilley's, for yarns and advice. Twilley's of Stamford Ltd, Roman Mill, Stamford, Lincolnshire PE9 1BG (0780 52661)

To Beryl Lee of Artisan, for special fabrics, Vilene Bondaweb and other craft items, as well as embroidery materials. Artisan, High Street, Pinner, Middlesex HA5 5PJ (081 866 0327)

To The Handicraft Shop, Northgate, Canterbury, CT1 1BE (0227 451188) for cream felt and turned paper balls

'French Knitting' machine from Frame Knitting Ltd., P.O. Box 21, Oakham, Leics, LE15 6XB (0572 723030)

COPYRIGHT

A DAVID & CHARLES BOOK
Copyright © Valerie Janitch 1991
First published 1992

Valerie Janitch has asserted her right to be identified as author of this work in accordance with the Copyright, Designs and Patents Act 1988.

A catalogue record for this book is available from the British Library.

ISBN 0 7153 9926 8

Typeset by ABM Typographics Limited Hull
and printed in Germany by Mohndruck GmbH
for David & Charles
Brunel House   Newton Abbot   Devon

Contents

Introduction

When I was six I watched in fascination as my mother cut out a dress for me. The fabric was a pretty lilac check. Then she placed the folded pieces on her sewing machine while she disappeared to prepare the evening meal. Left alone, I mused how nice it would be for my doll to have a dress just like mine. There was a length of fabric on top of the small shapes, so I cut the pieces out of that . . .

I still have a photograph of myself wearing a dress with a check top and plain skirt. I haven't a photo of the doll in her dress, but I do remember the excitement of making it – after my mother had re-cut my sad attempt and helped me sew it together.

In time I discovered that there were plenty more dollmaking enthusiasts out there, all finding a great deal of genuine pleasure and enjoyment in the inanimate yet personable little beings inhabiting their world. I hope that this book will inspire many more potential dollmakers, as well as extending the range of those who are already 'hooked'. Dolls are not just children's playthings. A glance at the illustrations shows that there is a doll for almost everyone. And the instructions tell you how to make it.

If you have never made a doll before, start with something simple and follow the directions closely. More experienced dollmakers will find that the basic patterns for each kind of doll offer a choice of re-creating the different examples shown in the book, or developing characters by altering and adapting the existing designs. Feel free to use the patterns as you please. There is only one stipulation. Dollmaking is fun: enjoy it!

Many of the dolls in the book are available as kits. For further details – or information about other books and patterns by Valerie Janitch – write to her at: 15 Ledway Drive, Wembley Park, Middlesex, England HA9 9TH. Please enclose a stamped self-addressed envelope.

Lucy Locket
(See page 57)

Knit 2 Together
(See page 117)

Workshop

EQUIPMENT AND ADHESIVES: TOOLS OF THE TRADE

BASIC SEWING EQUIPMENT

Medium/fine sewing needles
Large tapestry needle
Long darning needle (to sew on heads, limbs and hair, and move stuffing)
Pins
Two tiny safety pins (for threading elastic)
Tape measure
Paper clips

Cutting-out scissors
Small pointed scissors
Paper-cutting scissors

Household greaseproof paper
Sheet of graph paper
Pencil
Ruler

Not essential – but very useful

Small pair of tweezers
Pinking shears
Pair of compasses
Small craft knife

ADHESIVES

Clear, quick-drying all-purpose adhesive (UHU has a helpful long nozzle; stand the tube upright in a small mug whilst in use)
Dry glue stick (UHU Stic glues fabric as well as paper)

FELT AND FABRICS: HOW TO CHOOSE AND USE THEM

To make your dollmaking as enjoyable and trouble-free as possible, the major-ity of dolls in this book are made from felt. Felt avoids many problems, like awkward seams, tricky turnings and fraying edges, but it requires careful shopping. Look for a firm, smooth, even quality, without too much 'fluff' on the surface.

If you want to follow the photo-graphs of the dolls, look for a pale flesh-coloured felt. But beware: if you find that the 'flesh' tone that you are offered is too vivid, look for a rich *cream* shade instead (like that used for most of the dolls in the book). (Cream felt is avail-able by mail order from The Handicraft Shop, Northgate, Canterbury, CT1 1BE Tel: 0227 451188.) Choose a deep coffee-with-cream or nut-brown shade if you want a dark-haired sultry beauty with flashing jet-black eyes.

It is important to remember that felt has a certain amount of stretch, and this will become evident when the doll is stuffed, so be certain to place the arm and leg patterns in the same direction.

You will always find a suggestion as to the most suitable type of fabric to use for each garment. For easy identifica-tion, the colour of the fabric shown in the photograph is indicated in the list of materials. Avoid thick or knobbly fabrics, and large patterns; tiny floral prints, finely checked gingham or a very narrow stripe are far more suitable.

Always look for a firm fabric with a close weave; loosely woven or silky man-made fabrics mean trouble be-cause they fray easily. When a medium-weight material is recommended, choose a firmly woven cotton-type fab-ric, like poplin or a polyester-blend summer dress material. Cotton sheet-ing is a little heavier, but can be useful to make clothes for larger dolls. Fabrics described as 'lightweight' are similar in texture, but thinner and more delicate, like lawn.

For various reasons, it is often useful to be able to bond one fabric to another, or to paper or card. Although a dry glue stick can sometimes be used, a totally permanent bonding is achieved by using Vilene Bondaweb or Wunder-Under. This material also allows you to cut very accurate shapes – and can be used to prevent satin or silky fabrics fraying. It is easy to use, and you will find full instructions on the product.

PATTERNS AND CUTTING: THE SHAPE OF THINGS TO COME

Trace the patterns onto household greaseproof paper, or non-woven inter-lining (Vilene) if you intend to use them often. For pieces that are to be cut in felt, trace those patterns with a fold onto folded paper or interlining; cut through the double thickness, then open it out to cut flat in single felt. This precaution also ensures accuracy when you are cutting very small fabric pieces.

To make patterns from the diagrams, place tracing paper over graph paper or rule squares; then use a ruler to measure and rule the lines.

Trace the name of each piece and all the markings onto the pattern, then accurately transfer notches, circles and crosses to the wrong side of the pieces of fabric or felt when you have cut them out.

For patterns that are to be cut in thin card or paper, trace the patterns first onto greaseproof paper, then transfer them to the card. To do this, rub over the back of the tracing paper with a soft pencil, then fix this side flat on your card and retrace the lines with a firm point (ballpoint pen, hard pencil or fine knitting-needle). When you re-move the trace, a clear outline should remain on the card. (For patterns that are traced onto folded paper, turn the tracing over and trace your original outline through onto the other side before you open it up.)

An efficiently organised 'pattern library' will save you a lot of time in the future, whether you plan to repeat exactly the same doll, or to develop it in another way. Every time you trace a new pattern, put the pieces (with all the information and markings clearly copied onto them) into a transparent polythene bag. Close with a paper clip, label the outside for easy identification (and add the page number), then store the bags safely away in an envelope file for the next time you want to use them.

When the direction of fabric measurements is not specifically stated, the depth is given first, followed by the width: 10 × 20cm (4 × 8in) = 10cm (4in) deep × 20cm (8in) wide.

Arrows on fabric patterns indicate the straight grain of the fabric – ie, the 'up and down' of the weave. The arrow should be parallel to the selvedge when the pattern is placed on the fabric. Felt pieces may be placed in any direction, unless they are going to be stuffed. The arrows on fur-fabric patterns also indicate the direction of the pile.

When a pattern piece is marked 'reverse', you must turn the pattern over to cut the second piece of fabric; or you can cut both pieces together in folded fabric, right sides facing. Check carefully to ensure that stripes, checks and so on will match equally on both pieces.

Don't cut fur fabric with big scissors; use small, sharp, pointed ones – and cut only the jersey back of the fabric, *not* the pile.

Finally, when you cut the felt circles for the dolls' eyes – or any other small circle – it is much easier to cut them accurately if you mark the circle directly onto the felt. Find something with a circular rim the size you require – a thimble, the top from a pill container, pen cap or anything similar – but the sharper the edge of the rim, the better. Using a contrasting colour, rub a wax crayon, lead pencil, felt-tip pen or piece of chalk liberally over the rim. Press down onto the felt; then, still pressing the rim down very firmly, twist it, taking great care not to move the position – as if you were using a pastry-cutter. Lift off, and a clearly marked line should remain on the felt. Cut along it with small sharp scissors.

Alternatively, find – or cut – a self-adhesive label the size of the circle that you require; press it down lightly onto your felt, then cut round it. Remove the label carefully.

Note: Many instructions are briefly indicated on the patterns themselves. However, it is always wise to read the full directions, to obtain a complete picture of what you have to do.

SEWING AND STUFFING: THE SECRETS OF SUCCESS

Unless otherwise stated, you should always work with the right sides together. All the patterns allow for seams, and an indication of the actual measurement is usually given above the directions. For felt, this is always 1.5mm (¹⁄₁₆in). For fabrics, it is usually approximately 5mm (¹⁄₄in) for the larger dolls, or about 3mm (¹⁄₈in) for smaller ones. However, it is sensible to use one's own discretion: allow a little extra for a loosely woven fabric, or one that frays easily – whilst a light- or medium-weight fabric with a firm, close weave, permits slightly narrower seams.

To join felt, oversew (overcast) the edges very closely, either by hand or using the satin stitch on your sewing machine. The latter makes a very strong seam and looks neat and professional when it is turned to the right side and firmly stuffed. However, it is a little heavy for the smaller dolls, which benefit from hand-sewing.

Use your favourite brand of regular sewing thread for medium-weight fabrics, matching the colour as closely as possible. If you find that your thread breaks, knots or tangles, you may find it helpful to draw it through a block of beeswax before you begin to sew.

Try to avoid turning the raw edge under when you make a hem; a double hem can be bulky on small garments. Where possible turn the hem under only once and then sew it with a herringbone-stitch over the raw edge to prevent it from fraying. In such cases, it will help if you are able to cut your edge along the thread of the fabric.

Press all seams; when it is not practical to use an iron, and for oversewn felt, flatten the join with your finger or thumbnail.

When matching notches (especially if one side of the fabric or felt is gathered, as for a doll's head, or when you join a skirt to the bodice), it helps to mark each notch on one of the pieces (the gathered side) with a pin, so that the heads extend beyond the edge of the fabric. You can then line up each notch on the other side under a pin-head.

Buy the narrowest round elastic available – but not shirring elastic – and use a tiny safety-pin to thread the elastic through narrow hems for sleeves, waists, ankles and so on. Fix another safety-pin to the other end to prevent it from disappearing.

Herringbone-stitch can also be used to hold elastic in place – avoiding having to make a bulky channel to carry it. Simply pin the unstretched elastic into position, then herringbone-stitch over it using double thread. When you have finished sewing, draw the elastic up to fit and join it in your usual way.

Ladder-stitch is often used to sew on heads – and also limbs. This is simple to do. For instance, to ladder-stitch a head: first fix the head in position as instructed, and, beginning at the back, make a stitch in the neck or body, where you want the head to join it. Then take your thread straight up and make a stitch in the head; take your thread straight down to make another stitch in the neck or body – and up to make another stitch in the head. The thread between the stitches forms the 'ladder'.

Careful stuffing is the secret of a professional-looking doll. And the secret of successful stuffing is patience. Top-quality washable polyester is best. Tease out a little at a time, then push it well down before you insert the next piece; the eraser at the end of an unsharpened pencil makes a useful tool. A strong darning needle can prove invaluable: push the needle through the felt to move the filling around inside, or to pull it into hands and thumbs.

As each area fills up, mould it from the outside, squeezing and rolling it into shape. Make the head smooth and round and emphasise the face especially. Stuff very firmly, unless the instructions say otherwise. An under-stuffed doll can be a disaster because it will tend to get flatter and floppier the more it is cuddled – and end up hanging its head in shame!

HAIRSTYLES: BASIC METHODS – MALE AND FEMALE

For the majority of dolls, the hair is made by stitching and gluing small bunches or skeins of knitting yarn over the head. For some tiny ones, the sections are entirely glued on, and a thinner embroidery wool is used. Once the head is covered, you can add a bun, plait, top-knot, pony-tail, bunches of curls – the styling possibilities are endless.

To make a skein, cut a piece of stiff card 8-10cm (3-4in) wide by the depth specified in the directions. Wind the yarn smoothly and evenly around the card the number of times stated; this will be approximately correct for the thickness of yarn actually used for the doll illustrated, but have more if your own yarn is thinner than the example, less if it is thicker.

For a smooth, sleek hairstyle, tie the loops tightly at each edge with a 20cm (8in) length of yarn (figure 1). Slip the skein off the card and tie the centre, either loosely or tightly, as directed (figure 2).

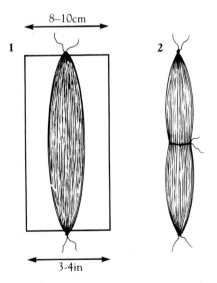

For male characters, or females with loose hair, fringes and so on, the skeins will be tied at the centre only (or elsewhere) and cut at the sides, then fixed in different ways.

Use matching double thread and a long darning needle to stitch the skein to the head, and spread a little glue underneath to hold the yarn in place. Trim off all the loose ends neatly.

Every time you cut a new card, store it away in an envelope, to avoid having to make another when you need that measurement again.

Curly Beards: To make a small curly beard, or a narrow fringe of hair like the tonsured friar in Chapter 10, cut a single strand of yarn about 12cm (5in) long. Lay it along a pencil and tape the ends to hold it taut (figure 3). Wind more yarn closely and evenly (but quite loosely) around the centre of the pencil, to cover an amount equivalent to the required width of the beard. Then cut the single strand at one end, close to the tape; fold it back and glue it neatly over the coiled yarn. Repeat at the other end. Slide the yarn off the pencil and glue it into place.

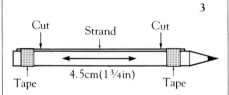

For a larger doll, replace the pencil with either a thicker cylinder or a strip of stiff card, the required depth of the beard.

FACES AND FEATURES: CHARACTERISATION STEP-BY-STEP

Creating a face that conveys your doll's personality is essential. So take as much time as it needs to get all the features exactly right and working together. Until you feel really comfortable with your doll, don't glue anything permanently into place ('sleep on it' if necessary!).

Generally, it is best to do the face last, so that you can see it in context. But you *must* have the hair in place. Pin felt or sequin eyes into place (use fine lace or wedding dress pins), positioning them about halfway down – experiment by bringing them closer together and then setting them wider apart to decide which expression is best.

Mark the nose with a pin, exactly central and level with the lower edge of the eyes. Or, if the nose is separate, pin it on. For a clearer idea of the finished effect, stitch the nose (and eyebrows) now, as it will be easy to remove them again later if you don't like it.

Now for the most important bit! Whether you want your doll to be cheerful, cheeky, demure or shy, the mouth will say it all. In fact there *are* occasions when one can give a doll a more sophisticated, or a rather mysterious, enigmatic expression by omitting the mouth altogether.

Many of the dolls' mouths are embroidered in stem (outline) stitch, or else with two straight stitches or a single fly-stitch. Use stranded embroidery cotton (floss); or ordinary sewing thread, either single or double, for smaller dolls. Suitable 'pinky-red' shades are Light Pimpernel, Light Pomegranate, Pomegranate and Geranium. For dark-skinned dolls, use either Scarlet, Geranium or Rose.

It is important to set up the whole face and mark the mouth before deciding anything. For a curved mouth, mark the shape with pins – setting them 2-3mm ($\frac{1}{16}$-$\frac{1}{8}$in) apart – beginning at the centre. If you don't like it, start again, re-positioning the eyes and nose too.

Make a knot at the end of your cotton or thread, then push the needle in somewhere at the side of the face and bring it out at one corner of the mouth; work in stem (outline) stitch, removing the pins one at a time, so that you can insert your needle into the hole left by the pin. When you reach the other corner, bring your needle out on that side of the face. To finish off, pull the ends taut and snip them close against the face, so that the thread disappears into the stuffing. When the doll is for a small child, begin and end at the side of the head, taking one or two tiny backstitches for extra security.

For a V-shaped mouth, use just three pins to mark the corners and centre, then work your straight stitches or fly-stitch in the same way.

If you are not entirely happy with the mouth, unpick it and start over again. When you are quite satisfied, complete the other features, and glue or stitch the eyes into place.

Sew sequin eyes with black thread. Make four straight stitches from the centre, forming an X or a +; or an eight-stitch star.

Trimming the hair leaves tiny fibres clinging to the face. To remove them, gently dab the surface with adhesive tape; it works like magic! Remove fluff from clothes in the same way.

TRIMMINGS: THE ESSENTIAL FINISHING TOUCHES

As the photographs show, the right trimmings *make* an outfit. As with the fabrics, the trimmings used for the original designs are described in detail in the list of materials. Do try to follow these guidelines, as trimmings that are out of proportion, or otherwise unsuitable, will spoil all your other work. It is a good idea to buy pretty lace edgings and narrow braids when you see them in the shops, as they might not be there a few months later.

It is usually fairly easy to find lace and beads which are in proportion to small dolls, but narrow braids are more difficult to come by. Soft-furnishing braids in particular are often stiff and heavy, making them unsuitable for delicate work. There are two solutions. The first is to find a lampshade or dress braid that can be cut down the centre to make two separate lengths half the width of the original. When you examine such a braid, you will see that a fine thread connects the two sides; if you cut along this they will come apart, completely undamaged.

The other alternative is to make your own braid from very narrow ribbon. This means that you can find the perfect colour match or contrast for the garment you are trimming, which adds an extremely professional finish.

Ribbon makes a wonderful trimming because it is so versatile. The narrowest width is only 1.5mm (¹/₁₆in); this is the one used for the braid described above. Made by Offray, it comes in such a rich palette of colours that your only problem will be deciding which shades to reject.

Beads and sequins come in a glamorous variety of tempting shapes and colours, but avoid them if the toy is for a very small child. You can buy shimmering tear-drop pearls as well as round ones, or they can be purchased in a long string by the metre or yard.

Flowers make a charming trimming for almost any feminine garment. Tiny forget-me-nots or rosebuds can look exquisite on a lacy collar or cap. Again, try to build up a collection of tiny bunches, because one usually needs only a few heads. Search cake decorating shops as well as haberdashers and department stores. Unfortunately, artificial flowers are seldom cheap, so try to make a few go a long way; or make your own ribbon roses.

MADE-TO-MATCH TRIMS: MAKING YOUR OWN

High quality trimmings with that 'touch of class' are often expensive. But you *can* make them yourself – without any danger of your work looking 'amateur' or 'home-made' in the disparaging sense of those terms. Top-quality Offray ribbons make sure your trimmings still have that professional look – without breaking the bank.

Here is a collection of 'finishing touches' . . . most of which you will recognise over and over again as you turn the pages of this book.

PLAITED BRAID

Offray ribbons come in a wonderful range of colours and subtle shades, and if you plait together three lengths of their 1.5mm (¹/₁₆in) wide satin, you can always make an attractive narrow braid in just the shade you want. Or you could plait two or three different ribbons for a multi-coloured braid.

1 The directions for the item that you are making will usually tell you how much ribbon you need to make the length of braid you require. For instance: 'Make a plait from three 25cm (10in) lengths of 1.5mm (¹/₁₆in) ribbon.' In this case, if you are making the braid in one colour only, cut one 25cm (10in) length of ribbon and one 50cm (20in) length. Fold the longer piece in half, smear a trace of glue inside the fold, place one end of the shorter piece between the fold, then pinch together (figure a).
2 Push a pin through the folded end and secure it to a drawing-board or something similar. Then begin to plait very evenly, making sure that the strands of ribbon are always flat – never fold them over. Keep the ribbon taut and draw the plait very firmly between your fingertips every 2 to 3cm (inch or so) to make it smooth and even (figure b). Hold the ends together with a paper-clip.
3 Glue the braid into place, spreading the glue just beyond the point where

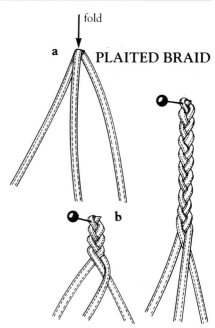

PLAITED BRAID

you intend to cut it, to ensure that it does not unravel. Press the cut ends down well, adding a little more glue if necessary.
4 If you are not following directions, you can calculate the amount of ribbon needed by measuring the length of braid you require and adding a third (then multiply by three for the total amount). For example, if you need a 30cm (12in) length of braid, plait three pieces of ribbon 40cm (16in) long. Which means you will need to buy 1.2m (48in or 1³/₈yd) of ribbon. If you want to make a multi-colour braid in two or three toning shades, calculate the amount of ribbon you will need in each colour accordingly.

RIBBON BOWS

The formal bow is extremely elegant, and looks wonderful in a wide satin or gauzy ribbon. The butterfly bow is quick, easy, and very dainty: single-face satin is best, in any width.

Formal Ribbon Bows
1 Fold under the cut ends of a piece of ribbon, so that they overlap at the centre back (figure a).
2 Gather the centre (figure b) and draw up, binding tightly several times with your thread to hold it securely (figure c).
3 Fold a scrap of ribbon lengthways into three and bind it closely around the centre: secure the ends at the back and trim off the surplus (figure d).
4 Gather across the centre of another piece of ribbon, then draw up tightly

and fold it around (as figure e) for the ties (streamers).

5 Stitch the ties behind the bow and trim the cut ends in an inverted V-shape (figure f).

RIBBON BOWS

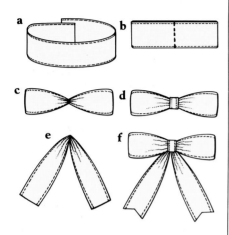

Butterfly Bows

1 Cut a piece of single-face satin ribbon (the directions will tell you the width and the length). On the wrong side, mark point A at the centre, close to the lower edge (figure g). On the right side, mark dots for points B on the top edge – see your individual directions for the distance points B should be from A. Then trim the cut ends in an inverted V-shape as figure h.

2 Hold the ribbon with the wrong side facing you. Using closely matching thread, bring your needle through point A from the back, close to the edge of the ribbon. Then curve the ends around and bring the needle through each point B. Draw up so that

both points B are over point A (figure i).

3 Make tiny gathering stitches up from points B to C (figure j). Take your thread over the top edge of the bow and gather right down from point C to point D. Draw up neatly, then wind the thread tightly around three or four times and secure at the back so that the result resembles figure k.

TINY TASSELS

A quickie novelty trimming made from the very narrowest ribbon; the result is surprisingly smart.

1 Take a length of 1.5mm (^{1}/16in) wide ribbon and fold it as figure a – the length and number of folds determine the size of the tassel.

2 Hold the folded ends neatly together and absolutely level (figure a), then make a knot at the centre (figure b). Take the two sides down so that all the ends are together, then bind very tightly with matching thread close under the knot (figure c).

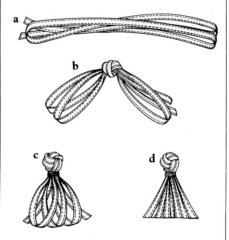

3 Snip off the folded ends and trim neatly to length (figure d).

SATIN ROSES

Artificial flowers – even the most un-realistic and poorly made ones – are always expensive. And the most popular flower of all, the romantic rose, is usually the *most* expensive. So why not make your own from a length of satin ribbon?

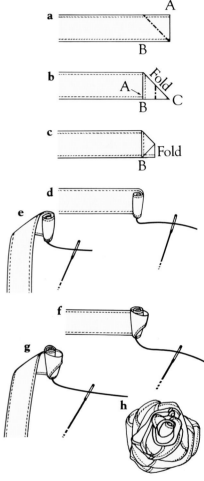

You'll be surprised at your own in-genuity when you produce your first rose. They can be anything from minia-ture to life-size, from bud to full bloom; and of course, you can match nature to exquisite perfection from the Offray ribbon shade card.

The width of the ribbon determines the size of the flower; the longer the ribbon, the more petals it will have. The directions will indicate the width and length that you should use for the design. Use single-face satin ribbon (except for miniature 3mm [^{1}/8in] roses).

1 Cut a length of ribbon as directed. Fold the corner as the broken line on

BUTTERFLY BOWS

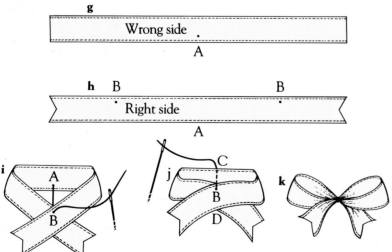

figure a and bring point A down to meet point B as figure b. Fold again as the broken line on figure b and bring point C over point A to meet point B as figure c. (Omit the second fold for 3mm [1/8in] ribbon).

2 Roll the ribbon round four times, with the folded corner inside, to form a tight tube, and make a few stitches through the base to hold (figure d). This forms the centre of the rose.

3 To make the petals, fold the ribbon down so that the edge is aligned with the tube (figure 3), then curve the ribbon around the tube to form a cone, keeping the top of the tube level with the diagonal fold. When the tube again lies parallel to the remaining ribbon, make two or three stitches at the base to hold the petal you have just made (figure f).

4 Continue to make petals with the remainder of the ribbon, sewing each one to the base of the flower before you start the next (figure g). Shape the rose as you work by gradually making the petals a little more open.

5 Finish with the cut end neatly underneath base of the completed rose (figure h).

RIBBON LEAVES

Sometimes the trimming itself needs a finishing touch; in the case of a flower – especially the satin roses – a leaf can set it off to perfection. These take only a moment to make; use a leafy green satin ribbon, or gold or silver metallic grosgrain ribbon. Have the ribbon a little wider than your proposed leaves.

1 For a satin leaf, cut off a length of single-face satin ribbon *twice* the length of your proposed leaf, plus 2cm (3/4in). Spread clear adhesive on the back of the ribbon with your fingertip, to cover *half* the length; then fold the ribbon in half with the glue inside and smooth over to flatten and ensure that the two pieces are firmly stuck. Cut out the leaf shape with sharp scissors.

2 For a gold or silver metallic grosgrain leaf, cut off a piece of ribbon a little more than the length of your proposed leaf. Spread clear adhesive over one side, rubbing it in well with your fingertip. When it is dry, cut out the leaf shape with sharp scissors. If the grosgrain ribbon is wide enough, turn your pattern so that the horizontal weave of the ribbon runs diagonally across the leaf: this looks very attractive, and also makes the leaf curl realistically.

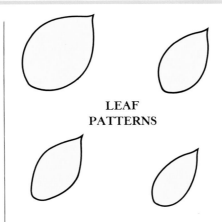

LEAF PATTERNS

WOOLLY POMPONS

The final finishing touch that everyone loves, and wants at one time or another – from Santa Claus to baby bunnies. You *can* buy them from craft shops but they're nearly always better if you make them yourself.

The directions are always the same, but the size of your card circle determines the size of your ball. This pattern makes a trimmed pompon about 4cm (1 1/2in) in diameter. For a larger or smaller pompon, simply adjust the size of the pattern.

You Will Need:
Knitting yarn: avoid anything *very* thick or thin or heavily textured
Strong thread or fine string (if your yarn is not strong, see step 3)
Thin card
A large tapestry needle
Small pointed scissors

1 Cut two circles of card as the pattern. Fold a 4m (4yd) length of yarn into four and thread a tapestry needle (have fewer strands if your yarn is thicker). Place the two card circles to-

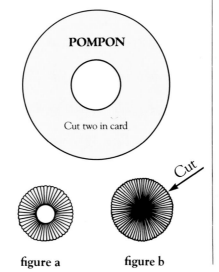

POMPON

Cut two in card

figure a   figure b

gether and wrap the yarn evenly over and over them as figure a, continuing until the central hole is full (figure b).

2 Push pointed scissors through the yarn and between the two card circles (see the arrow on figure b). Cut the yarn all round (keeping your scissors between the card).

3 Slip a 20cm (8in) length of double yarn between the two layers of card to surround the yarn in the centre; knot together, pulling as tight as you can (use thread or string if yarn is weak).

4 Cut away the card, then trim the pompon severely (but not the ties) to make a neat, round, firm ball.

5 Use the ties to fix the pompon in place – or snip them off if not needed.

LACE ROSETTES

These are quick-to-make, and very effective – especially when used in conjunction with other forms of decoration, like ribbon roses. The wider your lace, the more you will need. Cut the required length, then gather the straight edge with tiny stitches. Join the cut ends (glue or stitch), then draw up the gathers, to leave a hole in the centre; this may be as large or small as you wish, depending on how you plan to use the rosette.

FUR FABRIC EDGING

Cut a strip of fur fabric the required length (plus about 1cm/3/8in), and *twice* the required width. Fold it in half lengthways, wrong side inside; oversew the raw edges together, making long stitches which take up only the very edge of the fabric (figure a). Now flatten the strip so that the seam falls in the centre (this will be the back of the trimming – figure b); return along the seam, this time making long running stitches which catch up just enough of the underneath (front) fabric to keep the trimming flat.

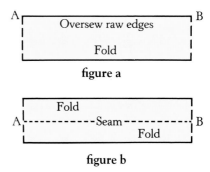

figure a

figure b

Dolls for Play

CHAPTER 1

Dolls in the Nursery

Y ou're never too young – or too old – for a doll. Dolls begin in the nursery. So what could be nicer than to greet a new baby with its very first doll.

Here are three: all designed to attract a small baby as it begins to take notice and become aware of its surroundings. One hangs in the cradle or pram, for Baby to watch. The same basic doll is tucked into a straw frame shaped like a Moses basket, to make an unusual wall decoration. And a smaller version of the same doll hasn't even arrived yet: the stork is still on its way, creating a most attractive mobile for the nursery.

The purpose of these little dolls is not just for new babies. They are intended for new dollmakers, too. The basic pattern is an ideal starter if you have never made a doll before, because it is so simple that your first doll can't fail to be a success.

ROCKING CRADLE BABY

Sugar and spice and all things nice are personified in a demure little girl wearing a candy-pink cotton frock. Choose a pretty, lightweight fabric to emphasise the dainty effect, adding another delicate touch with the crisp white broderie anglaise peeping below her hem.

MATERIALS

18cm (7in) square of cream felt
Scrap of brown felt
Lightweight pink cotton-type fabric: 15 × 60cm (6 × 24in)
20cm (8in) broderie anglaise (eyelet embroidery), 6cm (2in) deep
45cm (½yd) white lace, 15-20mm (⅝-¾in) deep
60cm (¾yd) very narrow pink braid (or 30cm/⅜yd cut in half, as illustrated)
40cm (½yd) pink satin ribbon, 3mm (⅛in) wide
15cm (6in) pink single-face satin ribbon, 15mm (⅝in) wide
Polyester stuffing
Brown double-knit yarn, for hair
Pinky-red stranded embroidery cotton (floss)
Matching and black sewing threads
Clear adhesive

1. Cut the face once, and the body and head twice each, in cream felt.
2. Join the two head pieces to form the centre back seam, leaving open between the notches. Open out flat and join to the face, leaving the neck edge open between the lower notches. Turn to the right side.
3. Join the two body pieces, leaving the top and bottom straight edges open. Push a knife handle or something similar up through the body until it protrudes about 2-3cm (approx 1in) above the edge of the neck: now fit the head over the handle and down over the neck until the lower edge is level with the broken line on the pattern.

Stitch the head to the neck across the back only. Making tiny stitches close to the edge, gather across the neck edge of the face: draw up to fit, distributing the gathers evenly, and stitch to the front neck.
4. Stuff the body quite firmly, up to the neck, then oversew (overcast) the lower edges.
5. Stuff the head very firmly, beginning by pushing the filling down into the chin and lower part of the face, then pushing forward into the rest of the face from the back. Slip-stitch the centre back seam.

6. Cut the dress, cape and mob cap in pink fabric.

7. Join the centre back seam of the dress and press open. Turn up the hem as indicated and herringbone-stitch over the raw edge. Turn to the right side and glue braid over the hem stitching line.

8. Turn the top edge under as indicated, and gather close to the fold: mark the centre front, then fit the dress on the doll, pinning the centre front and drawing up tightly around the neck: catch the centre front to hold in place. Distribute the gathers evenly.

9. Lift the skirt and pin the broderie anglaise around the body, join overlapping at the centre back, so that the broderie anglaise extends about 1.5cm (5/8in) below the skirt. Stitch into place: trim and join the overlap.

10. Turn under and stitch a very narrow hem around the sides and lower edge of the cape. Turn the top edge under as indicated, and gather 1cm (3/8in) below. Glue braid all round the edge, below gathers. Mark the centre back, then fit the cape on the doll, pinning the centre back and drawing up tightly around the neck. Catch the front edges together, then stitch through the doll's neck to hold the centre back in place. Distribute the gathers evenly. Make a tiny butterfly bow (see Made-to-Match Trims) at the centre of a 15cm (6in) length of narrow ribbon, then stitch over join at centre front, trimming the ends neatly.

11. Turn under and tack a very narrow hem around the mob cap. Pin lace over this edge, so that most of the lace extends beyond (it won't lie flat: don't worry). Sew the lace to the cap with a gathering stitch: mark the edge into quarters (as *notches*), then draw up around the head, distributing the gathers so that they are mainly around the sides and top. Catch into place.

12. Make a curl by winding yarn tightly around the tip of your little finger (or a pencil) four or five times, according to thickness: catch the loops together with matching thread before removing. Stitch curls around top of forehead, close under the cap frill, then stitch another row below, adding more as required (see the illustration).

13. Cut the eyes in brown felt and pin to the face, about 1.5cm (5/8in) apart. Using double black sewing thread, stitch into place with eight straight stitches from the centre to just beyond the edge of the eye, forming a star. Make a tiny (3mm/1/8in) straight stitch between for the nose. Embroider the mouth in stem (outline) stitch, using two strands of cotton).

14. Make the wide ribbon into a butterfly bow (points b 5cm/2in from a), and stitch to centre front of cap, just above the lace. Make the remaining narrow ribbon into a loop and stitch the cut ends just behind the bow.

MOSES BASKET BABY

The little girl in the previous design becomes a baby boy for the Moses basket version. But if you're making the wall decoration in preparation for the Big Event, choose lemon, lavender, apricot or a pale creamy-brown colour-scheme for the babe and bedding.

MATERIALS

18cm (7in) square of cream felt
Scrap of brown felt
Felt to back: 23 × 15cm (9 × 6in)
Pale blue spotted voile (dotted Swiss), or alternative:
   11 × 20cm (4½ × 8in) for nightgown
   8 × 20cm (3¼ × 8in) for pixie hood
Mid-blue lightweight cotton-type fabric to cover:
   30 × 40cm (12 × 16in)
50cm (½yd) blue lace, 10mm (3/8in) deep, to trim nightgown
20cm (8in) broderie anglaise (eyelet embroidery), 5cm (2in)
   deep, for sheet
15cm (6in) blue satin ribbon, 3mm (1/8in) wide, to hang
Polyester stuffing
Medium-thickness wadding (see steps 8 and 11)
Nine 76cm (30in) strands Twilley's stranded brown
   embroidery wool (shade No. 49), or fine knitting yarn,
for the boys' hair
Natural garden raffia
Stiff card (double cereal carton)
Pinky-red stranded embroidery cotton (floss)
Matching and black sewing threads
Glue stick
Clear adhesive

1. Make the doll as directed for the Cradle Baby, steps 1-5 inclusive.

2. Put three 76cm (30in) strands of embroidery wool (or fine knitting yarn) together: fold in half and cut the fold. Repeat twice more – so that you have twenty-four 9.5cm (3¾in) lengths. Fold these in half and stitch the fold to the centre top of the head, just behind the seam, so that the cut ends fall over the forehead. Prepare three more strands of wool in the same way: stitch the folded centre 1.5cm (5/8in) to one side of the centre bunch, again just behind the seam. Repeat at other side of head.

3. Cut the nightgown and pixie hood in voile.

4. Fold the hood in half, right side inside, and join the centre back seam. Turn the lower edge under 1cm (3/8in) and gather, but don't draw up. Turn the front

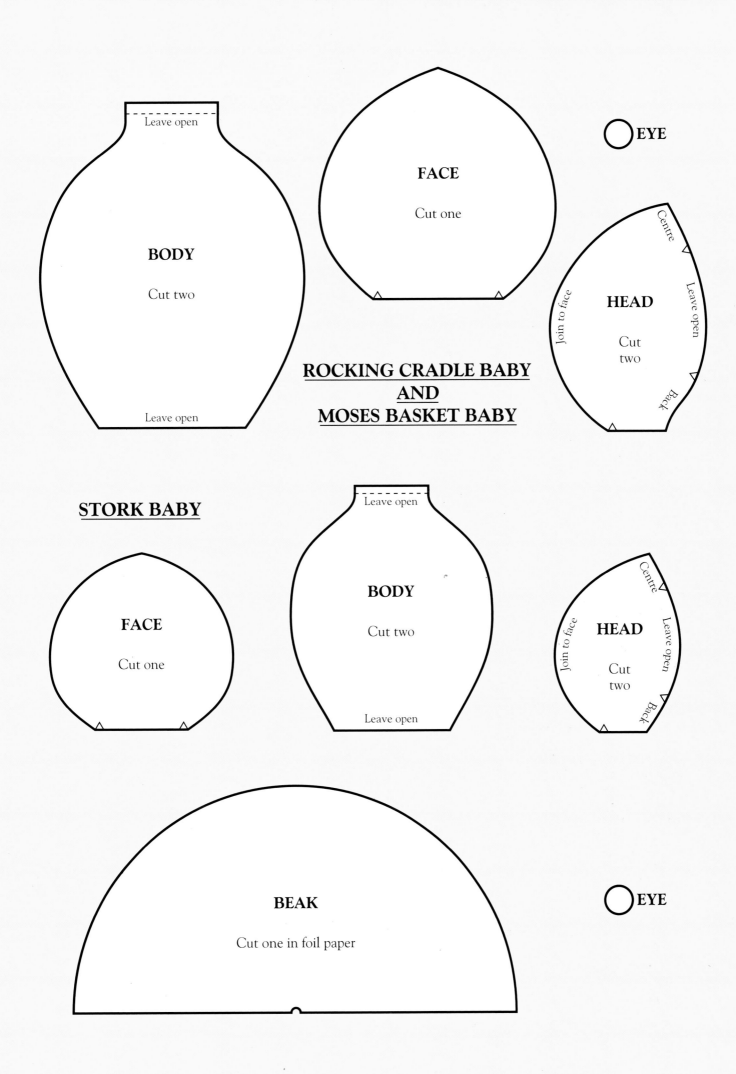

EYE

BODY

Cut two

Leave open

Leave open

FACE

Cut one

HEAD

Cut two

Centre

Leave open

Join to face

Back

ROCKING CRADLE BABY
AND
MOSES BASKET BABY

STORK BABY

FACE

Cut one

Leave open

BODY

Cut two

Leave open

HEAD

Cut two

Centre

Leave open

Join to face

Back

BEAK

Cut one in foil paper

EYE

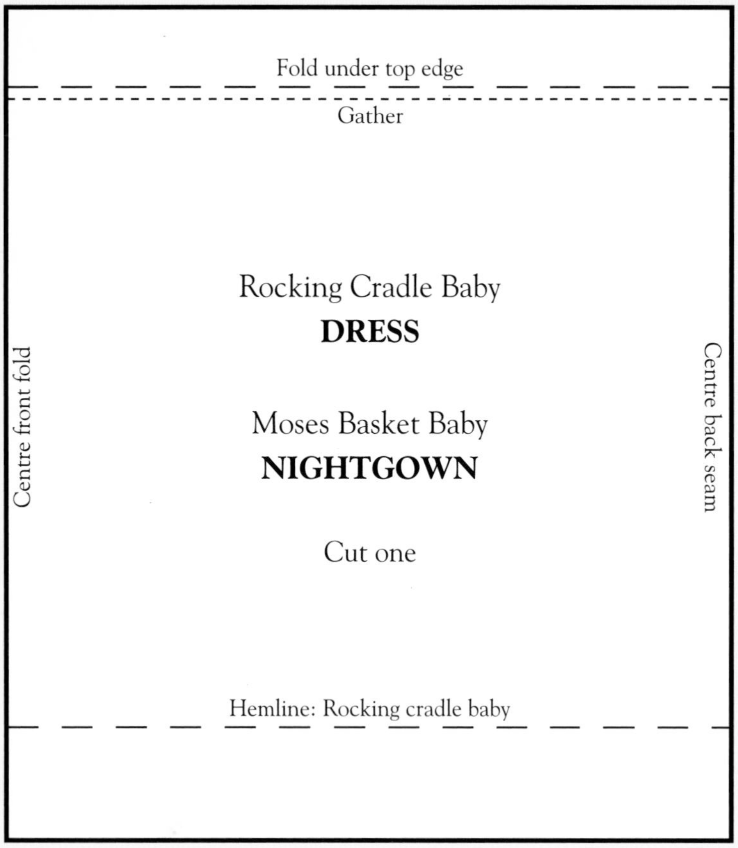

Fold under top edge

Gather

Rocking Cradle Baby
DRESS

Moses Basket Baby
NIGHTGOWN

Cut one

Centre front fold

Centre back seam

Hemline: Rocking cradle baby

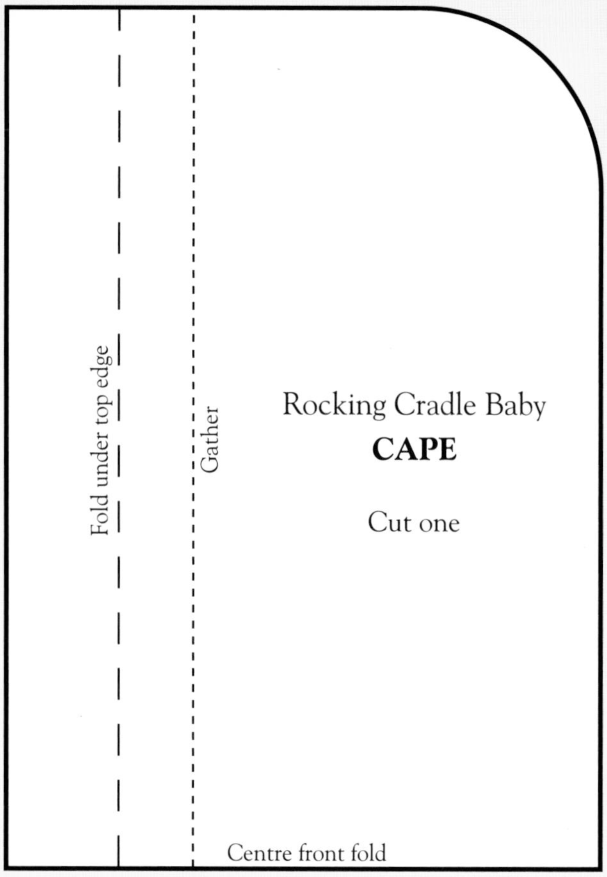

Fold under top edge

Gather

Rocking Cradle Baby
CAPE

Cut one

Centre front fold

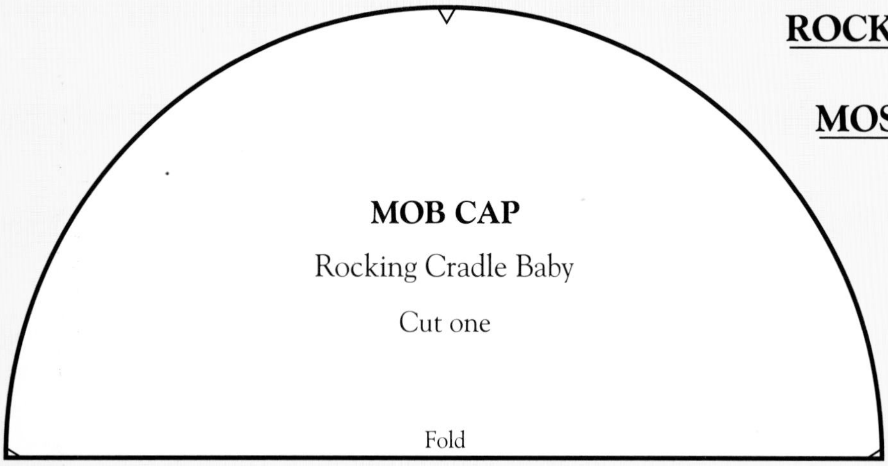

MOB CAP

Rocking Cradle Baby

Cut one

Fold

ROCKING CRADLE BABY
AND
MOSES BASKET BABY

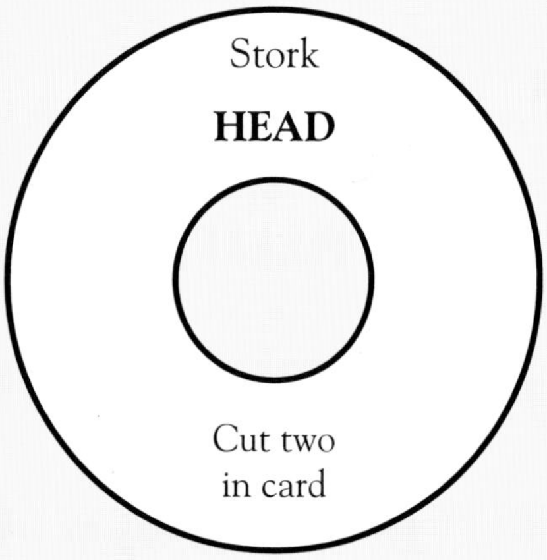

Stork

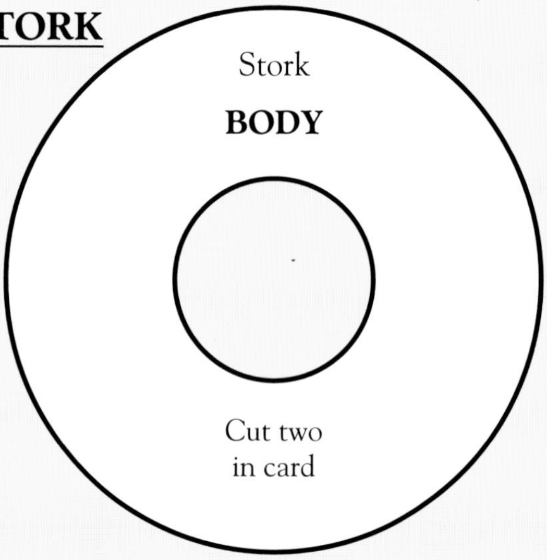

HEAD

Cut two
in card

STORK

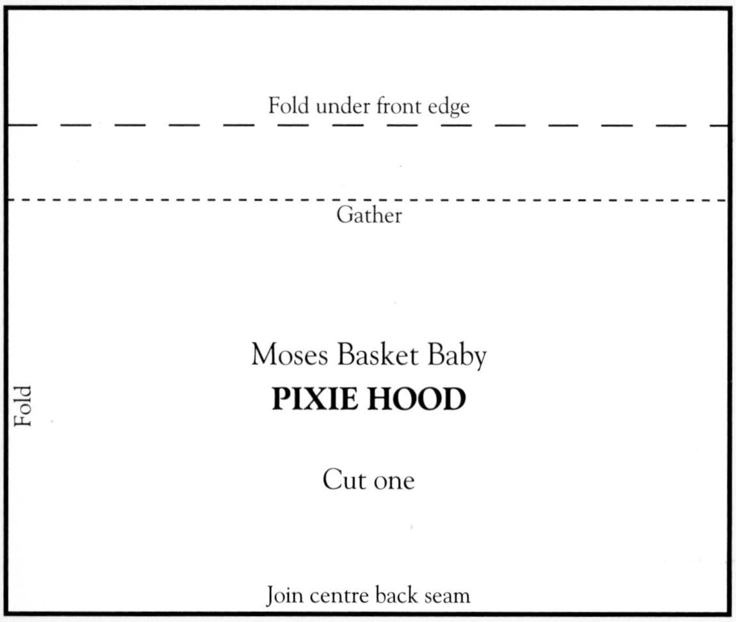

Fold under front edge

Gather

Fold

Moses Basket Baby
PIXIE HOOD

Cut one

Join centre back seam

Stork

BODY

Cut two
in card

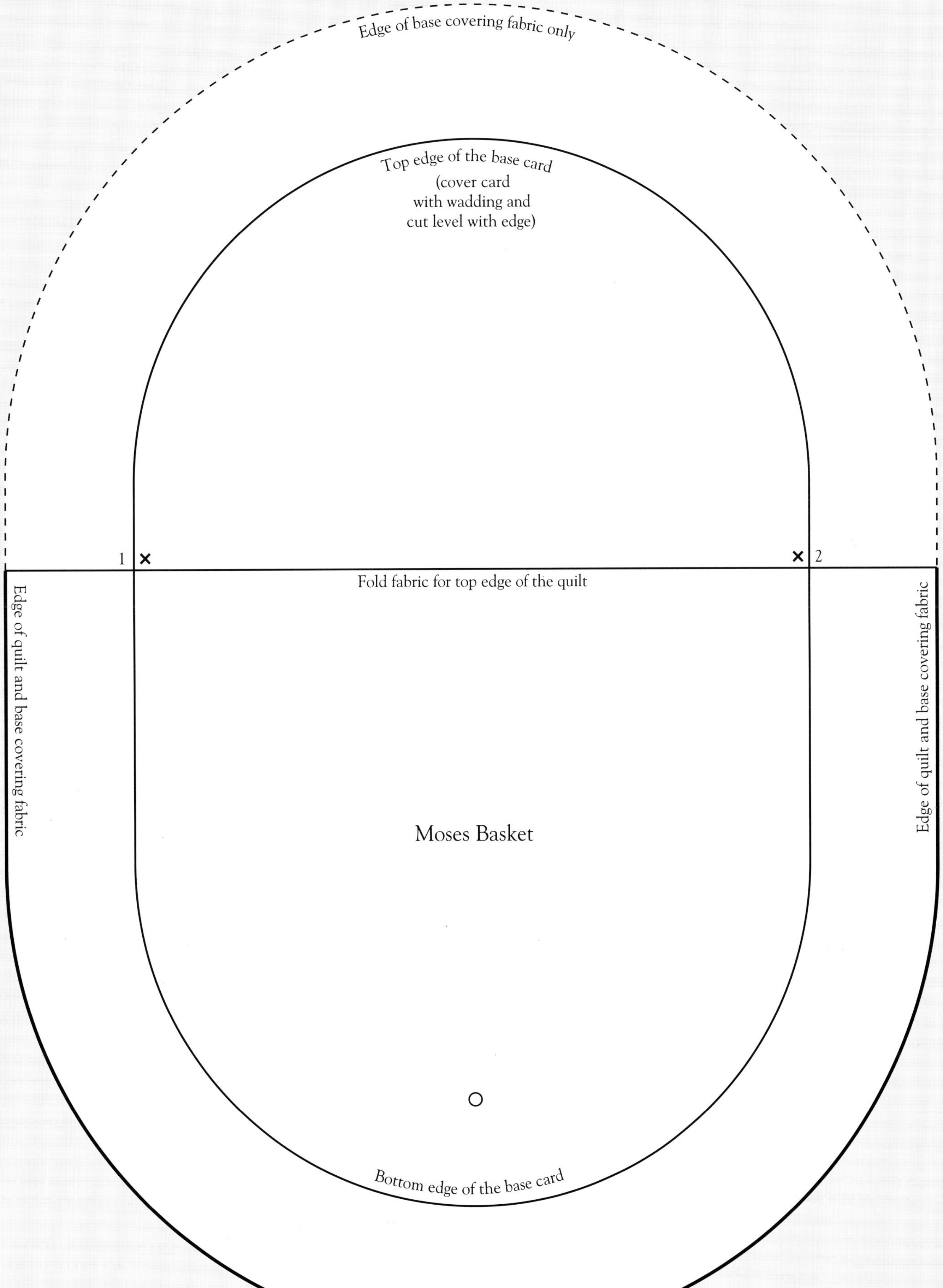

Edge of base covering fabric only

Top edge of the base card
(cover card
with wadding and
cut level with edge)

1 ✕   ✕ 2

Fold fabric for top edge of the quilt

Edge of quilt and base covering fabric

Edge of quilt and base covering fabric

Moses Basket

O

Bottom edge of the base card

edge under 1.5cm (⅝in) and gather 1cm (⅜in) from the fold, but don't draw up. Fit the hood on the doll and draw up the gathers to fit around the face and neck, fastening off both threads securely and catching them to the doll to hold in place. Distribute the gathers evenly round the neck, but have them mostly around the sides of the face.

5. Join the centre back seam of the nightgown and press open. Turn up and stitch a very narrow hem, trimming the edge with overlapping lace.

6. Turn the top edge under as indicated, and pin lace close to the edge so that most of it overlaps, then gather. Mark the centre front, then fit the nightgown on the doll, pinning the centre front and drawing up tightly round the neck: catch the centre front to hold in place. Distribute the gathers evenly.

7. Trim the hair neatly, gluing to hold in place if necessary. Cut the eyes in brown felt and pin to the face. Make a tiny (3mm/⅛in) straight stitch in double black sewing thread for the nose. Using three strands of embroidery cotton, make two straight stitches to form a V-shaped mouth.

8. Cut the complete base in stiff card. Spread the glue stick on one side and press wadding down on top, then cut level with the edge of the card.

9. Cut the base again in your covering fabric, but adding a 2.5cm (1in) overlap all round, as indicated. Gather quite close to the edge, with double thread.

10. Place the card base, wadding side down, on the wrong side of the fabric: draw up the gathers tightly round the back of the card and secure the thread.

11. Cut the quilt section of the pattern in wadding. Then cut the pattern again in *folded* fabric, adding a 2.5cm (1in) overlap all round the curved edge as indicated. With the right side of the folded fabric outside, place the straight edge of the wadding centrally inside the fold, then tack the two layers of fabric together just beyond the wadding.

12. Fold the top edge of the broderie anglaise over the folded edge of the quilt: catch to the back of the quilt and stitch the ends to the front at each side, forming a 'sheet'.

13. Place the doll in position on the base, then cover with the quilt, pinning it to the edge of the card so that it fits snugly over the baby. Oversew the quilt to the edge of the base, taking the raw edges round to the back: trim off excess, leaving about 1-1.5cm (⅜-½in).

14. Glue the back of the base to the felt and trim it level all round, then oversew the felt to the edge of the card.

15. Knot nine fairly thick strands of raffia together at one end: have more if the raffia is thin, but the number of strands should be divisible by three. Divide the strands evenly and plait smoothly together to form a long braid.

16. Beginning at the left side of the base, at the top of the sheet (IX on the pattern), oversew the plaited raffia round the top of the base, placing one *side* edge of the plait on top of the base fabric, right against the edge, and taking your stitches through the edge of the base and the raffia. Continue all round the base to IX, then take the plait up and stitch it to the top edge of the first row – around the top of the 'basket' only, ending at X2 on the pattern. Take the cut ends of the raffia smoothly round to the back and sew them down neatly.

17. Loop the ribbon in half and stitch the cut ends at the top of the felt back, to hang.

18. Coil the remaining plaited raffia round to form a 'button', and stitch to hold. Glue this to the back of the base, near the bottom (O on pattern), so that the decoration hangs at an attractive angle.

'SPECIAL DELIVERY' STORK MOBILE

An enchanting gift for the mother-to-be preparing a nursery for the new arrival. The stork is simplicity itself to make from two woollen pompons, and the cream-clad infant is just a scaled-down version of the two previous dolls.

MATERIALS

15cm (6in) square of cream felt
Scrap of black felt
Lightweight cream cotton-type fabric with fancy weave:
    15cm (6in) square for robe
    9 × 25cm (3½in) × 10in) for bonnet
20cm (8in) square of fine white net, for shawl
2m (2¼yd) cream lace, 15mm (⅝in) deep

50cm (½yd) cream striped organdie ribbon, 23mm (1in) wide
35cm (14in) cream single-face satin ribbon, 9mm (⅜in) wide
Polyester stuffing
Wadding, cotton wool (absorbent cotton) or stuffing (see step 12)
Six 76cm (30in) strands Twilley's stranded embroidery wool (shade No. 81), or fine knitting yarn, for hair
Ball of white double-knit or thick-knit baby yarn
2 pipe cleaners (chenille stems), 16.5cm (6½in) long
Gold foil paper (see step 14)
Thin card
Small paper clip
Small curtain ring
Matching and black sewing threads
Clear adhesive

1. Using the 'Stork Baby' pattern pieces, make the doll as directed for the Cradle Baby, steps 1-5 inclusive.

2. Put six 76cm (30in) strands of embroidery wool (or fine knitting yarn) together; fold in half and cut the fold. Repeat twice more – so that you have twenty-four 9.5cm (3¾in) lengths. Tie the centre tightly with a single strand, then fold in half again and stitch the tied centre to the centre top of the head, 1cm (⅜in) behind the seam, so that the cut ends overlap the face.

Run some glue along the seam, right across the top of the head, then bring the wool smoothly down over it, spreading it out to cover the whole forehead.

3. Cut the robe and bonnet once each in cream fabric: arrow shows direction of fabric only if it has a vertical weave or stripe, as that used in the photograph.

4. Turn under a narrow hem along the short side edges of the bonnet, and tack.

Turn the front edge of the bonnet under 1.5cm (⅝in) and tack. Pin lace on top, slightly overlapping the fold, then gather the front edge, but don't draw up yet.

Gather the back edge of the bonnet and draw up as tightly as possible, stitching through the gathers to form a rosette.

Gather the lower edge of the bonnet, between the front gathering line (omitting the front frill), but don't draw up yet.

5. Fit the bonnet on the doll and draw up both sets of gathers to fit round the face and neck. Secure threads and catch the bonnet to the head to hold it in place.

6. Bend a pipe cleaner in half and stitch the cut ends to the back of the body, so that the bent end extends about 5cm (2in) below the lower edge.

7. Right side inside, join the side edges of the robe to form the centre back seam: press open, then turn to the right side. Stitch lace around the raw lower edge, overlapping 1cm (⅜in): try to avoid turning up a hem, if possible. Stitch two more rows of lace above, each slightly overlapping the previous one.

8. Turn the top edge under 1cm (⅜in) and tack. Pin lace on top, overlapping the edge 1cm (⅜in): gather along the straight edge of the lace.

Mark centre front, then fit the robe on the doll and draw up tightly around the neck, distributing the gathers evenly all round.

9. Make three small straight stitches in black thread, one on top of the other, about 4mm (5/16in) long, for each eye, with another single, very tiny stitch between, using only one strand of thread, for the nose. (Try to sew the eyes so that the outer ends are angled slightly down.)

10. Cut a 20cm (8in) square of fine net for the shawl. Fold it diagonally in half and catch the corners at each end of the fold together. Place the baby inside, with the centre of the fold under the head: pin, but don't fix.

11. Using the appropriate patterns for the card circles, and white knitting yarn, make two pompons (see Made-to-Match Trims) for the stork's head and body.

12. Fold a pipe cleaner in half for the neck, and bind it to about 5mm (¼in) from the end with wadding, stuffing or cotton wool: then bind it closely with the white yarn.

Divide the strands of yarn to make deep indentations in the head and body into which to fit the neck: fill these 'holes' generously with glue before inserting each end of the bound cleaner and pressing the strands of yarn closely round it to hold in place. When quite dry, bend the neck as illustrated. (You may find it easier to visualise the finished effect if you bend the neck before making the holes and gluing it to the body and head.)

13. Wind the yarn 25-30 times around your forefinger. Pass a piece of yarn through the centre and tie tightly as you slip the yarn off your finger, then fold the tied section and cut the loops. Bind tightly just below the tie, and trim to form a fat tassel.

Make another indentation at the back of the body and glue the head of the tassel inside to form the tail. Trim to shape.

14. Cut the beak in foil paper and roll it round tightly to form a very narrow cone; glue the open end into the front of the head, following the photograph.

15. Cut the eyes in black felt and glue at each side of the beak, as illustrated.

16. Stitch the joined corners of the shawl to the centre of the beak, so that the baby hangs as illustrated.

17. Stitch one end of a length of black thread through the shawl/beak, then take down through the centre of the body, securing it underneath to leave about 40cm (16in) of thread above.

Slip the paper clip onto the thread between the head and body. Then fix another thread through the head, taking it up and tying it to the paper clip so that the stork is suspended as illustrated.

Fix the curtain ring to the top of the paper clip.

18. To make the heading decoration, make a butterfly bow from 50cm (½yd) of organdie ribbon (points b 13.5cm/5in from a).

Stitch the straight edges of two 40cm (16in) lengths of lace together to form a double-width piece; then make this into a butterfly bow (points b 12cm/4½in from a), and bind it to the centre of the first bow.

Make another bow from a 20cm (8in) length of satin ribbon (points b 6cm/2⅜in from a), and bind it on top of the other bows.

Stitch to the front of the paper clip.

Make a rosette from 20cm (8in) of lace, and stitch another satin bow, made from 15cm (6in) of ribbon (points b 4cm/1½in from a) in the centre.

Glue the rosette over the back of the paper clip.

19. Pin the ring to a curtain or suspend it in any other way that allows you to adjust the position of the baby so that it hangs as illustrated (bend the pipe cleaner to hold the dress down). When this is satisfactory, catch the back of the head, the body, and the end of the pipe cleaner, to the shawl.

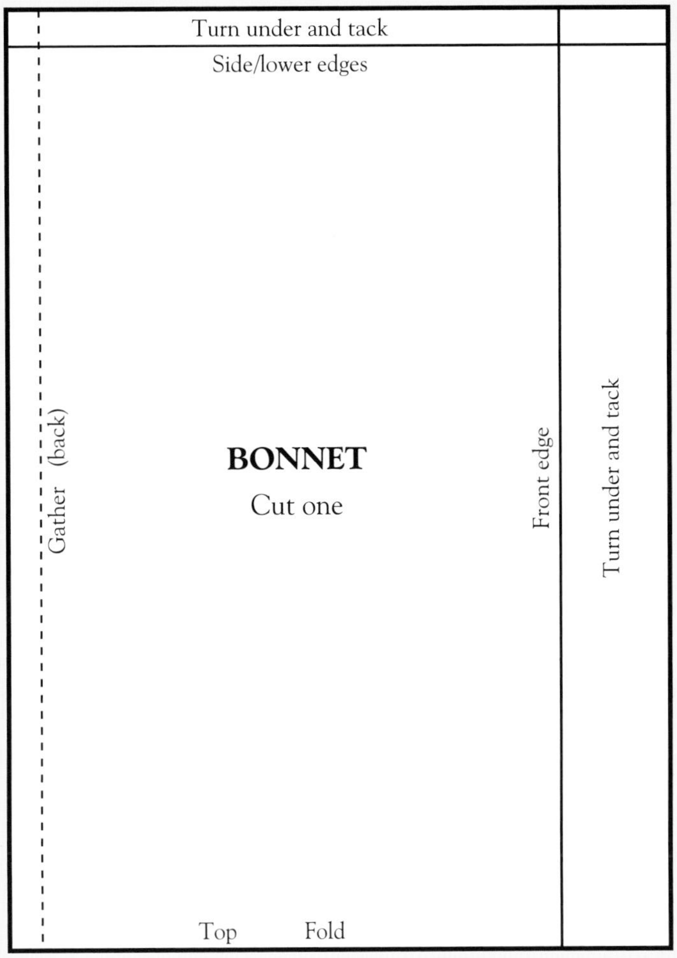

Turn under and tack

Side/lower edges

BONNET

Cut one

Gather (back)

Front edge

Turn under and tack

Top   Fold

STORK BABY

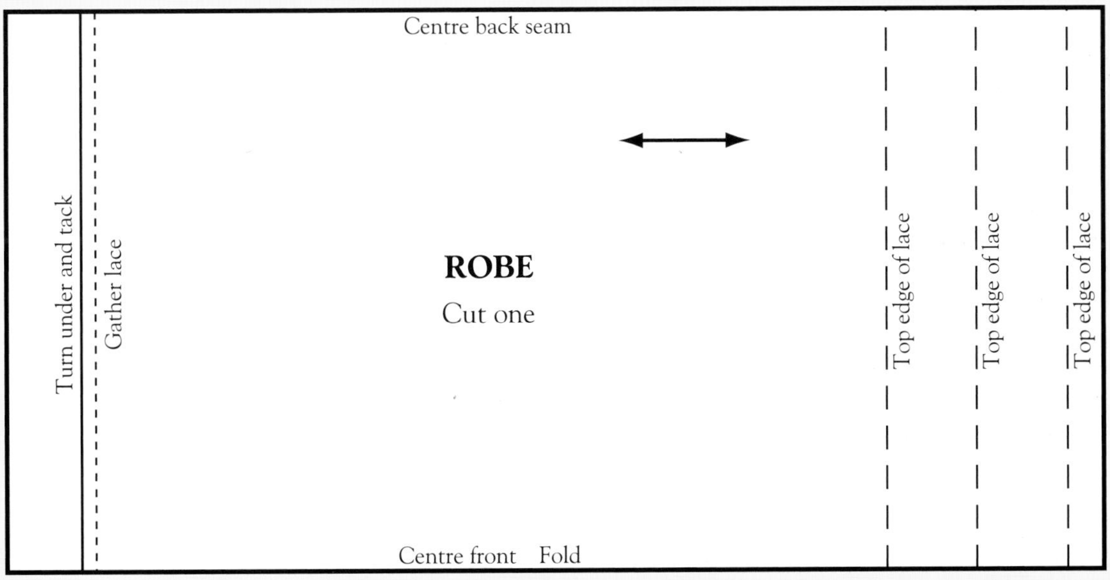

Centre back seam

Turn under and tack

Gather lace

ROBE

Cut one

Top edge of lace

Top edge of lace

Top edge of lace

Centre front   Fold

CHAPTER 2

Rough-and-Tumble Twins

As soon as a child is old enough to play with a doll, it wants something bright and cheerful – and a little larger than life. And like all toys for very small children, they not only need to be very safe, with no dangerous bits and pieces to come adrift, but they also need to be tough enough to stand up to the kind of treatment that they are likely to encounter from their young owners. Thomas and Thomasina fill the bill perfectly; a thoroughly modern boy and girl dressed in eye-catching colours, with long limbs and friendly grins.

If you wish to adapt the pattern to make a doll with flesh colour arms, use the complete arm/hand pattern.

SEAMS: Oversew (overcast) edges of felt to join. Seam allowance on fabric is 5mm (1/4in).

ROUGH-AND-TUMBLE THOMAS

Thomas wears a T-shirt underneath his denim-look dungarees: a suitably workmanlike outfit to prepare him for a busy life in the nursery.

MATERIALS

30cm (12in) square of cream felt
Two 20cm (8in) squares of yellow felt (body and sleeves)
Two 20cm (8in) squares of red felt (legs)
10 × 20cm (4 × 8in) dark brown felt for shoes and eyes
30 × 60cm (12 × 24in) blue medium-weight cotton-type fabric for dungarees
Polyester stuffing
Ball of very thick knitting yarn for hair
Pinky-red stranded embroidery cotton (floss)
Matching and black sewing threads
Stiff card
Clear adhesive

1. Cut the face once, the head twice, and the hand four times, in cream felt. Cut the front and back body pieces and the collar once each, the cuff twice and the sleeve four times, all in yellow felt. Cut the leg and sole twice each in red felt.

2. Right sides together, join the centre back seam of the head, leaving open between the notches. Gather the lower edge between X's, then right sides together, join to the top edge of the body back, easing the gathers in to fit.

3. Gather and join the lower edge of the face to the body front in the same way. Then gather all round, close to the outer edge, beginning and ending at X's.

4. Right sides together, pin the face to the head, matching notches. Then draw up the gathers to fit, distributing them evenly between the pins, and oversew (overcast) together.

5. Join the side edges of the body below the head. Turn to the right side.

6. Stuff the body firmly, pushing the filling well up into the neck; pin the lower edges together. Then stuff the head very firmly, pushing the filling smoothly into the face, and down into the neck. Close the centre back seam, stitching firmly.

7. To make each arm, pin two sleeve pieces together near the top, and pin two hand pieces together near the bottom; now join the hands to the sleeves along the wrist edges. Then join the hands and sleeves all round, leaving open between the notches. Turn to the right side.

8. Stuff the hands and sleeves firmly, then oversew round the top edge.

9. Stitch the tops of the arms securely to the top corners of the body.

10. Right side inside, join the centre front seam of each leg. Then pin the sole to the lower edge, notches matching at centre front and back; oversew together. Turn to the right side. Stuff firmly. Pin the top edge, matching the seam to the centre back; then gather across the top, drawing up slightly before securing the thread.

11. Pin the lower edge of the body front over the tops of the legs (toes forward); stitch securely. Then pin and stitch the body back over the backs of the legs in the same way; push a little more stuffing inside before you finally close the seam.

12. To make the collar, fold the top edge under along the broken line and glue it lightly to hold in place. Run some more glue on top of this edge, then wrap the collar smoothly round the neck. Trim the cut ends to length and stitch the join.

To make the cuffs, fold the lower edge under and glue as for the collar, gluing it again in the same way before wrapping around the arm (centre of strip at front of arm), the folded edge just overlapping the wrist seam. Trim and stitch the cut ends over the seam at the back of the arm.

13. To make the dungarees, cut the trouser leg, the pocket and the strap twice each, and the bib once, in blue fabric.

14. Right side inside, join each trouser leg between A-B. Then, right sides together, join the two pieces between C-A, for the centre front seam, and between A-D for the centre back. Turn the raw edges between D-C to the wrong side and tack. Clip curves and press seams open. Turn to the right side.

15. Turn the top edge of the bib under and herringbone-stitch neatly over the raw edge. Place each strap on top of the bib, right sides together and side and lower edges of straps and bib level; stitch 5mm (¼in) from the side edges (figure 1). Then fold the

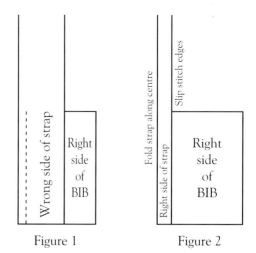

Figure 1   Figure 2

straps along the centre broken line, round to the back; turn the raw edge under 5mm (¼in) and slip-stitch it over the previous seam – thus binding the side edge of the bib. Turn the raw side edges of the remainder of each strap inside and slip-stitch the edges neatly together (figure 2). Press.

16. Right sides together and points C matching, join the lower edge of the bib to the top edge of the trousers; note stitching line.

17. Turn the top edge of the trousers under as indicated, and herringbone-stitch the raw edge.

18. Turn under and tack a narrow hem around the sides and lower edge of each pocket. Turn the top edge under and herringbone-stitch the raw edge. Pin the pockets to the trousers, positioning as indicated, then stitch neatly into place.

19. Fit the dungarees on the doll and turn up the leg hems to the required length. Then stitch.

20. Fit the dungarees on the doll again. Take the straps over the shoulders, crossing them at the back before pinning the ends inside the waist edge of the trousers 2-2.5cm (¾-1in) from the centre back; stitch securely to the top edge and trim off any excess inside.

21. Slip-stitch the edges of the centre back seam neatly together.

22. Cut the shoe upper twice in brown felt. Cut the sole twice in card and glue to felt; cut the felt just outside the card, leaving a 2-3mm (⅛in) surplus all round.

23. Right side inside, join the centre front seam of each shoe and turn to the right side. Pin the upper to the sole, card inside and notches matching at centre front and back; oversew neatly together.

24. Gather close to the top edge of each shoe before fitting it on the doll; then draw up the gathers and catch the shoe securely into position.

25. *Note:* The following amounts are for a *very* thick, chunky yarn. The style will work equally well with an ordinary thick-knit yarn – but you will need to use more strands to cover the head; judge the number according to the thickness of your yarn.

Cut fifty 30cm (12in) strands of yarn and place them neatly together, cut ends level. Place the strands smoothly over the top of the head, across the seam, so that they overlap the face about 10cm (4in); spread the strands out over the centre of the seam to cover about 6cm (2½in), then stitch securely over the seam, using double matching thread.

Cut fifty 40cm (16in) strands of yarn and tie them loosely together at the centre with a single strand. Place the tied centre on top of the head over the seam, to hang down equally at each side; stitch the centre securely over the first set of strands.

Lift the hair, one section at a time, and spread glue liberally underneath, then lower it down into position, patting and smoothing it into place.

Trim the cut ends to the required length all round; but remember that little boys are never very tidy, so don't make the ends *too* even!

26. Cut the eyes in brown felt and pin to the face. Make four straight stitches, one on top of the other, about 4mm (³⁄₁₆in) long, level with the bottom of the eyes, for the nose.

Mark the mouth with pins and when you are satisfied with the expression, embroider it in stem (outline) stitch, using three strands of cotton.

Finally, glue the eyes into place.

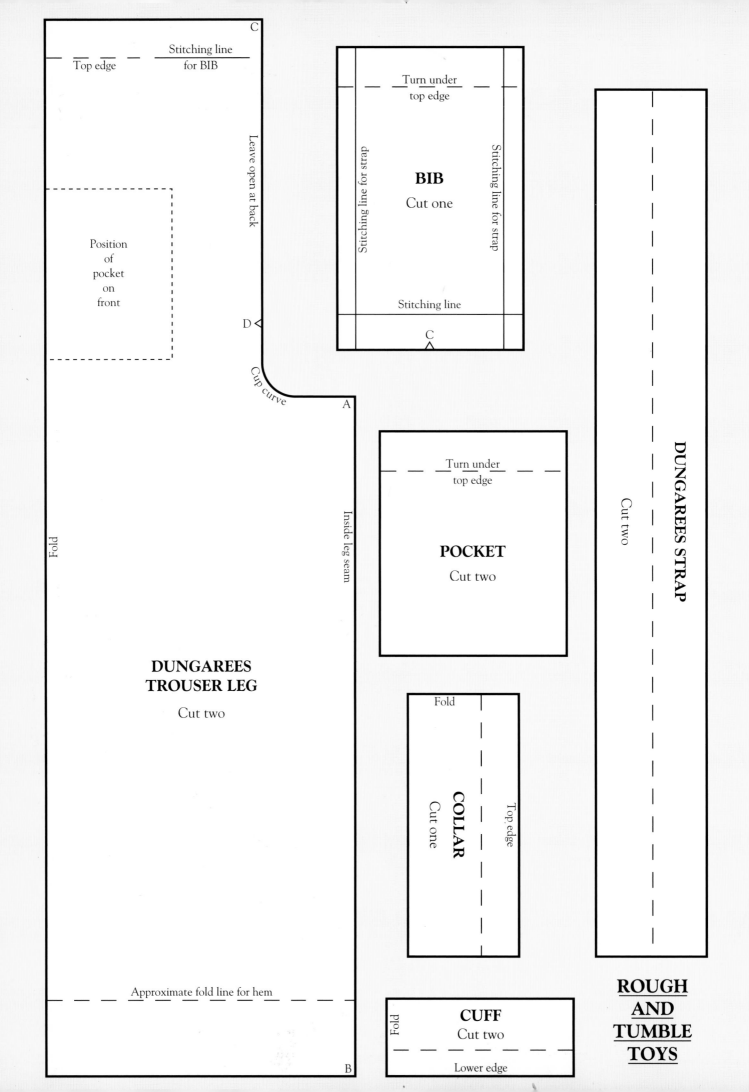

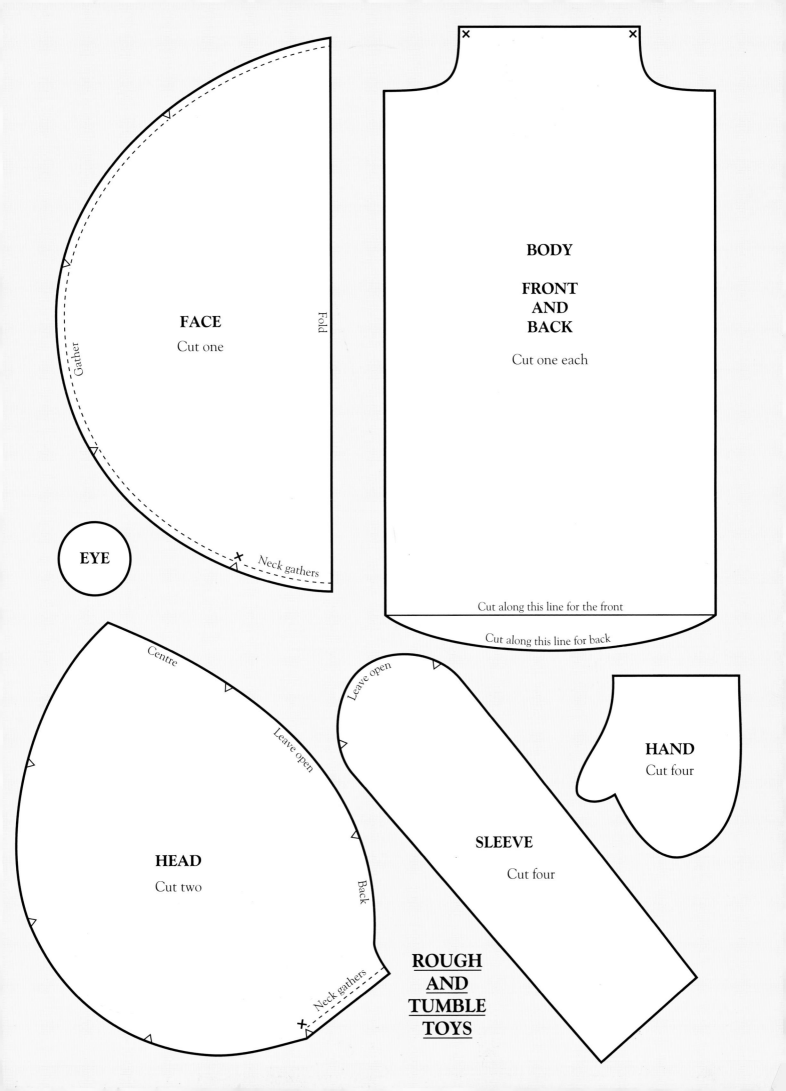

FACE

Cut one

Fold

Gather

Neck gathers

EYE

BODY

FRONT
AND
BACK

Cut one each

Cut along this line for the front

Cut along this line for back

Centre

Leave open

HEAD

Cut two

Back

Neck gathers

Leave open

SLEEVE

Cut four

HAND

Cut four

ROUGH
AND
TUMBLE
TOYS

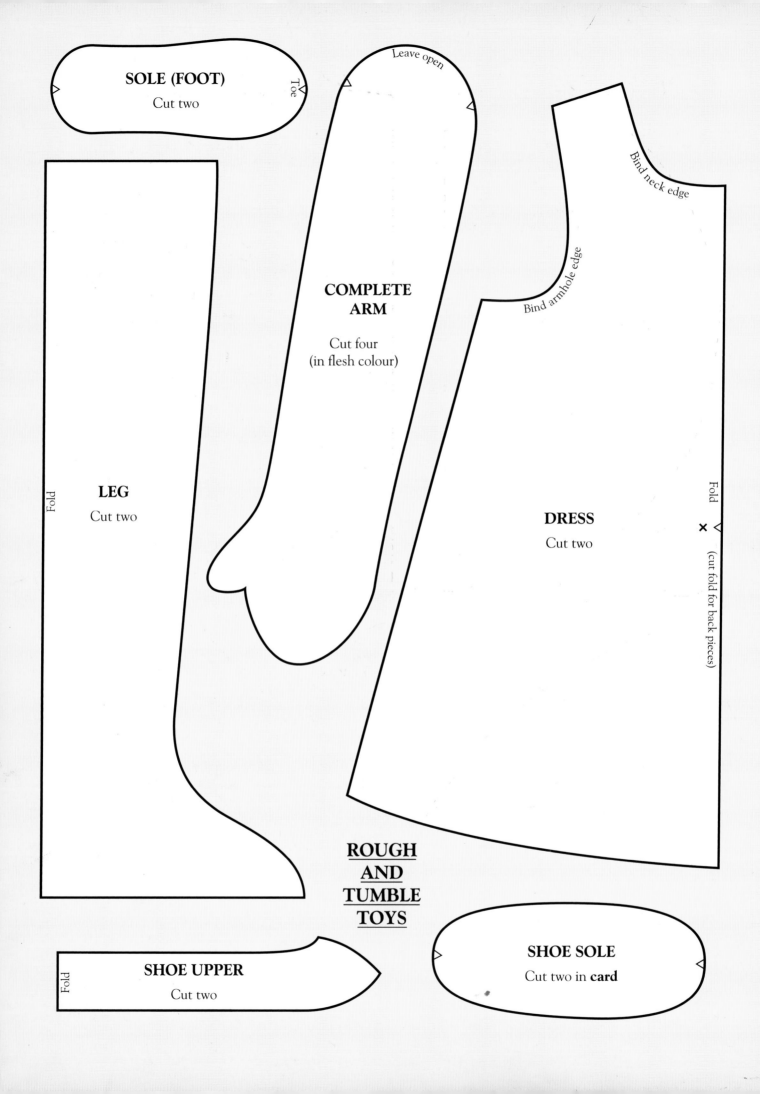

SOLE (FOOT)

Cut two

Toe

Leave open

Bind neck edge

Bind armhole edge

COMPLETE ARM

Cut four
(in flesh colour)

Fold

LEG

Cut two

Fold

DRESS

Cut two

× (cut fold for back pieces)

ROUGH AND TUMBLE TOYS

Fold

SHOE UPPER

Cut two

SHOE SOLE

Cut two in **card**

ROUGH-AND-TUMBLE THOMASINA

When planning a striking colour-scheme, remember that very dark backgrounds always create a more dramatic effect than pale shades and pastels. In this case, the felts used for the body and legs were chosen to pick up the vivid orangey-red and lime green pattern on the black dress fabric. Colour-matching in this way makes your doll look carefully co-ordinated, and gives it a very professional appearance.

MATERIALS

30cm (12in) square of cream felt
Two 20cm (8in) squares of red felt (body and sleeves)
Two 20cm (8in) squares of green felt (legs)
10 × 20cm (4 × 8in) black felt for shoes
3 × 5cm (1¼ × 2in) dark brown felt for eyes
25 × 45cm (10 × 18in) medium-weight cotton-type fabric for dress
Polyester stuffing
Large ball of very thick knitting yarn for hair
35cm (⅜yd) narrow white lace edging
70cm (⅞yd) green single-face satin ribbon, 15mm (⅝in) wide
50cm (½yd) bias binding, to match fabric
Pinky-red stranded embroidery cotton (floss)
Matching and black sewing threads
Stiff card
Clear adhesive

1. Cut the face once, the head twice, and the hand four times, in cream felt. Cut the front and back body pieces once each in red felt, and the sleeve four times. Cut the leg and sole twice each in green felt.
2. Make the doll as directed for the boy, steps 2-11 inclusive.
3. Cut the shoe upper twice in black felt. Cut the sole twice in card and glue to felt; cut the felt just outside the card, leaving a 2-3mm (⅛in) surplus all round.
4. Make the shoes as directed for Thomas, steps 23-24 inclusive.
5. Stitch lace over the neck and wrist seams.
6. *Note:* The following amounts are for a *very* thick, chunky yarn. The style will work equally well with an ordinary thick-knit yarn – but you will need to use more strands to cover the head: judge the number according to the thickness of your yarn.

Cut twenty 60cm (24in) lengths of yarn and place the strands across the centre of the seam joining the face and head, one end extending 10cm (4in) down over the forehead; catch over the seam with double matching thread, spreading the yarn out over about 2cm (¾in). Take the strands smoothly down over the centre back seam and catch them just above the nape of the neck, covering about 4cm (1½in).

Place another set of twenty 60cm (24in) lengths of yarn across the top of the head, over the top seam, hanging down equally at each side; stitch at the centre top, and then catch over the seam low down at each side, as illustrated.

Stitch twenty more 60cm (24in) lengths of yarn to the top of the head, immediately in front of, and against, the previous set, hanging down equally at each side; take the sides smoothly down over the face and catch them directly in front of the previous strands.

Stitch twenty 50cm (20in) lengths of yarn to the top of the head, immediately *behind* the previous two. Spread glue over each side of the back of the head and bring the strands smoothly down over it, so that the head is covered, then catch them into position.

Divide the strands at the centre back and catch them tightly together at each side to form bunches.

Trim the fringe level across the forehead, and trim the cut ends at each side neatly.
7. Cut the eyes in brown felt and pin to the face. Make four straight stitches, one on top of the other, about 4mm (³⁄₁₆in) long, level with the bottom of the eyes, for the nose.

Mark the mouth with pins, and when you are satisfied with the expression, embroider it in stem (outline) stitch, using three strands of cotton.

Finally, glue the eyes into place.
8. Cut the dress twice in fabric. Cut one piece in half, as indicated, for the back.
9. Join the shoulder and side seams; press open. Join the centre back seam below the notch. Turn under and tack the raw edges of the centre back opening; press.
10. Bind the neck and armhole edges neatly. Turn up a small hem, turning the raw edge under, and stitch.

Fit the dress on the doll and slip-stitch the edges of the centre back opening together.
11. Cut the ribbon in half and tie round the bunches, securing the bows to the hair to prevent them from coming undone.

CHAPTER 3

The Cuddle-and-Hug Basic Doll

Small children soon begin to take an enquiring interest in everything they see and hear. Here is another very easy-to-make felt doll, with a little more detail to satisfy that increased awareness. This is a very useful basic figure: it is more in proportion than the previous doll, and can be developed to create almost any character you like.

NOTE: Before cutting out, note any special instructions for the individual doll you are making. In particular, check the amount of flesh (and any additional) felt required; if this differs, it will appear in the list of materials.

MATERIALS
20cm (8in) cream/flesh-colour felt, 90cm (36in) wide
Scrap of felt for eyes (see individual doll)
Wool, yarn or alternative for hair (see individual doll)
Polyester stuffing
Pinky-red stranded embroidery cotton (floss) or alternative, for mouth
Matching and black sewing threads
Clear adhesive
SEAMS: Oversew (overcast) edges of felt to join. Seam allowance on fabric is 5mm (¼in).

1. Cut the face and the body front and back once each in felt, the head, leg and sole twice each, and the complete arm four times.
2. With right sides facing, join the centre back seam of the head pieces at top and bottom, leaving open between the notches. Then gather across the base between X's and join to the neck edge of the body back, matching X's, easing the gathers in to fit.
3. Gather the lower edge of the face and join to the body front in the same way.
4. Gather all round the remaining edge of the face; with right sides facing, pin the face and head together, matching notches and X's. Then stitch, drawing up the gathers to fit, and distributing them evenly between the pins.
5. Join the side edges of the neck and body below X's.
6. Turn, first the head and then body, to the right side.

7. Stuff the head very firmly, pushing the filling well forward into the face and chin, and down into the neck. Then stuff the body firmly, pushing the filling up into the neck from below. Pin the lower edges of the body, but stitch the centre back seam of the head, adding more stuffing if necessary.
8. To make each arm, join two pieces all round, leaving open between the notches. Turn to the right side and stuff, pushing well down into the hand and thumb (use a strong darning needle to draw the filling into the thumb from outside). Oversew (overcast) the top edges together.
9. To make each leg, join the centre front seam, then fit the sole round the lower edge, matching centres at back and front, and stitch together. Turn to the right side and stuff firmly. Gather across the top edge, matching the centre front seam to the centre back, and draw-up slightly.
10. Pin the lower edge of the body front over the top edge of each leg (toes forward), then stitch securely. Stitch the lower edge of the body back over the backs of the legs in the same way, but add a little more stuffing just before you finish stitching. Oversew the body between the legs.
11. Stitch the tops of the arms securely across the shoulders (thumbs forward), allowing natural freedom of movement.
12. Follow the individual directions for the hair and features of the doll you are making.

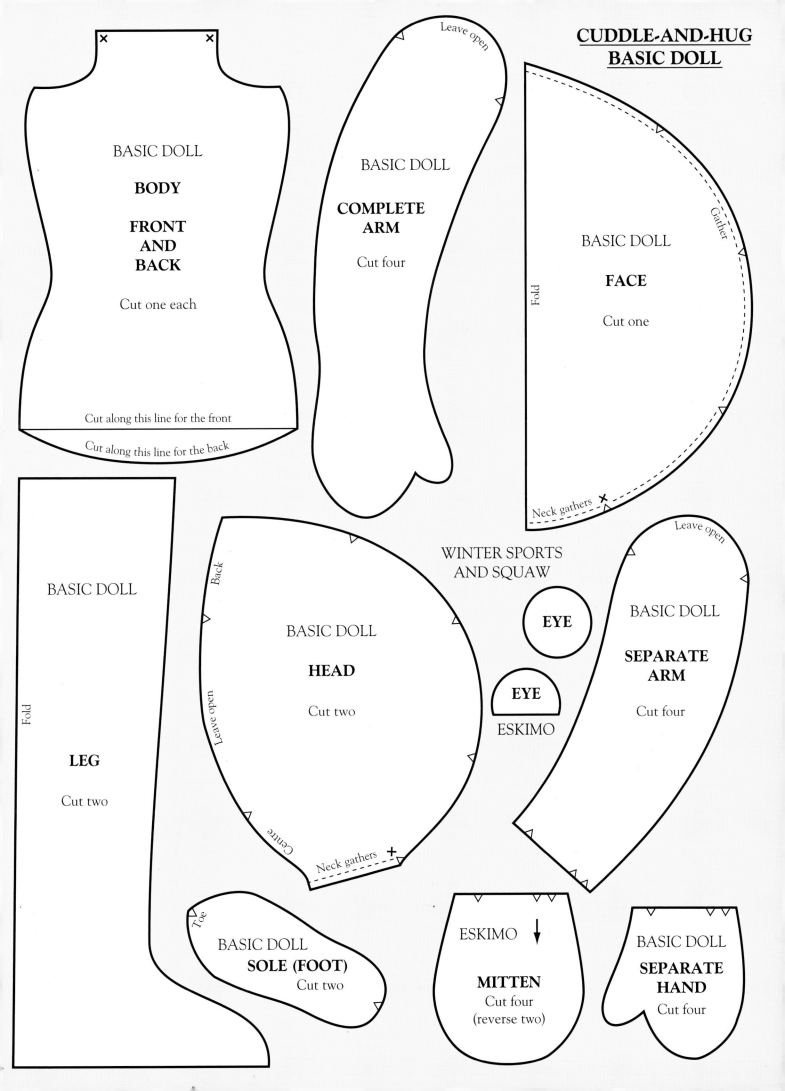

BASIC DOLL

BODY

**FRONT
AND
BACK**

Cut one each

Cut along this line for the front

Cut along this line for the back

Leave open

BASIC DOLL

**COMPLETE
ARM**

Cut four

CUDDLE-AND-HUG
BASIC DOLL

Fold

Gather

BASIC DOLL

FACE

Cut one

Neck gathers

BASIC DOLL

LEG

Cut two

Fold

Back

Leave open

Centre

BASIC DOLL

HEAD

Cut two

Neck gathers

WINTER SPORTS
AND SQUAW

EYE

EYE

ESKIMO

Leave open

BASIC DOLL

**SEPARATE
ARM**

Cut four

Toe

BASIC DOLL
SOLE (FOOT)

Cut two

ESKIMO

MITTEN

Cut four
(reverse two)

BASIC DOLL
**SEPARATE
HAND**

Cut four

Someone to Talk to

Once a child begins to treat its toys as friends, and not just playthings to be hurled around, it will appreciate a doll with a definite personality of its own. Here are three interesting and colourful cuddle-and-hug characters who look happy enough to chum up with any small boy or girl.

WINTER SPORTING BOY OR GIRL

A unisex doll with a *very* warm personality! The basic garments are extremely simple – all made from felt for quick and easy cutting and stitching. Then you add the style with knitted strips, colour-matching the yarn to your felts, for a smart outfit to greet the snow.

ADDITIONAL MATERIALS

Three 23cm (9in) squares of bright pink felt for tunic and hat
Two 20cm (8in) squares of purple felt for trousers and gloves
One 20cm (8in) square of black felt for boots
2 × 4cm (³⁄₄ × 1¹⁄₂in) dark brown felt for eyes
A ball each of matching pink and purple double-knit yarn
Double-knit yarn for hair
30cm (12in) narrow round elastic
Matching sewing threads
Thin card

1. Make the Basic Doll as directed in Chapter 3, *but* cut the arm and hand separately; the arm four times in cream felt and the hand four times in purple (it is a good idea to cut the trousers first [step 3] and then use the remaining felt for the hands).

To join them together, pin two arm pieces together near the top and pin two hand pieces together near the bottom: join the hands to the arms along the wrist edges. Leave pinned together ready for step 8 of the Basic Doll.

2. Cut about fifty (according to thickness) 20cm (8in) long strands of yarn for the hair. Tie them together loosely with a single strand 8cm (3in) from one end. Place the yarn over the top of the head, the tied area over the meeting point of the seams, and the shorter end hanging down over the forehead: spread the strands out over the seam to cover about 3cm (1¹⁄₄in),

then stitch them securely into place.

Cut about one hundred 30cm (12in) long strands and tie them tightly together at the centre. Place across the first section, so that they hang down equally at each side: stitch the centre securely.

Spread the strands out evenly around the head, but don't trim them to length until the hat is in position (they may be glued lightly to the head to hold them in place, if you wish, but this is not necessary).

3. Cut the tunic front once, and the back and sleeve twice each, from *two* squares of pink felt. Cut the trousers twice in purple. Cut the boot and sole twice each in black.

4. Right side inside, join each trouser leg between A-B. Then, right sides together, join the two pieces between C-A-C. Turn to the right side.

Fold the top edge over 1cm (³⁄₈in) and gather close to the edge. Gather close to the bottom of each trouser leg.

Fit the trousers on the doll; draw up the gathers round the waist and legs and fasten off securely.

5. Join the front of the tunic to the back pieces across the shoulders.

Set the sleeves into the armholes, matching the side edges and centre top of the sleeve to the shoulder seam. Then join the side and sleeve seams of the tunic.

Knit (see page 38) a strip 3cm (1¹⁄₄in) wide by 12cm (4³⁄₄in) long for each cuff. Join the short ends, then stitch neatly over the lower edge of each sleeve.

Fit the tunic on the doll: overlap the centre back edges, pin and then slip-stitch the join.

Knit another strip for the collar, 5cm (2in) wide by 12cm (6in) long. Wrap it around the neck, wrong side outside; join the ends at the centre back. Wrong side

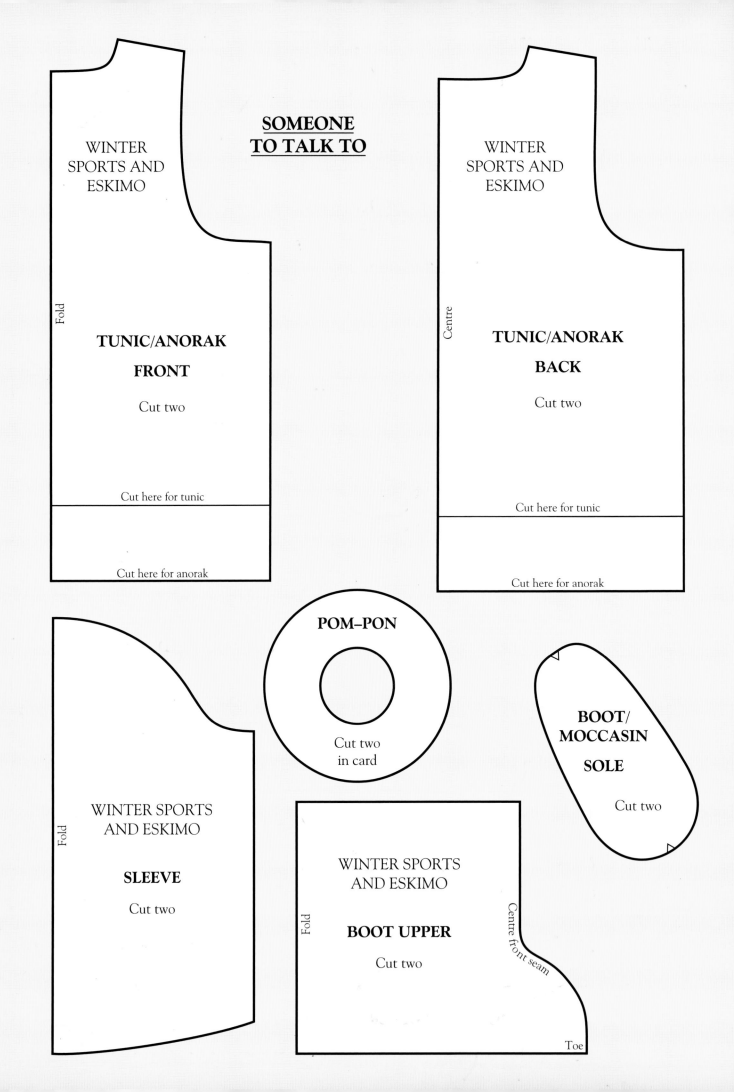

SOMEONE
TO TALK TO

WINTER SPORTS AND ESKIMO

TUNIC/ANORAK FRONT

Cut two

Fold

Cut here for tunic

Cut here for anorak

WINTER SPORTS AND ESKIMO

TUNIC/ANORAK BACK

Cut two

Centre

Cut here for tunic

Cut here for anorak

POM–PON

Cut two in card

BOOT/ MOCCASIN SOLE

Cut two

WINTER SPORTS AND ESKIMO

SLEEVE

Cut two

Fold

WINTER SPORTS AND ESKIMO

BOOT UPPER

Cut two

Fold

Centre front seam

Toe

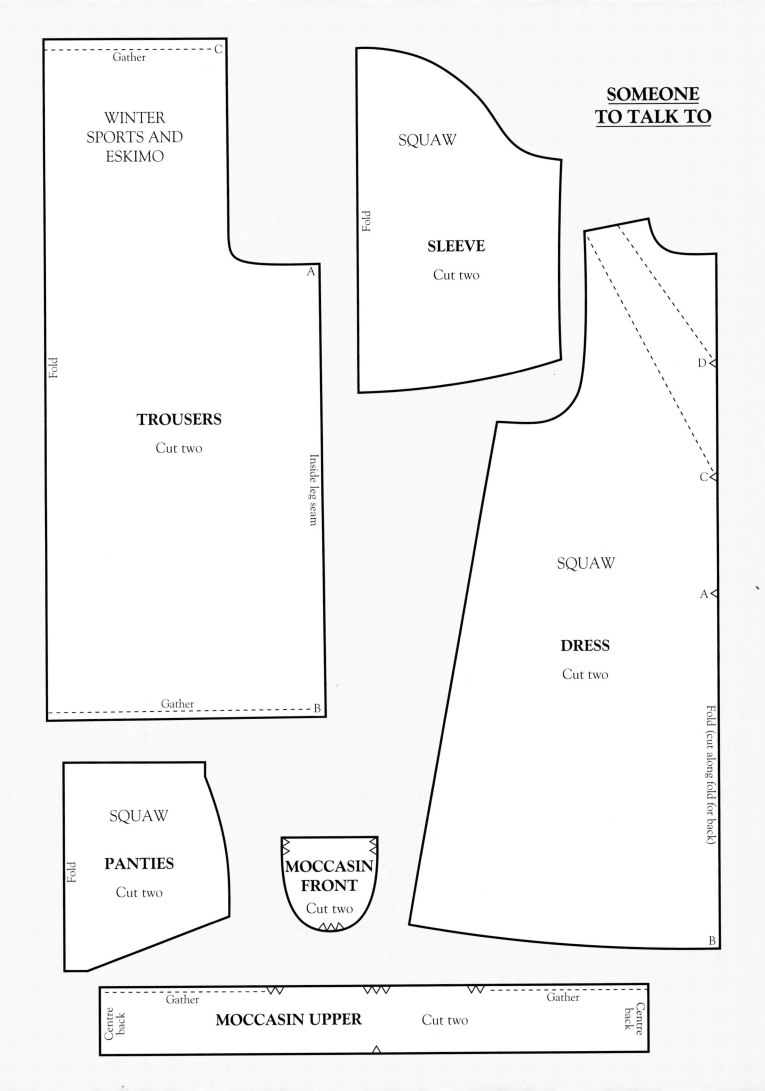

WINTER
SPORTS AND
ESKIMO

Gather C

Fold

TROUSERS

Cut two

Inside leg seam

A

Gather B

SQUAW

Fold

SLEEVE

Cut two

D

C

SQUAW

A

DRESS

Cut two

Fold (cut along fold for back)

B

SQUAW

Fold

PANTIES

Cut two

**MOCCASIN
FRONT**

Cut two

Centre back

Gather

MOCCASIN UPPER

Gather

Cut two

Centre back

inside, fold the collar over to make it double thickness.

6. To make the hat, cut the remaining square of pink felt in half. Join the two pieces along the two short edges to form the side seams. Gather all round one long edge and draw up tightly for the crown. Turn under and stitch a 1cm (³/₈in) hem around the lower edge.

Knit a strip as directed, approximately 4cm (1¹/₂-³/₄in) wide and long enough to encircle the head (about 36-7cm/14¹/₄in). Join the two short ends, then pin it round the lower edge of the hat, right side of band to wrong side of hat and lower edges level, stretching the band to fit. Oversew the edges together, then turn the band over to the right side. Thread elastic through the hem and draw up to fit the head.

Make a pompon, cutting your card circles from the patterns shown here, and using both yarns together in your needle. Use the ties to fix it securely over the hole in the crown, stitching and tying them inside.

Fit the hat on the doll. Using a long darning needle, catch the hat securely to the head, hiding your stitches underneath the band.

7. Join the centre front seam of each boot upper, then stitch the sole to the lower edge, matching centres at front and back. Turn to the right side.

Knit two strips 2.5cm (1in) wide by 12cm (4³/₄in) long. Join the short ends of each and stitch over the top of the boots before fitting them on the doll.

8. Cut the eyes in dark brown felt and pin them to the face. Make two straight stitches, one on top of the other, about 4mm (³/₁₆in) long, level with the bottom of the eyes, for the nose.

Mark the mouth with pins and, when you are satisfied with the expression, embroider it in stem (outline) stitch, using three strands of cotton.

Finally, glue the eyes into place.

9. Trim the hair neatly all round, as illustrated.

To knit the strips: The striped bands illustrated were knitted in double-knit yarn, but as long as you knit the strips to the correct width and length, you can use any yarn and size of needle; just experiment to find the number of stitches needed to produce the required width, and then continue knitting until the strip is the correct length.

As an indication, the number of stitches used for the doll in the photograph were as follows:

Boots:	6 stitches
Cuffs:	8 stitches
Hat:	10 stitches
Collar:	12 stitches

To make the strips, cast on the correct number of stitches and knit two rows. Then join in the second colour and knit two rows. Knit two more rows in the first colour, then two more rows in the second colour. Continue until the strip is the required length and then cast off.

COSY ESKIMO

Another unisex doll dressed to beat the cold. Once again, choose a clear, bright colour-scheme to please a small child. Add some attractive ribbon and braids to make the design even more eye-catching.

ADDITIONAL MATERIALS

18cm (7in) blue felt, 90cm (36in) wide, for anorak and hood
20 × 32cm (8 × 13in) green felt for trousers
20cm (8in) square of beige felt for boots
2 × 4cm (³/₄ × 1¹/₂in) black felt for eyes
Piece of silver-grey fur fabric for mittens and trims (see step 2)
Ribbon and braids to trim the anorak and boots
   (see steps 8 and 14)
Very dark brown double-knit yarn for hair
Matching and black sewing threads
Clear adhesive (optional)

1. Make the Basic Doll as directed in Chapter 3, *but* cut the arm only in flesh felt; see step 2 (below) to cut the mittens.

2. Cut strips of fur fabric as follows, *all with the pile run-ning lengthways:* 10cm (4in) wide × 30cm (12in) long for the hood; 6cm (2¹/₂in) wide × 18cm (7in) long for the collar; 4cm (1¹/₂in) wide × 25cm (10in) long for the hem. From the remaining fur, cut the mitten four times, direction of pile as arrow, reversing the pattern for two pieces.

3. Join the mittens to the arms as follows. Pin two arm pieces together near the top and pin two mittens, right sides together, near the bottom: join the mittens to the arms along the wrist edges and then oversew the mittens all round. Leave the arm pinned, ready for step 8 of the Basic Doll (ignore directions for thumb).

4. Cut about twenty (according to thickness) 18cm (7in) long strands of yarn for the hair; tie tightly at the centre with a single strand. Fold in half and stitch the tied area to the centre top of the head, over the point where the seams meet, so that all the cut ends hang down over the face.

Prepare two more bunches of twenty tied strands, but this time cut them 17cm (6⁵/₈in) long. Stitch each over the seam, 2cm (³/₄in) from the first bunch, so that they hang over the face in the same way.

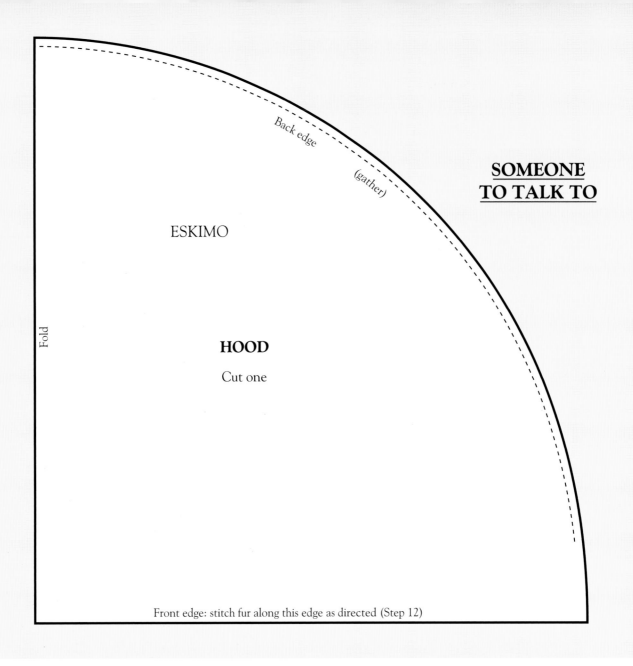

Back edge

(gather)

ESKIMO

Fold

HOOD

Cut one

Front edge: stitch fur along this edge as directed (Step 12)

Prepare two final bunches of only *ten* strands each, this time 16cm (6¼in) long. Stitch each over the seam, 2cm (¾in) from the previous bunches.

Trim the cut ends neatly, as illustrated.

5. Cut the anorak front and the hood once each, and the back and sleeves twice each, in blue felt. Cut the trousers twice in green. Cut the boot and sole twice each in beige.

6. Right side inside, join each trouser leg between A-B. Then, right sides together, join the two pieces between C-A-C. Turn to the right side.

Fold the top edge over 1cm (⅜in) and gather close to the edge. Gather close to the bottom of each trouser leg.

Fit the trousers on the doll; draw up the gathers round the waist and legs and fasten off securely.

7. Join the front of the anorak to the back pieces along the shoulder seams.

Set the sleeves into the armholes, matching the side edges and centre top of sleeve to the shoulder seam.

Then join the sleeve and side seams of the anorak. Turn to the right side.

8. Trim the anorak with ribbon and braid, as you wish. In the photograph, two rows of 1cm (⅜in) wide ribbon are stitched side-by-side down the centre front, with a band of 7mm (¼in) wide grey braid glued between them; the same braid, but in green, has been cut in half lengthways to make the very narrow trim glued over the outer edges of the ribbon.

The green braid, un-cut, is glued around the bottom of each sleeve, with a band of ribbon stitched immediately above.

9. Prepare the strip of fur fabric for the hem as directed in Made-to-Match Trims. Then stitch it around the lower edge of the anorak.

10. Fit the anorak on the doll. Overlap the centre back edges and slip-stitch together.

Trim off excess fur fabric and join the cut edges.

11. Cut the eyes in black felt and pin them to the face. Make two straight stitches, one on top of the other,

about 4mm (³/₁₆in) long, level with the bottom of the eyes, for the nose.

Mark the mouth with pins and, when you are satisfied with the expression, embroider it in stem (outline) stitch, using three strands of cotton.

Finally, glue the eyes into place.

12. To make the hood, place the strip of fur fabric along the straight edge of the felt, right sides together; but have the fur overlapping the felt 2cm (³/₄in). Stitch together 5mm (¹/₄in) from the edge of the felt. Now bring the fur over, wrong side inside, and turn it under, pinning the other long edge so that it overlaps the felt 5mm (¹/₄in). Slip-stitch the edge neatly over the previous stitching line.

Gather the curved edge of the felt, between the fur.

Fit the hood on the doll, catching the front corners under the chin, as illustrated. Fix the front edge around the face as shown, and catch in place at the top and sides, just behind the fur.

13. Prepare the fur fabric for the collar as before, then wrap it around the neck and join the ends at the back.

14. Join the centre front seam of each boot upper. Turn to the right side and stitch and/or glue trimming over the seam; allow it to overlap 1cm (³/₈in) at the top and turn this surplus inside, but cut the trimming level with the felt at the bottom of the seam. The doll illustrated has a central band of ribbon edged with green braid as used on the sleeves.

Turn to the wrong side again and stitch the sole to the lower edge, matching centres at front and back. Turn to the right side and fit on the doll.

REDSKIN SQUAW

Use a slightly darker felt – camel or a very light brown – for the Basic Doll, to give the correct flesh tone, and embroider the mouth in a brighter red than the fairer-skinned dolls. The hair of the doll in the photograph is a 'chunky' yarn, which is extra thick and specially effective for this particular doll. However, if you prefer to substitute an ordinary double-knit yarn, just use more strands; double the number given should be about right. Choose your own braids and trimmings; but have bright, warm colours to contrast with the deep brown of her dress.

ADDITIONAL MATERIALS

20 × 60cm (8 × 24in) red-brown felt for dress and panties

8 × 16cm (3 × 6¹/₂in) light sandy-brown felt for moccasin uppers

8cm (3in) square darker brown felt for soles

2 × 4cm (³/₄ × 1¹/₂in) black felt for eyes

Very thick chunky (or double-knit) black yarn for hair

1m (1¹/₈yd) silky red-brown lampshade fringe, 2.5cm (1in) deep

70cm (³/₄yd) ric-rac braid EACH in yellow, orange and red

1.5m (1³/₄yd) satin ribbon, 1.5mm (¹/₁₆in) wide, EACH in yellow, orange and red

30cm (12in) yellow grosgrain ribbon, 15mm (⁵/₈in) wide, for the headband

Matching and black sewing threads

Stiff card

Clear adhesive

1. Make the Basic Doll as directed in Chapter 3 (see above for colour of felt).

2. Cut the dress, sleeve and panties twice each in red-brown felt; cut one dress piece in half along the fold line to form the two back pieces. Cut the moccasin upper and front twice each in light brown felt, and the sole twice in darker brown.

3. Join the two pantie pieces along the side edges and between the legs. Turn to the right side and gather round the top edge.

Fit on the doll and draw up the gathers evenly round the waist.

4. *Overlap* the centre back edges of the dress 5mm (¹/₄in), and slip-stitch together between A-B. Then oversew the shoulder seams to join the back and front.

Set the sleeves into the armholes, matching the side edges and centre top of sleeve to the shoulder seam. Then join the sleeve and side seams of the dress. Turn to the right side.

5. Stitch the top edge of the fringe *under* the lower edges of the sleeves and skirt, so that the loops hang below as illustrated.

Then stitch three rows of ric-rac braid above, as illustrated.

Stitch a yoke of fringe to the back and front of the dress, in a V-shape, beginning and ending at the back at point C, taking over the shoulders level with the sleeve seam and turning at point C on the centre front.

6. Plait the narrow ribbons to make braid. Glue over the top edge of the fringed yoke. Then glue round the edge of the neck. And finally, glue between the fringe and neck in another V-shape, beginning, turning and ending at point D.

7. Fit the dress on the doll, overlap the upper half of the centre back and slip-stitch together.

8. Join the two short edges of the moccasin upper for the centre back seam, then turn to the right side. Wrong sides together, oversew the lower edge of the upper all round the sole, matching notches at the front and seam at centre back.

Wrong sides together, oversew the front piece to the top edge of the upper, matching double and triple notches. Gather round the remaining top edge of the upper, then fit the moccasin on the doll and draw up the gathers to fit; secure to doll at each side of the foot.

Glue ribbon braid along straight edges of fronts.

9. Wind the yarn ten times around a 23cm (9in) deep card; tie tightly at each end, then remove and place smoothly across the top of the head, pinning the tied ends over the seam at each side. Using double black thread, stitch the centre of the skein to the top of the face with long stitches extending between the point where the seams meet and 3cm (1¼in) in front of the seam. Then stitch the pinned ends into place.

Wind the yarn ten times around a 20cm (8in) deep card; tie and remove the skein as before. Pin the ends to the back of the head, directly behind the previous ends, then stitch the centre as before, close behind the first skein, but covering only 1.5cm (⅝in). Stitch the pinned ends.

Wind yarn ten times around a 17cm (6¾in) deep card. Stitch directly behind the previous skein in the same way, but make your centre stitches cover only 1cm (⅜in).

Wind yarn ten times around a 15cm (6in) deep card. Repeat as for previous skein.

This should cover the back of the head; if not, continue with more skeins in the same way until the felt is completely covered.

Cut fifteen 50cm (20in) lengths of yarn. Stitch the centre to the forehead, close against the first skein, covering 2cm (¾in). Then take each side smoothly down over the face and stitch to the side of the head, over the ends of the first skein.

Divide the hanging strands at each side into three and plait neatly into braids, binding the ends tightly with thread and then trimming level.

10. Cut the eyes in black felt and pin to the face. Make four straight stitches, one on top of the other, about 4mm (³⁄₁₆in) long, level with the bottom of the eyes, for the nose.

Mark the mouth with pins and, when you are satisfied with the expression, embroider it in stem (outline) stitch, using three strands of cotton.

Finally, glue the eyes into place.

11. Pin the wider yellow ribbon around the head as illustrated, join at back. Stitch into place along the centre, then glue remaining ribbon braid over the stitches.

CHAPTER 5

Nursery Rhyme Favourites

T he basic cuddle-and-hug doll featured in the previous chapter appears again here. But the designs for the characters are more developed and detailed, and fabric replaces felt for most of the garments. Look for firmly woven cotton-type fabrics unless otherwise instructed, as you will find these easier to cut and sew than loosely woven or silky materials.

As they are based on traditional nursery rhymes which have been repeated and loved for generations, the characters are deliberately dressed in old-fashioned styles. This nostalgia contrasts with the dolls in the previous chapters, widening your range still more.

SEAM ALLOWANCE on fabric is approximately 5mm (¹/4in). Always work with right sides together, unless otherwise instructed. Oversew (overcast) edges of felt to join.

Old Mother Hubbard
Went to the cupboard,
    To get her poor Dog a bone;
But when she got there
    The cupboard was bare,
And so the poor Dog had none.

LITTLE MISS MUFFET

Do you recognise the fabric from which Miss Muffet's demurely Victorian dress is made? It is exactly the same as the one used for Thomasina, the thoroughly modern miss in Chapter 2. In that case the dark background was chosen for dramatic effect, picking up the bright colours of the flowers to match them in felt for the arms and legs. Here, the black background is used in quite a different way: to emphasise Miss Muffet's crisp white pinafore.

This is an excellent example of a carefully chosen fabric doing two completely different jobs – and succeeding in both cases. Do take time when choosing the fabrics for your dolls. The weight and texture are important, as described above; but finding appropriate patterns and attractive colour-schemes must also be an essential part of your planning.

MATERIALS

15 × 70cm (6 × 28in) cream felt for body, arms, face and head

20 × 30cm (8 × 12in) black felt for legs

See Chapter 3 for Basic Doll, excluding felt (above)

6 × 17cm (2½ × 6¾in) coloured felt (to tone with dress) for shoes

8cm (3in) square of beige felt for soles

2 × 4cm (¾ × 1½in) dark brown felt for eyes

30cm (12in) medium-weight flower-printed cotton-type fabric, 90cm (36in) wide, for dress (with dark background)

23 × 50cm (9 × 18in) white spotted voile (dotted Swiss) for pinafore

20 × 60cm (8 × 24in) lightweight cotton-type fabric for undies

40cm (½yd) white lace, 3cm (1¼in) deep, for pinafore yoke

45cm (½yd) very narrow white lace for pinafore hem

70cm (¾yd) lace, 10mm (⅜in) deep, to trim undies

4cm (1½in) approximately, guipure lace daisies, or alternative, to trim hair

15cm (6in) bias binding to match dress fabric

50cm (½yd) white bias binding

30cm (12in) bias binding for panties (optional)

Narrow round elastic

Double-knit yarn for hair

Matching and black sewing threads

Stiff card

1. Make the Basic Doll as directed in Chapter 3, using black felt for the legs and soles.
2. Cut the bodice front and skirt once each in dress fabric, and the bodice back and sleeve twice each. Cut the petticoat once in lightweight fabric, and the panties twice. Cut the pinafore once in spotted voile (or alternative).

3. Join the two pantie pieces along the side edges and between the legs. Make a hem along the top, as indicated, turning under the raw edge. Bind the leg edges (or make a very narrow hem), then turn to the right side and trim with lace. Thread elastic through the channel at the top and draw up to fit the waist.
4. Join the centre back seam of the petticoat and press open. Make a hem along the top, as indicated, turning under the raw edge. Make a narrow hem along the lower edge, then turn to the right side and trim with lace. Thread elastic through the channel at the top and draw up to fit the waist.
5. To make the dress, join the bodice front to the back pieces at each shoulder. Press the seams open.
6. Gather round the top edge of each sleeve, as indicated. Then set into the armholes, matching the sides, notches and centre top of sleeve to the shoulder seam. Draw up the gathers to fit, then stitch into place, distributing the gathers evenly. Clip the curved seam carefully.
7. Join the sleeve seams and the side seams of the bodice.
8. Turn up the lower edge of each sleeve along the line indicated: turn the raw edge narrowly under and hem.
   Then herringbone-stitch elastic against the hemline and draw up to fit the arm, knotting securely.
9. Gather the top edge of the skirt. Then pin it to the lower edge of the bodice, matching the centre fronts, sides, notches and circles. Draw up the gathers to fit, distributing them evenly between the pins, and stitch together. Press the seam up.
10. Join the centre back seam of the skirt below X.
11. Turn under the centre back edges of the bodice as indicated, and also the edges of the skirt above X; herringbone-stitch over the raw edges.
12. Bind the neck edge neatly.
13. Fit the dress on the doll to determine the length; pin the hem of the skirt, then remove and stitch.
14. Fit the dress on the doll again; overlap and pin the centre back edges, then slip-stitch neatly together.
15. Turn under and stitch a very narrow hem down each back edge of the pinafore. Turn the raw lower edge up to form a very narrow hem, then stitch narrow lace on the right side.
16. Join the shoulder seams, matching notches, and press open.
17. Bind the armhole edges; then turn the binding inside and catch down to form an interfacing.
18. Gather the neck edge as indicated, across the front, and at each side of the back. Fit the pinafore on the doll, pinning the top corners at the centre back, and then pinning the shoulder seams level with those of the dress. Draw up the front and back gathers to fit.

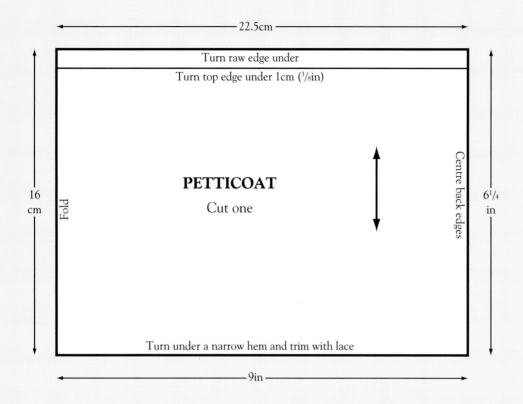

22.5cm

Turn raw edge under

Turn top edge under 1cm (³⁄₈in)

PETTICOAT

Cut one

16 cm

Fold

Centre back edges

6¹⁄₄ in

Turn under a narrow hem and trim with lace

9in

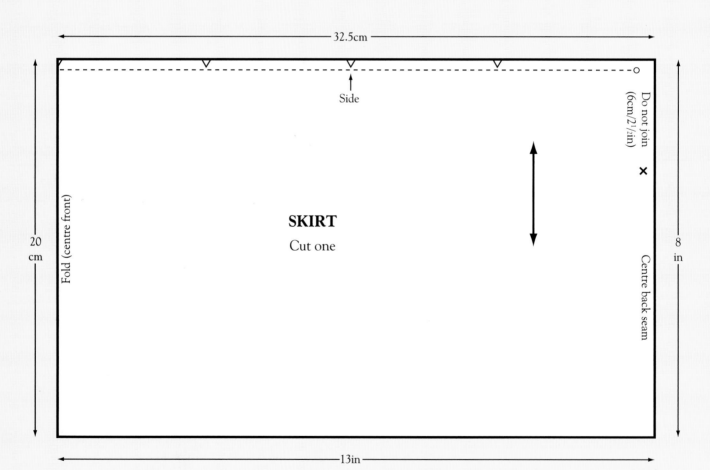

32.5cm

Side

Do not join (6cm/2¹⁄₂in)

SKIRT

Cut one

20 cm

Fold (centre front)

8 in

Centre back seam

13in

LITTLE MISS MUFFET

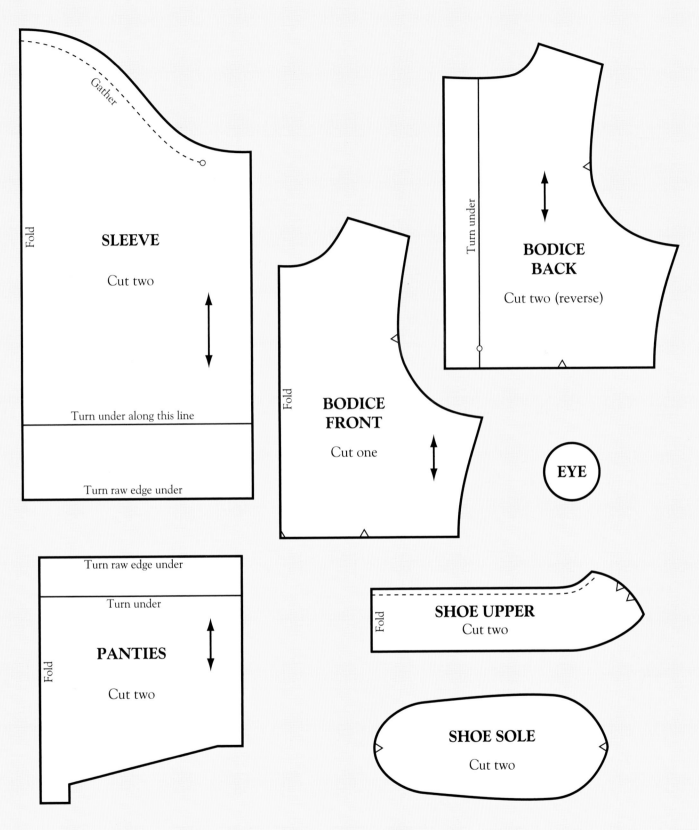

SLEEVE

Cut two

Gather

Fold

Turn under along this line

Turn raw edge under

BODICE BACK

Cut two (reverse)

Turn under

BODICE FRONT

Cut one

Fold

EYE

PANTIES

Cut two

Turn raw edge under

Turn under

Fold

SHOE UPPER
Cut two

Fold

SHOE SOLE

Cut two

LITTLE MISS MUFFET

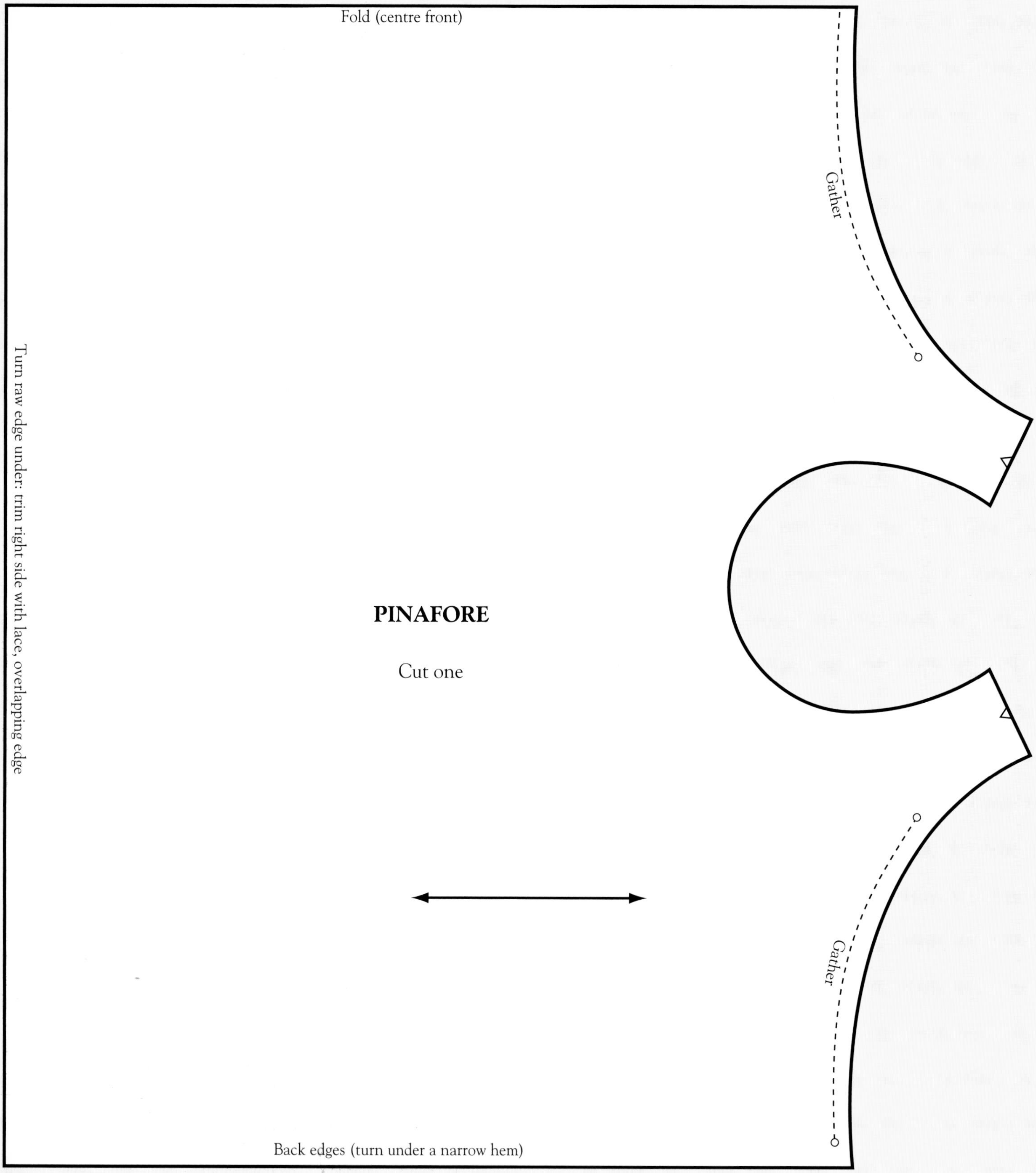

Fold (centre front)

Gather

Turn raw edge under; trim right side with lace, overlapping edge

PINAFORE

Cut one

Gather

Back edges (turn under a narrow hem)

LITTLE MISS MUFFET

Remove the pinafore and bind the top edge, distributing the gathers evenly. If necessary, gather the folded top edge of the binding and draw up so that it lies flat.

19. Gather the straight edge of the wide lace, then pin it evenly round the neck edge of the pinafore, level with the top edge of the binding; draw up to fit, then oversew (overcast) neatly into place. Catch the lace down over the shoulder seams.

20. Fit the pinafore on the doll and stitch the top corners together at the centre back.

21. Cut the shoe upper and sole twice each in the appropriate felts.

To make each shoe, oversew the centre front of the upper, matching the double notches. Then pin the lower edge to the sole, matching the centre front and back of the upper to the notches. Oversew together. Turn to the right side.

Beginning at the centre back, make a row of tiny gathering stitches very close to the top edge. Fit the shoe and draw up these gathers to fit, catching the shoe to the back of the foot as you secure the thread.

22. Wind the yarn twenty-five times around a 30cm (12in) deep card; tie tightly at each edge with a single strand, then remove the skein from the card and tie the centre loosely (this centre tie may be snipped away as soon as you have sewn the skein to the head). Using double thread and a long darning needle, stitch the centre of the skein at the nape of the neck, over the centre back seam; bring the ends up at each side and round to the front, taking them smoothly over the face to the top of the head, following the photograph for guidance. Stitch securely into position.

Wind the yarn twenty times around the same 30cm (12in) deep card and tie the skein in the same way. Stitch the centre to the back of the head, close against the first skein; then bring each side up behind the first skein and stitch the ends *over* the previous ends.

Wind the yarn twenty times around a 25cm (10in) deep card and tie the skein as before. Stitch to the head as you did the previous skein.

Wind the yarn twenty times around a 20cm (8in) deep card and tie as before. Stitch the centre close against the centre of the last skein, but bring the sides up together to cover the back of the head, and stitch the ends to the centre top of the head, between the previous ends.

To make the fringe, wind the yarn twenty-five times around an 8cm (3in) deep card. Tie tightly at *one* edge only; cut along the other edge. Stitch the tied section to the top of the head so that the cut ends fall over the forehead.

To make her top-knot, wind the yarn thirty times around your 30cm (12in) deep card; tie the ends tightly, then remove the skein from the card and tie it in a loose knot, knotting the ties together securely to hold it in shape. Stitch to the top of the head, covering all the previous ends.

Tuck in, or snip off, any stray ends neatly, and trim the fringe to the required length.

23. Fix trimming to front of top-knot, as illustrated.

24. Cut the eyes in brown felt and pin to the face. Make two straight stitches, one on top of the other, about 4mm ($\frac{3}{16}$in) long, level with the bottom of the eyes, for the nose.

Mark the mouth with pins and when you are satisfied with the expression, embroider it in stem (outline) stitch, using three strands of cotton.

Finally, glue the eyes into place.

Little Miss Muffet
Sat on a tuffet,
Eating her curds and whey;
There came a big spider,
Who sat down beside her
And frightened Miss Muffet away.

OLD MOTHER HUBBARD

Notice how easy it is to adapt a basic pattern to give a totally different appearance. Mother Hubbard wears a long-sleeved blouse and a skirt in which the arrangement of the stripes gives added interest. Her outfit looks very different from Miss Muffet's 'little girl' dress. But in fact it is made in almost exactly the same way – only the interpretation and small details are changed.

Of course the novelty feature of *this* doll is the old lady's dog!

MATERIALS

15 × 70cm (6 × 28in) cream felt for the body, arms, face and head

20 × 30cm (8 × 12in) wine felt for legs

See Chapter 3 for Basic Doll, excluding felt (above)

10 × 17cm (4 × 6¾in) black felt for shoes

2 × 4cm (¾ × 1½in) dark brown felt for eyes

35cm (14in) lightweight flower-printed cotton-type fabric, 90cm (36in) wide, for blouse, petticoat and drawers

20cm (8in) medium-weight wine striped cotton-type fabric, 90cm (36in) wide, for skirt

40 × 60cm (16 × 24in) medium-weight plain white cotton-type fabric for mob cap and apron

2m (2yd) lace, 10mm (⅜in) deep, to trim blouse, apron and undies

50cm (⅝yd) white ribbon, 9mm (⅜in) wide, for apron strings

25cm (10in) single-face satin ribbon, 15mm (⅝in) wide, to trim the mob cap

15cm (6in) bias binding to match blouse

Narrow round elastic

Double-knit yarn for hair

Matching sewing threads

Stiff card

1. Make the Basic Doll as directed in Chapter 3, using wine felt for the legs and soles.
2. Cut the blouse front and the petticoat once each in the lightweight fabric, and the blouse back and sleeve and the drawers, twice each.

Cut the main skirt once, and the hem four times, in striped fabric, noting the vertical and horizontal arrows indicating the direction of the stripes.

Fold a sheet of tracing paper into four to trace the mob cap pattern. Cut the mob cap, apron and waistband once each in plain white fabric.

3. Join each leg of the drawers between A-B. Then, right sides together, join the two pieces between C-A-C. Clip the curved seam carefully. Make a hem along the top, as indicated, turning under the raw edge. Make a narrow hem around the lower edge of each leg, then turn to the right side and trim with lace.

Thread elastic through the channel at the top and draw up to fit the waist.

4. Join the centre back seam of the petticoat and press open. Make a hem along the top, as indicated, turning under the raw edge. Thread elastic through this channel and draw up to fit the waist.
5. Join the blouse front to the back pieces at each shoulder. Press the seams open.
6. Gather round the top edge of each sleeve, as indicated. Then set into the armholes, matching the sides, notches and centre top of sleeve to the shoulder seam. Draw up the gathers to fit, then stitch into place, distributing the gathers evenly. Clip the curved seam carefully.
7. Join the sleeve seams and the side seams of the bodice.
8. Make a narrow hem around the lower edge of each sleeve, turning the raw edge inside. Then stitch lace on the right side so that it overlaps the edge. Turn to the wrong side again and herringbone-stitch elastic against the hemline; draw up to fit the wrist and knot securely in place.
9. Gather the top edge of the main skirt piece. Then pin it evenly to the lower edge of the blouse, matching the centre fronts, sides, notches and circles. Draw up the gathers to fit, distributing them evenly between the pins, and stitch together. Press the seam up.
10. Join the centre back seam of the skirt below X.
11. Join the short edges of the hem sections to form a circle. Right sides together, stitch one long edge to the lower edge of the skirt. Turn the seam down and press; then turn up the lower edge of the hem level with the stitching line and herringbone-stitch over the raw edge.
12. Turn under the centre back edges of the blouse as indicated, and also the edges of the skirt above X; herringbone-stitch over the raw edges.
13. Bind the neck edge, then stitch lace on top to form a stand-up collar.
14. Fit the blouse and skirt on the doll; overlap and pin the centre back edges, then slip-stitch neatly together.
15. Turn up the lower edge of the petticoat so that it is 1cm (⅜in) shorter than the skirt; make a hem and trim the right side to match the drawers.
16. Turn the raw edge under round the sides and lower edge of the apron, and trim with overlapping lace.

Gather the top edge.

17. Turn under and tack the short side edges of the waistband. With right sides together and raw edges level, pin the waistband to the top edge of the apron, drawing up the gathers to fit and distributing them evenly. Fold the waistband in half lengthways, over the top of the apron; turn the raw edge under and slip-stitch over the gathers.
18. Cut the white ribbon in half and insert one piece

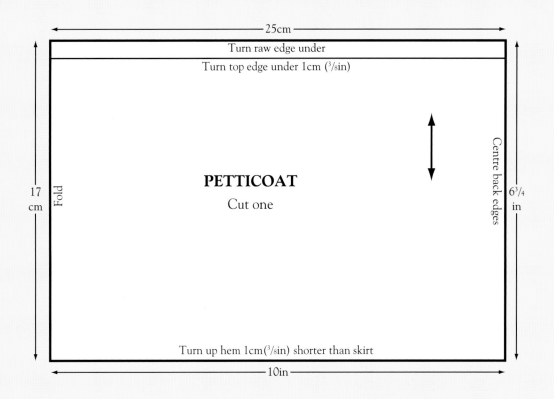

25cm

Turn raw edge under

Turn top edge under 1cm (³/₈in)

Fold

PETTICOAT

Cut one

Centre back edges

17 cm

6³/₄ in

Turn up hem 1cm(³/₈in) shorter than skirt

10in

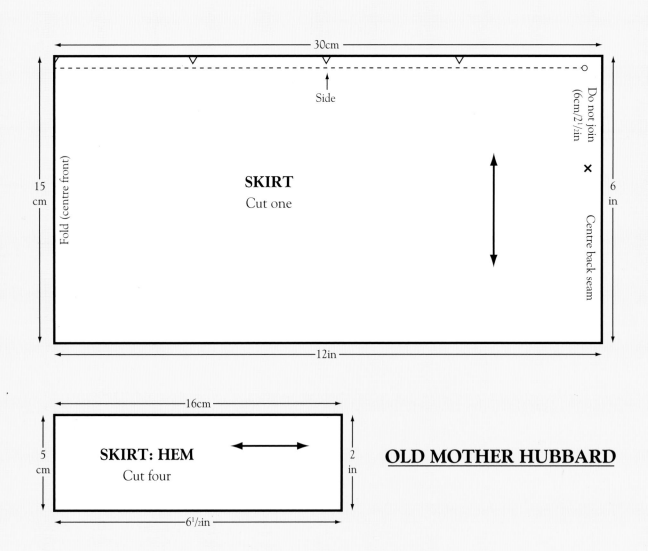

30cm

Side

Fold (centre front)

SKIRT

Cut one

Do not join (6cm/2¹/₂in)

✕

Centre back seam

15 cm

6 in

12in

16cm

SKIRT: HEM

Cut four

5 cm

2 in

6¹/₂in

OLD MOTHER HUBBARD

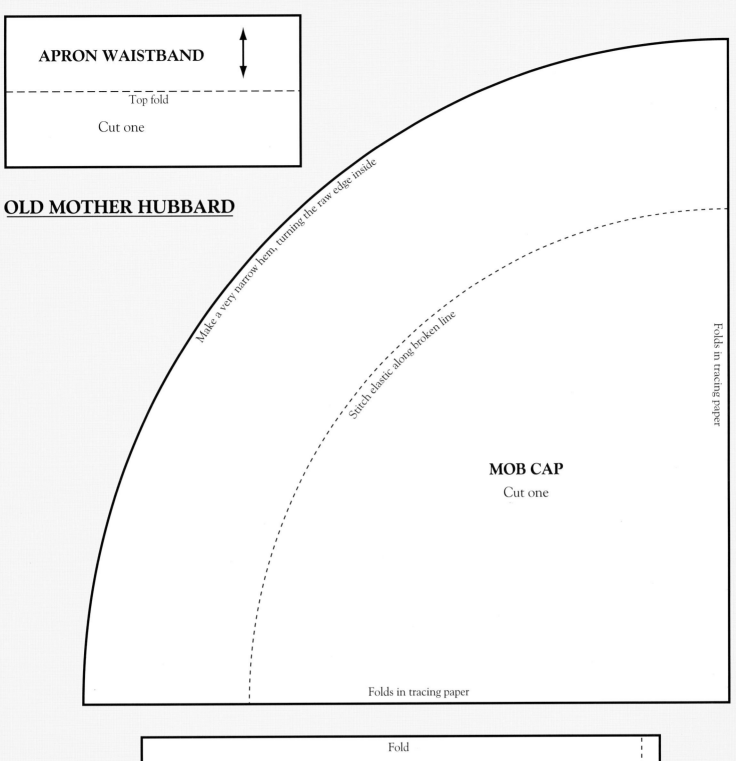

APRON WAISTBAND

Top fold

Cut one

OLD MOTHER HUBBARD

Make a very narrow hem, turning the raw edge inside

Stitch elastic along broken line

Folds in tracing paper

MOB CAP

Cut one

Folds in tracing paper

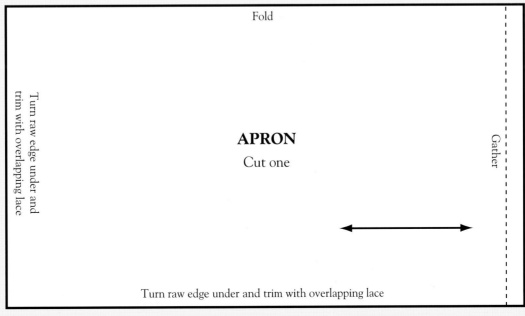

Fold

Turn raw edge under and trim with overlapping lace

APRON

Cut one

Gather

Turn raw edge under and trim with overlapping lace

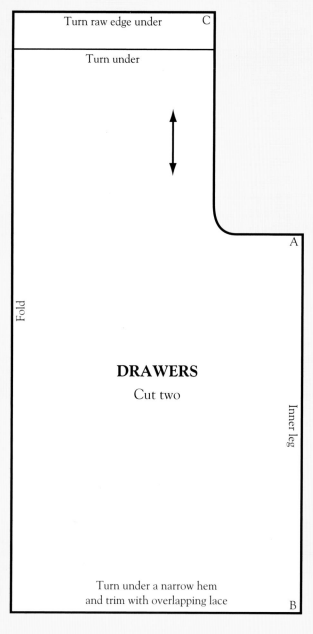

Turn raw edge under   C

Turn under

Fold

DRAWERS

Cut two

Inner leg

Turn under a narrow hem
and trim with overlapping lace   B

A

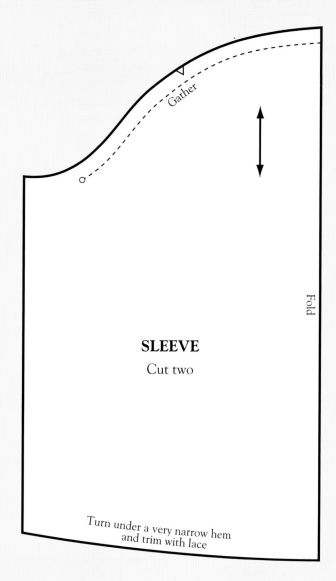

Gather

Fold

SLEEVE

Cut two

Turn under a very narrow hem
and trim with lace

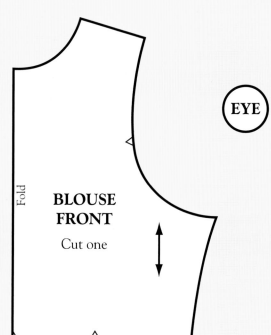

Fold

**BLOUSE
FRONT**

Cut one

EYE

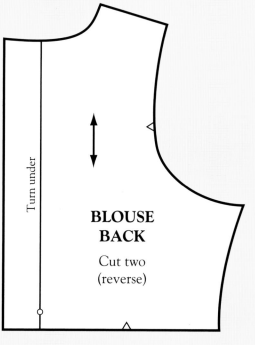

Turn under

**BLOUSE
BACK**

Cut two
(reverse)

OLD MOTHER HUBBARD

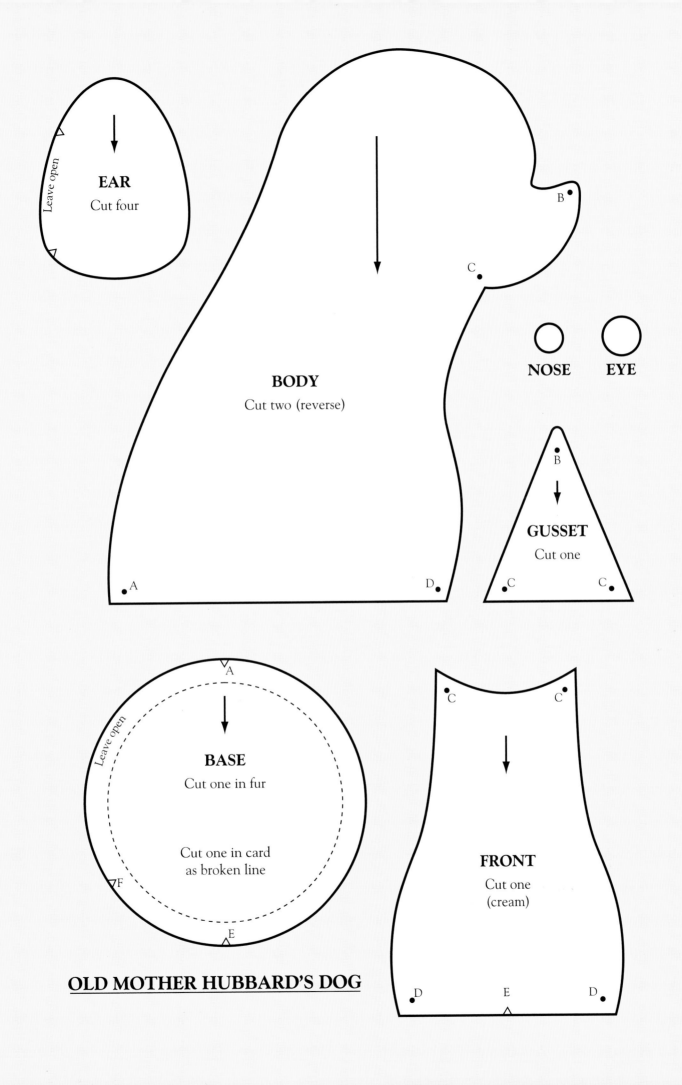

EAR
Cut four

Leave open

BODY
Cut two (reverse)

B

C

A

D

NOSE

EYE

GUSSET
Cut one

B

C

C

BASE
Cut one in fur

Cut one in card
as broken line

Leave open

A

F

E

FRONT
Cut one
(cream)

C

C

D

E

D

OLD MOTHER HUBBARD'S DOG

at each end of the waistband, stitching them securely. Tie apron round waist.

19. Cut the shoe upper and sole twice each in black felt.

Follow the directions for Miss Muffet's shoes: step 21.

20. Wind the yarn twenty times around a 25cm (10in) deep card; tie tightly at each edge with a single strand, then remove the skein from the card and tie the centre loosely (this centre tie may be snipped away as soon as you have stitched the skein to the head).

Pin the tied centre of the skein to the forehead so that the front edge is 5cm (2in) in front of the seam and the strands are spread out to cover 2.5cm (1in) behind the front pin. Take the sides down so that they cover the face as illustrated, and pin the ends to the back of the head, behind the seam.

Prepare another skein in the same way and pin the centre behind the first skein, so that it covers the remaining 2.5cm (1in) between the first skein and the seam. Take the sides down behind, but close against the previous skein and pin the ends behind the first ones.

Wind the yarn twenty times around a 23cm (9in) deep card. Tie as before and then pin the centre behind the second skein, over the centre back seam. Take the sides down behind the previous skein and pin as before.

Wind the yarn twenty times around a 20cm (8in) deep card. Tie the edges *and* the centre tightly, then pin the centre behind the third skein and take the sides down together, pinning the ends at the nape of the neck to cover the back of the head.

Adjust the pins if necessary, then stitch the centres and ends of the skeins securely to the head, using a long darning needle and double thread.

21. Make a *very* narrow double hem all round the edge of the mob cap.

Mark the broken line indicated on the pattern; the easiest way to do this is to cut a 26cm (10in) circle out of stiff paper and pin it to the fabric, centres exactly matching. Then use the circle as a template, drawing lightly round the edge with a pencil. Herringbone-stitch elastic over the marked line, then draw up to fit the head.

Make a butterfly bow from the wide ribbon, points b 7.5cm (3in) from a. Stitch to centre front of cap, just above the elastic.

22. Cut the eyes in brown felt and pin to the face.

Mark the mouth with pins and when you are satisfied with the expression, embroider it in stem (outline) stitch, using three strands of cotton.

Finally, glue the eyes into place.

MOTHER HUBBARD'S DOG

Looking sadly forlorn about the lack of bones, he remains devoted to his loving mistress! If you haven't any cream fur fabric, you will have enough brown for the front as well, to make him one colour all over.

Seam allowance on fur fabric is 4mm (just under ³/₁₆in). *Cutting note:* Arrows indicate *smooth* direction of pile (and straight of fabric).

MATERIALS

Brown fur fabric, 20cm (8in) deep × 50cm (20in) wide
Cream fur fabric, 10cm (4in) deep × 8cm (3in) wide (optional)
Scrap of black felt
Polyester stuffing
Matching sewing threads
Stiff card
Clear adhesive

1. Cut the body twice (reversing the second piece), the ear four times, and the gusset and base once each, in brown fur fabric. Cut the front once in cream (or brown).

Cut the base again, slightly smaller as the broken line, in card.

2. Join the body pieces between A-B.

3. Join the lower edge of the gusset to the top of the front between C-C.

4. Join the gusset and front to each side of the body, matching points B, C and D.

5. Stitch the base round the lower edge, matching points A and E; leave open between A-F, but turn under a narrow hem along both raw edges. Turn to the right side.

6. Stuff firmly, pushing the filling well up into the nose. Slip the card base inside before completing the stuffing, then slip-stitch the edges of the opening together.

7. To make each ear, *oversew (overcast)* two pieces together, leaving open between the notches. Turn to the right side and oversew the raw edges of the opening neatly together.

Stitch to each side of the head as illustrated.

8. Cut the eyes and nose in black felt and glue them into position as illustrated.

9. Release all the fur trapped in the seams by stroking firmly with a pin.

LUCY LOCKET

Very demure in her high-waisted dress patterned with tiny rosebud sprigs, Lucy happily swings her pocket. (It isn't known whether this photograph was taken before or after she lost it!)

You will need a lightweight fabric for this outfit; the fashions of the early nineteenth century, on which this design is based, made much use of very fine cottons and delicate pastel shades.

Once you have found a suitable fabric, always exploit it. For example, Lucy's purple rosebuds on a lilac ground are picked up in the ribbons and her shoes; the fabric for her apron, which has a woven stripe, is in a slightly deeper shade of lilac – and her felt 'pocket' matches it.

MATERIALS

See Chapter 3 for Basic Doll

50cm (⅝ yd) flower-printed lightweight cotton-type fabric for dress, pantalettes and bonnet

16 × 10cm (6¼ × 4in) medium-weight plain or fancy-weave fabric for apron

6 × 17cm (2½ × 6¾in) coloured felt for shoes

8cm (3in) square of beige felt for soles

5 × 10cm (2 × 4in) felt for pocket

2 × 4cm (¾ × 1½in) dark brown felt for eyes

4cm (1½in) diameter circle of heavyweight Vilene or Pellon interlining for bonnet

1.2m (1⅜yd) lace, 10mm (⅜in) deep

1m (1yd) single-face satin ribbon, 6mm (¼in) wide

70cm (⅞yd) satin ribbon, 3mm (⅛in) wide

15cm (6in) bias binding to match dress

Narrow round elastic

Double-knit yarn for hair

Matching and black sewing threads

Stiff card

1. Make the Basic Doll as directed in Chapter 3.
2. Cut the bodice front, the skirt, the bonnet front and the bonnet back, once each in flowered fabric; cut the bodice back, sleeve and pantalettes twice each. Cut the apron once in plain fabric. Cut the bonnet back interlining once in Vilene or Pellon.
3. Join each leg of the pantalettes between A-B. Then, right sides together, join the two pieces between C-A-C. Clip the curved seam carefully. Make a hem along the top, as indicated, turning under the raw edge. Make a narrow hem around the lower edge of each leg, then turn to the right side and trim with two rows of lace, as illustrated.

Thread elastic through the channel at the top and draw up to fit the waist.
4. Join the bodice front to the back pieces at each shoulder. Press the seams open.

5. Gather the top edge of the skirt, across the front and each side of the back, as indicated. Then pin the skirt to the lower edge of the bodice, at front and back, matching side edges, centre fronts, notches and circles. Draw up the gathers to fit, distributing them evenly between the pins, and stitch together. Press the seam up.
6. Join the side edges of each sleeve and press the seam open. Then gather round the top edge as indicated.

Set the sleeves into the armholes, matching the centre top to the shoulder seam and the notches and other points indicated on the pattern. Draw up to fit

Lucy Locket lost her pocket
Kitty Fisher found it;
There was not a penny in it,
But a ribbon round it.

and stitch into place, distributing the gathers evenly.

7. Turn up the lower edge of each sleeve along the line indicated; turn the raw edge narrowly under and hem.

Then herringbone-stitch elastic against the hemline and draw up to fit the arm, knotting securely.

8. Join the centre back seam of the skirt below X.

9. Turn under the centre back edges of the bodice as indicated, and also the edges of the skirt above X; herringbone-stitch over the raw edges.

10. Bind the neck edge, then stitch lace on top to form a stand-up collar. Finally, stitch 3mm (⅛in) wide ribbon over the lower edge of the collar, as illustrated.

11. Fit the dress on the doll to determine the length; pin the hem of the skirt, then remove and herringbone-stitch over the raw edge.

Turn to the right side and trim the hem with one row of lace, over the stitching line.

12. Make a very narrow hem down each side of the apron, then turn the bottom edge under and herringbone-stitch the raw edge.

Trim the right side with a double row of overlapping lace topped with a band of narrow ribbon, as illustrated.

13. Turn the top edge of the apron under, then gather very close to the folded edge and draw up to measure 4cm (1½in).

Pin the apron immediately below the bodice, matching centre fronts and distributing the gathers evenly. Stitch neatly into place.

14. Stitch 6mm (¼in) wide ribbon along the lower edge of the bodice front, as illustrated.

15. Make a butterfly bow to trim each sleeve, using 10cm (4in) of the wider ribbon, and marking points b 3cm (1¼in) from a.

16. Make the shoes as directed for Miss Muffet; step 21.

17. Follow the directions for Mother Hubbard's hair; step 17.

Then wind the yarn twenty-five times around a 4cm (1½in) deep card. Tie tightly at one edge only, then slip the loops off the card. Stitch the tied section to the side of the head under the hair, so that the loops fall as illustrated.

Repeat for the other side of the face.

Make a curl by winding the yarn ten times around your forefinger; catch the loops tightly together with matching thread, then remove from your finger and stitch at the centre top of the forehead, against the hair.

Make three more curls and stitch them across the forehead, below the first one.

Make another three curls and stitch them across the forehead, close under the second row.

Make four curls and stitch them close under the previous row.

Make a final curl and stitch it in the centre of the forehead, close under the last row.

18. Right side inside, fold the bonnet front in half as indicated by the heavy broken line. Make a seam along each short side edge and turn to the right side. Tack the raw back edges together, then press the side seams. Now oversew (overcast) the side edges together between the back edge and X to form the centre back seam.

19. Tack the interlining to the wrong side of the bonnet back, centres matching.

Gather the back edge of the bonnet front. Then, right sides together and raw edges level, pin round the edge of the back piece, centre back seam and notches matching. Draw up the gathers to fit, distributing them evenly between the pins, and stitch into place. Turn the gathers towards the centre of the back, then top-stitch neatly all round the edge of the back circle to hold them in place.

20. Stitch one end of a 15cm (6in) length of the narrower ribbon inside the bonnet at each end of the gathering line, extending beyond the edge to form ties. Then, using a double thread, gather along this line as indicated.

21. Fit the bonnet on the head (mark the centre of the gathering line and pin this point temporarily to the top of the head). Bring the ties round and make a bow under the chin, catching the knot to hold it in place. Draw up the gathers and secure the thread, catching the centre to the top of the head and then distributing the gathers evenly at each side so that the brim frames the face as illustrated.

Stitch a band of the wider ribbon over the gathers.

22. Cut the eyes in brown felt and pin to the face. Make four straight stitches, one on top of the other, about 4mm (³⁄₁₆in) long, level with the bottom of the eyes, for the nose.

Mark the mouth with pins and, when you are satisfied with the expression, embroider it in stem (outline) stitch, using three strands of cotton.

Finally, glue the eyes into place.

23. Cut the pocket twice in felt.

Make a rose (see Made-to-Match Trims) from 20cm (8in) of the wider ribbon, and stitch to the right side of one pocket piece, the centre of the rose at 0, as illustrated.

Wrong sides together, oversew the two pieces neatly all round the curved edge.

Gather 15cm (6in) lace and stitch round the straight top edge.

Stitch the ends of a 15cm (6in) length of the narrow ribbon inside, at each end of the top opening, to form a handle. Stitch the handle securely around her wrist and hand, as illustrated.

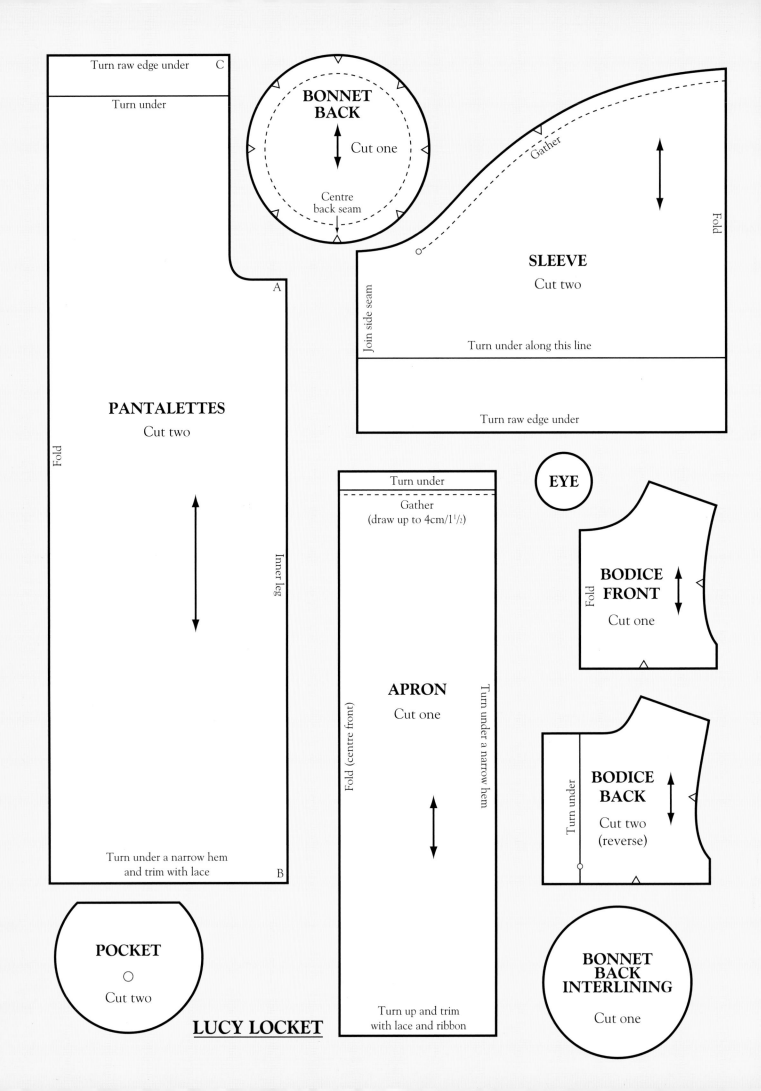

Turn raw edge under   C

Turn under

BONNET BACK

Cut one

Centre back seam

Gather

SLEEVE

Cut two

Join side seam

Turn under along this line

Turn raw edge under

PANTALETTES

Cut two

Fold

Inner leg

Turn under

Gather
(draw up to 4cm/1½)

EYE

BODICE FRONT

Cut one

Fold

A

Fold (centre front)

APRON

Cut one

Turn under a narrow hem

BODICE BACK

Cut two
(reverse)

Turn under

Turn under a narrow hem
and trim with lace   B

POCKET

○

Cut two

Turn up and trim
with lace and ribbon

LUCY LOCKET

BONNET BACK INTERLINING

Cut one

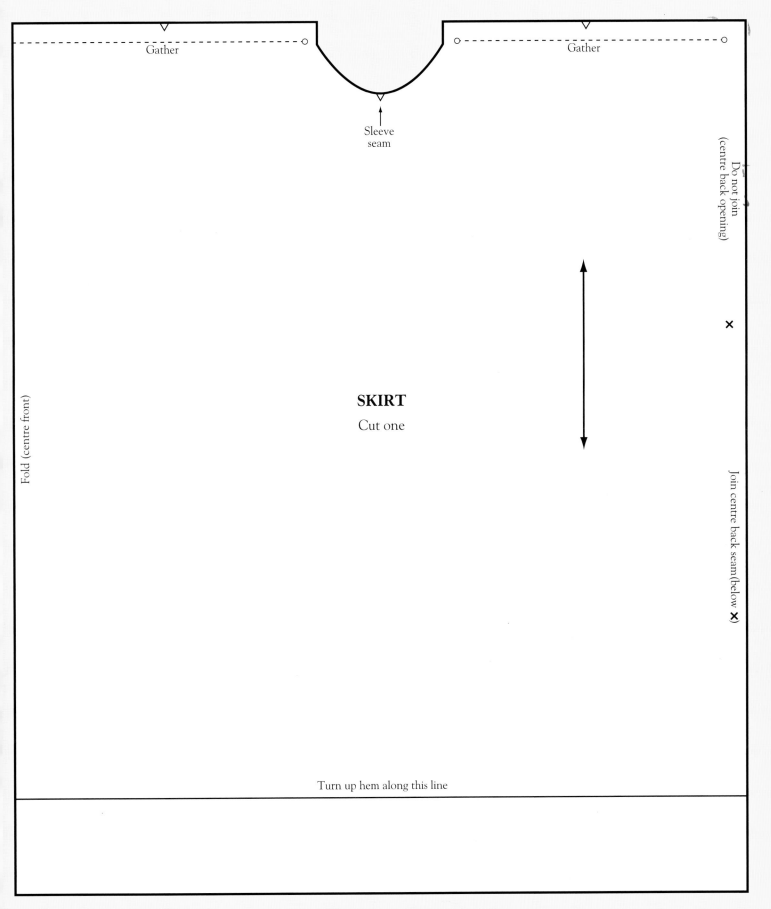

Gather

Sleeve
seam

Do not join
(centre back opening)

×

Fold (centre front)

SKIRT

Cut one

Join centre back seam(below ×)

Turn up hem along this line

LUCY LOCKET

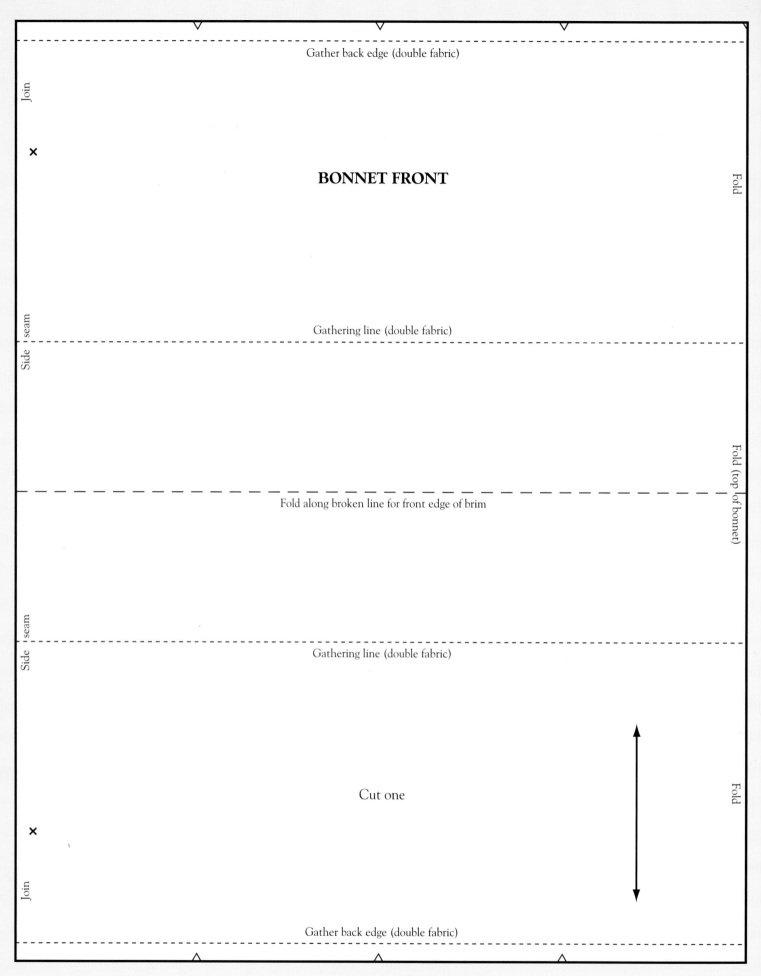

Gather back edge (double fabric)

Join

Fold

BONNET FRONT

Side seam

Gathering line (double fabric)

Fold (top of bonnet)

Fold along broken line for front edge of brim

Side seam

Gathering line (double fabric)

Cut one

Fold

Join

Gather back edge (double fabric)

LUCY LOCKET

CHAPTER 6

Storybook Favourites

A trio of very different cuddle-and-hug characters with one thing in common: they're all the stuff that the best bedtime stories are made of! A happy-go-lucky cowboy, a daffy scarecrow and a bloodthirsty pirate combine to give you a wide choice. But you will still be using the same basic doll pattern; just see what can be done with clever characterisation! Using these examples to stimulate your imagination, think of other fictional heroes and villains for which the basic doll would adapt equally well.

COWBOY JOE

Men never seem to lose their obsession with the Wild West. So to start off the youngest male in the family, here's Cowboy Joe, who might have stepped out of any classic Western. When he remembers where he left his horse, he'll be rounding up cattle with the best of them!

His hair is a particularly thick (Aran) yarn, but if you prefer to use ordinary double-knit, simply increase the number of strands accordingly. Use an extra thick felt for his hat; if you can't find any, bond two pieces together for the brim (using Bondaweb/Wunder-Under) before cutting it out. Choose a very fine cotton for his scarf. Ideally, use the corner of an inexpensive handkerchief, as in the photograph. If the doll is for a *very* young child, omit the belt buckle, just neatly gluing the ends of the ribbon.

MATERIALS

See Chapter 3 for Basic Doll
15 × 60cm (6 × 24in) check gingham for shirt
12cm (4¾in) square of lightweight cotton-type fabric for scarf (see above)
20 × 30cm (8 × 12in) mid-blue felt for jeans
15cm (6in) square of green felt for waistcoat (vest)
25 × 40cm (10 × 16in) mid-brown felt for hat
20cm (8in) square of dark brown felt for boots and eyes
25cm (10in) dark brown grosgrain ribbon, 15mm (⅝in) wide, for belt
35cm (14in) striped grosgrain ribbon, 15mm (⅝in) wide, for hat-band
1m (1⅛yd) satin ribbon, 1.5mm (1/16in) wide, in each of three colours, to trim waistcoat
or 90cm (1yd) very narrow braid
10cm (4in) narrow gold braid, for belt buckle
Thick-knit Aran yarn (or alternative) for hair
Matching and black sewing threads
Scrap of thin card
Clear adhesive

1. Make the Basic Doll as directed in Chapter 3.
2. Cut the shirt front once, and the back and sleeve twice each, in gingham. Cut the jeans twice in blue felt. Cut the waistcoat (vest) back once, and the front twice, in green felt. Cut the boot upper four times, and the sole twice, in dark brown felt. And cut the hat brim once, and the crown twice, in mid-brown felt.
3. Wrong side inside, fold the front of the shirt along the central fold line and stitch through the double fabric along the line indicated. Open out the tuck you have just made, aligning the centre fold line with the seam; top-stitch neatly along this line, then press.
4. Join the front to the back pieces at each shoulder. Press the seams open.

5. Gather round the top edge of each sleeve, as indicated. Then set into the armholes, matching the sides, notches and centre top of sleeve to the shoulder seam. Draw up the gathers to fit, then stitch into place, distributing the gathers evenly. Clip the curved seam carefully.
6. Join the sleeve and side seams of the shirt.
7. Turn under the centre back edges of the shirt as indicated; herringbone-stitch over the raw edges.
8. Bind the neck neatly.
9. Fit the shirt on the doll to determine the length of the sleeves. Then turn the raw edges under accordingly and herringbone-stitch over them.
10. Fit the shirt on the doll again; overlap the centre back edges and slip-stitch together.
11. Pull the shirt smoothly down and catch the lower edge all round the body.
12. Join the inner leg seam of each jeans piece between A-B. Then, right sides together, join the two pieces between C-A-C. Turn to the right side.
13. Turn the top edge under, as indicated, and pin. Fit the jeans on the doll to check that the top edge is positioned around the hips, as illustrated. If not, adjust the pins.
14. Gather round the top edge, close to the fold; draw up the gathers to fit, then catch the top edge of the jeans to his shirt.
15. Gather the lower edge of each leg and draw the jeans up neatly around the ankles.
16. Glue a ribbon belt over the top edge of the jeans, ends meeting in a wide V-shape at the front.

Glue a square of ribbon to thin card, then cut the card about 1.5mm (1/16in) larger all round. Glue narrow gold braid around the edge to form a buckle, then glue over the ribbon ends, as illustrated.
17. To make each boot, join two uppers between the notch and the lower edge. Then join the centre front seam, matching the double notches.
18. Fit the sole around the lower edge, matching the notches to the centre front and back seams, then oversew (overcast) together. Turn to the right side.
19. Fit the boot on the doll, over the jeans. Then oversew the remainder of the centre back seam neatly.
20. Join the waistcoat (vest) fronts to the back, oversewing the shoulder and side seams. Turn to the right side and press the seams flat.

Make plaited braid, or use very narrow purchased braid (cut in half, if necessary). Glue all round the outer edge, then glue a second band just inside the first one, as illustrated (leaving a space between that is approximately the width of the braid itself).

Fit waistcoat on doll and catch the shoulder seams to the figure to hold in position.

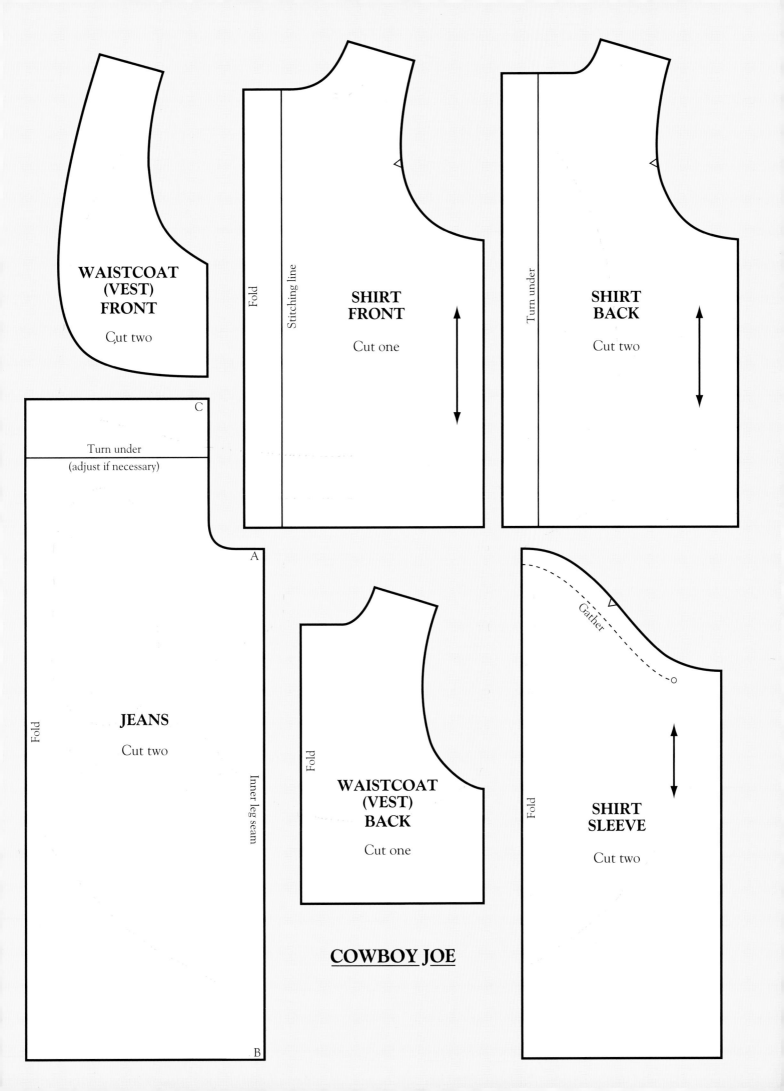

**WAISTCOAT
(VEST)
FRONT**

Cut two

Fold

Stitching line

**SHIRT
FRONT**

Cut one

Turn under

**SHIRT
BACK**

Cut two

C

Turn under
(adjust if necessary)

A

Fold

JEANS

Cut two

Inner leg seam

B

Fold

**WAISTCOAT
(VEST)
BACK**

Cut one

Gather

Fold

**SHIRT
SLEEVE**

Cut two

COWBOY JOE

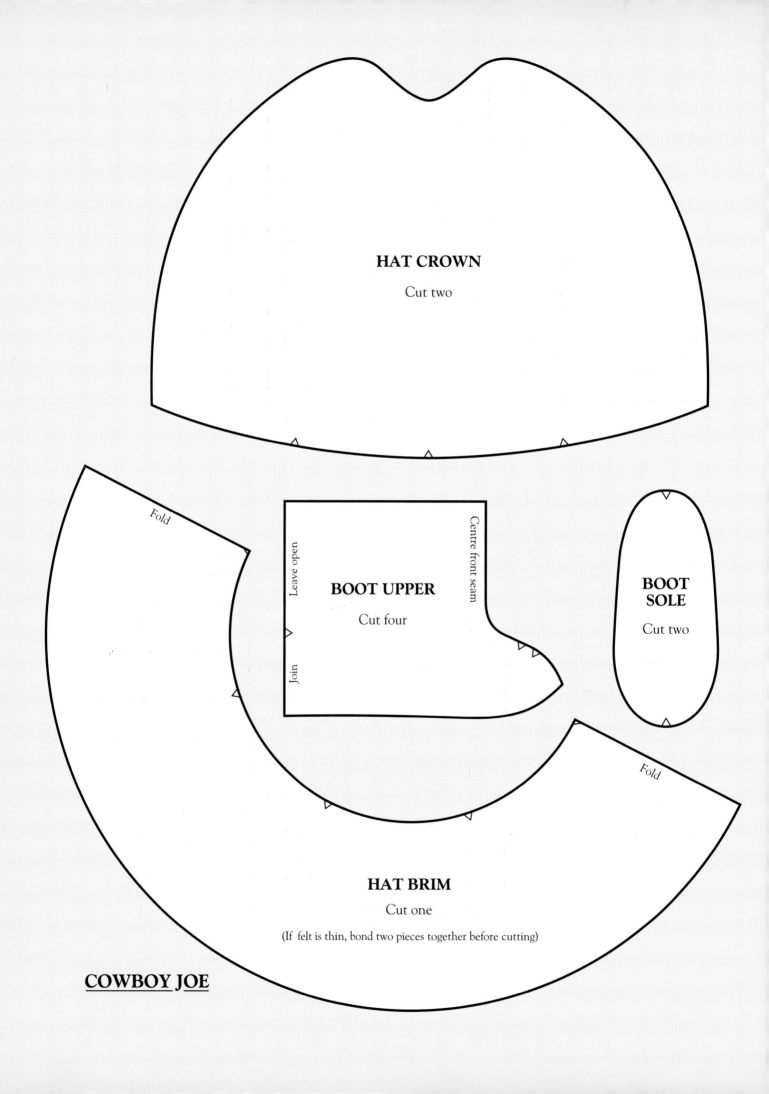

HAT CROWN

Cut two

Fold

BOOT UPPER

Cut four

Leave open

Centre front seam

Join

BOOT SOLE

Cut two

HAT BRIM

Cut one

(If felt is thin, bond two pieces together before cutting)

Fold

COWBOY JOE

21. Make a very narrow hem along two adjoining edges of a 12cm (4³/₄in) square of fabric: if using the corner of a handkerchief, cut it slightly smaller and use the existing hem on two sides, leaving the other edges raw.

Fold in half diagonally, wrong side inside, and drape round the neck as illustrated, catching the corners together at the back.

22. Cut about fifty 23cm (9in) long strands of thick-knit yarn (you will need more if using double-knit). Place the strands over the top of the head so that they hang down 8-9cm (3¼-3½in) over the forehead (in front of the seam), with the remainder hanging down over the back of the head.

Cut a 30cm (12in) long strand of yarn and place it across the strands, level with the seam, the ends hanging down equally at each side. Pin this strand to the head, over the seam, 11cm (4½in) from each end, leaving 8cm (3in) taut across the top of the head: spread the strands out evenly under this single strand. Then, using double matching thread, stitch everything securely to the head, over the seam.

Cut fifty more strands (or the same number as be-fore), but this time 30cm (12in) long. Tie them loosely at the centre. Place the strands across the first set, so that they hang down equally at each side; stitch the tied centre to the crown of the head, just behind the seam.

Spread all the strands out evenly over the head, gluing lightly to hold in place. Trim the ends neatly all round (but not *too* neatly; remember he's an energetic cowboy!).

23. Cut the eyes in brown felt and pin to the face. Make four straight stitches, one on top of the other, about 4mm (³/₁₆in) long, level with the bottom of the eyes, for the nose.

Mark the mouth with pins and, when you are satisfied with the expression, embroider it in stem (out-line) stitch, using three strands of cotton.

Finally, glue the eyes into place.

24. Join the two crown pieces of the hat, leaving the lower curved edge open. Pin the lower edge around the inner edge of the brim, matching notches and seams. Oversew together and turn to the right side.

Glue ribbon around base of crown, join at back.

PERCY PARSNIP – THE SCARECROW

A hotch-potch of clothes and colours characterises the traditional scarecrow (see page 73), so of course Percy Parsnip should look as if he's escaped from a jumble sale! Surprisingly, this makes careful planning even more important: so put all your proposed fabrics together in order to study the effect before you cut anything out. Whilst you want to avoid matching and toning colours and textures, an attractive doll needs clever design to achieve a harmonious mix; make sure all your colours and fabrics work well together, how-ever casual and unplanned Percy's garments may *appear* to be.

Obviously, his clothes will have been old and drab before he inherited them – faded still further by exposure to all kinds of weather out in the fields. So if you're going for the authentic scarecrow look, his gar-ments will be in dull, muted tones. To this generally sombre background, add bright flashes of contrasting colour – for his patterned waistcoat, silk scarf and handkerchief, and the felt flower and ribbon band on his hat.

Make the basic doll in a muddy shade of beige – not forgetting to add his button nose! Use black felt for the eyes, and embroider his broad grin in a brighter shade of red than usual.

MATERIALS

See Chapter 3 for Basic Doll (use beige felt – as above)
25 × 40cm (10 × 16in) medium-weight cotton-type, or lightweight wool, check fabric for trousers
15 × 30cm (6 × 12in) medium-weight cotton-type striped fabric for shirt sleeves
12cm (5in) square of medium-weight cotton-type flowered fabric (or use felt) for waistcoat (vest)
5 × 25cm (2 × 10in) lightweight silky fabric for scarf
5cm (2in) square of lightweight silky fabric for handkerchief
20 × 60cm (8 ×24in) wine felt for coat
25 × 45cm (10 × 18in) grey felt for hat
15 × 20cm (6 × 8in) black felt for boots and eyes
6cm (2½in) square of bright pink and a scrap of yellow felt, for flower
Scraps of felt for patches
20 × 35cm (8 × 14in) heavyweight Vilene or Pellon interlining for hat and fabric waistcoat
Vilene Bondaweb or Wunder-Under for hat and fabric waistcoat
40cm (½yd) narrow braid (about 5mm/¼in wide) for waistcoat
40cm (½yd) grosgrain ribbon, 20mm (³/₄in) wide, for hat
40cm (½yd) thin string
Rough-textured double-knit yarn for hair
Matching sewing threads
Clear adhesive

1. Make the Basic Doll as directed in Chapter 3 (see above for colour of felt).

2. Cut the trousers twice in check fabric. Cut the shirt sleeve twice in striped fabric. Cut the coat front, back, sleeve and pocket flap twice each in wine felt. Cut the boot upper four times, and the sole twice, in black felt.

3. Join each trouser leg between A-B. Then, right sides together, join the two pieces between C-A-C. Clip the curved seam, then turn to the right side. Turn under the top edge as indicated and gather close to the fold.

4. Fit the trousers on the doll to determine the length; turn up leg hems and herringbone-stitch over the raw edges.

5. Cut square patches in felt and glue to the knees.

6. Fit trousers on doll again; draw up gathers around the waist and secure.

7. Tie string around each leg, knotting at the sides, as illustrated.

8. To make each boot, join two uppers between the notch and the lower edge. Then join the centre front seam, matching the double notches. Turn to the right side.

9. Fit the sole around the lower edge, matching the notches to the centre front and back seams, then oversew (overcast) together.

10. Fit the boot on the doll. Then oversew the remainder of the back seam neatly.

11. Draw threads to fray the lower edge of each sleeve, as indicated. Then join the side seam. Turn to the right side. Gather the top edge as indicated.

12. Fit the sleeves on the arms and draw up the gathers; stitch to body to hold in place.

13. Bond the waistcoat fabric to Vilene or Pellon, or felt, and cut out. Glue braid over the neck and lower edges, and down the centre front.

14. Pin the waistcoat into position, then stitch the shoulder and side seams to the body.

15. Knot the scarf around the neck, tucking the ends into the waistcoat.

16. Join the centre back seam of the coat. Then join the front pieces to the back at the shoulders.

17. Gather the top edge of each sleeve as indicated. Set the sleeves into the armholes, matching the side edges, notches and centre top of sleeve to the shoulder seam. Draw up the gathers to fit, then stitch into place, distributing the gathers evenly.

18. Join the sleeve and side seams of the coat. Press all the seams, then turn to the right side.

19. Pin the pocket flaps to the coat as indicated, then appliqué along the top edge.

20. Cut a slit in the coat under one pocket flap, as indicated. Fray the edges of the handkerchief, then draw one corner through the slit and catch it inside the coat so that the remainder protrudes as illustrated.

21. Cut oval felt patches and glue to elbows.

22. Fit coat on doll.

23. The yarn used for the hair of the doll in the photograph is a rough-textured double-knit, which gives a very pleasing effect for this particular character. However, if you can't find anything similar, just use a plain double-knit; but *don't* trim the ends level – the untidier it is, the better!

Cut about sixty 25cm (10in) long strands of yarn and tie loosely at the centre with a single strand. Place on top of the head, the ends hanging down at each side; spread the tied centre out to cover about 4cm (1½in), then stitch securely into place with double thread.

Spread the strands out evenly to cover the sides and back of the head, gluing lightly to hold in place.

24. Cut the hat side and crown in grey felt and bond to Vilene or Pellon, cutting it level with the edge of the felt.

Cut the brim in felt and bond it to another piece of felt. Cut the outer edge level, but cut a smaller circle in the centre, as indicated by the broken line on the pattern. Cut the surplus felt into small tabs, as shown.

25. Glue the tabs to the back of the side strip, along the lower edge, curving it round to fit; glue the overlap.

26. Pin the crown to the top edge of the side piece, then oversew neatly together.

27. Cut the nose in the felt you used for the basic doll and gather with tiny stitches close to the edge. Place a tiny ball of stuffing in the centre, then draw up the gathers tightly round it and secure the thread.

28. Cut the eyes in black felt. Then fit the hat on the head to determine the position of the nose and eyes, pinning them into place. At the same time mark the mouth with pins.

29. When you are satisfied, remove the hat and stitch the nose into place. Embroider the mouth in stem (outline) stitch, using three strands of cotton, and glue the eyes into position.

30. Replace the hat and stitch it securely all round the head, just above the brim, using double thread and a long darning needle.

31. Glue ribbon around the hat, join at the back.

32. Cut five flower petals in pink felt, and the centre circle in yellow. Glue the inner points of the petals to the back of the circle, meeting in the middle and evenly spaced.

Glue the flower to the hat, as illustrated.

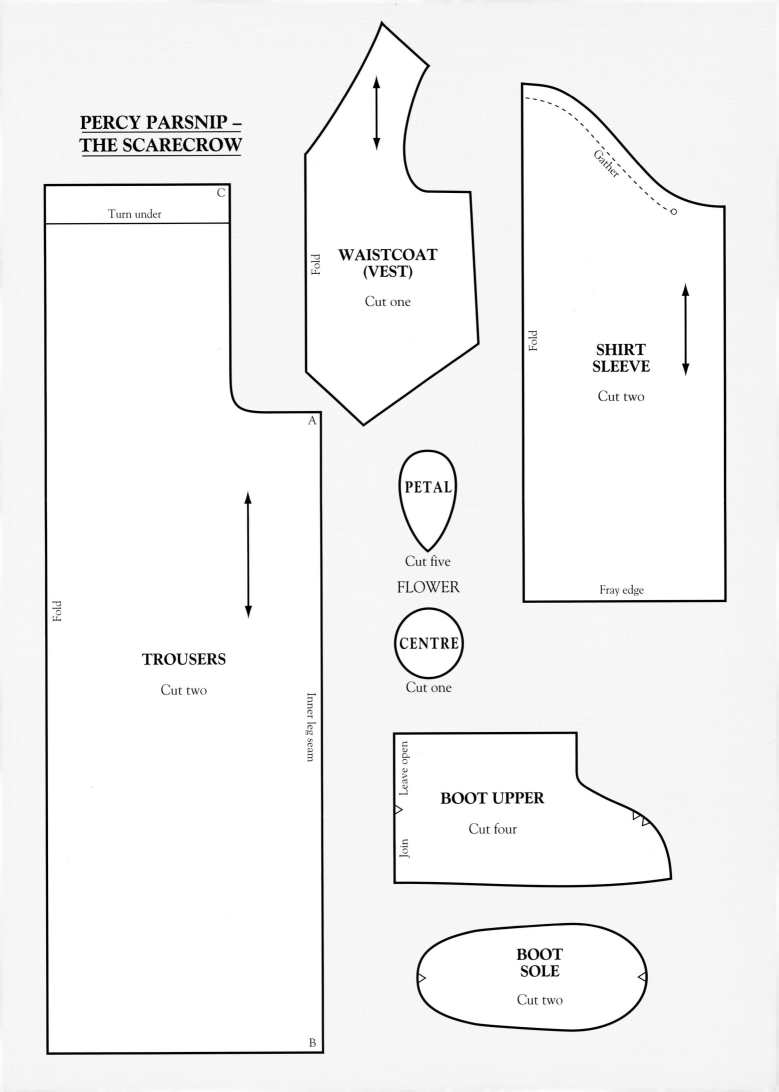

**PERCY PARSNIP –
THE SCARECROW**

Turn under

C

A

Fold

TROUSERS

Cut two

Inner leg seam

B

Fold

**WAISTCOAT
(VEST)**

Cut one

PETAL

Cut five

FLOWER

CENTRE

Cut one

Gather

Fold

**SHIRT
SLEEVE**

Cut two

Fray edge

Leave open

Join

BOOT UPPER

Cut four

**BOOT
SOLE**

Cut two

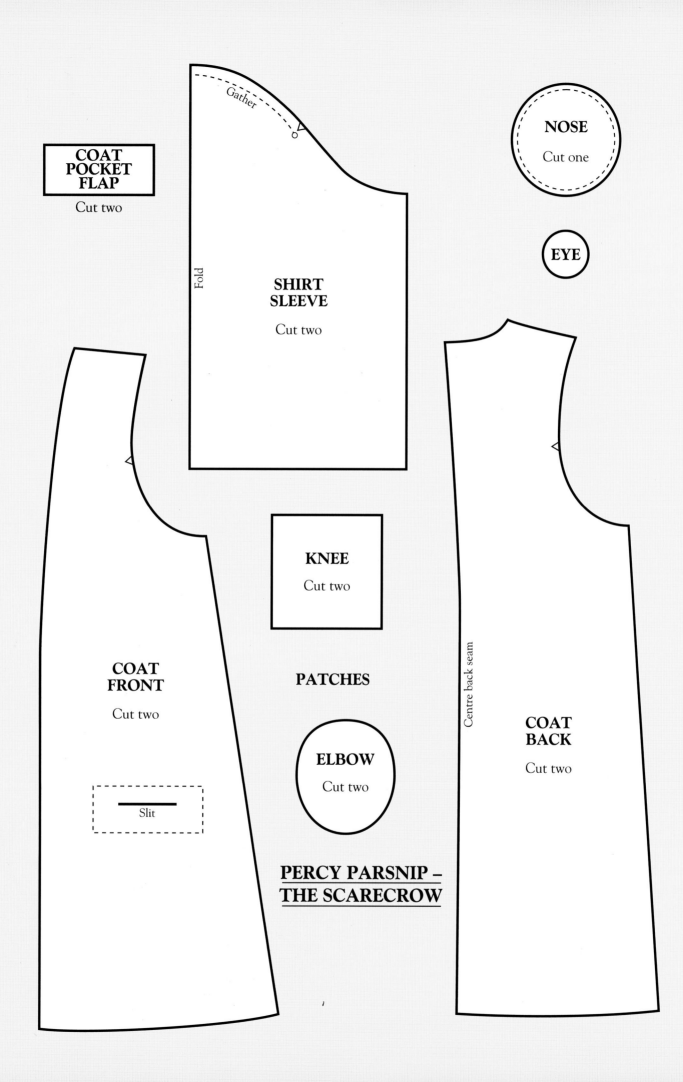

COAT POCKET FLAP

Cut two

Gather

Fold

SHIRT SLEEVE

Cut two

NOSE

Cut one

EYE

KNEE

Cut two

COAT FRONT

Cut two

Slit

PATCHES

ELBOW

Cut two

Centre back seam

COAT BACK

Cut two

PERCY PARSNIP – THE SCARECROW

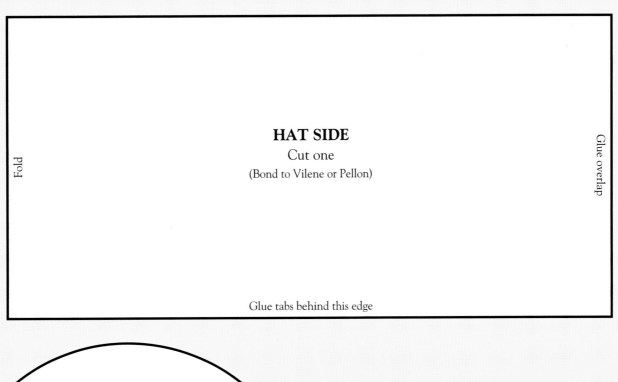

HAT SIDE
Cut one
(Bond to Vilene or Pellon)

Fold

Glue overlap

Glue tabs behind this edge

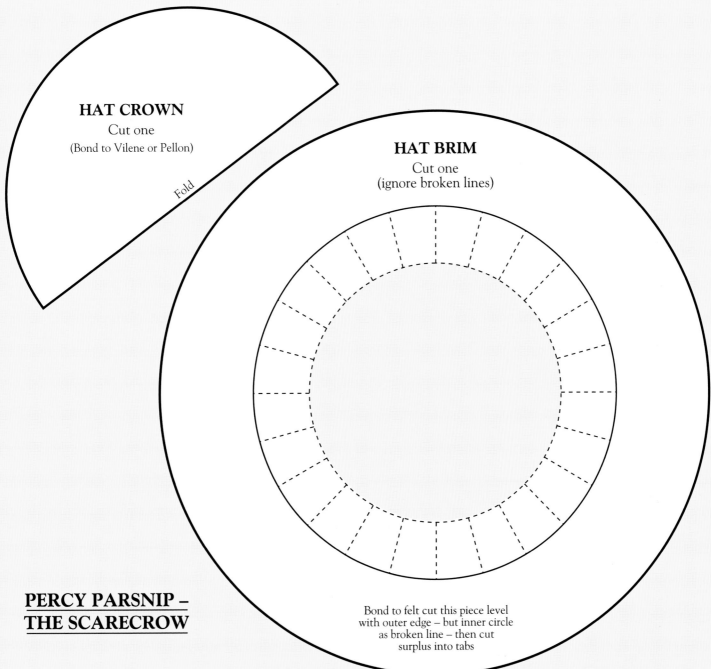

HAT CROWN
Cut one
(Bond to Vilene or Pellon)

Fold

HAT BRIM
Cut one
(ignore broken lines)

Bond to felt cut this piece level
with outer edge – but inner circle
as broken line – then cut
surplus into tabs

**PERCY PARSNIP –
THE SCARECROW**

BLACK JAKE – THE PIRATE

Make up the Basic Doll pattern in the usual way, but cut the hand and arm separately and make the figure up using different felts as indicated below. Combine felt and fabric in an assortment of strong colours, dramatised by his curly black beard.

MATERIALS

20 × 30cm (8 × 12in) cream felt for the head and hands
13 × 40cm (5 × 16in) red felt for the body and arms
20 × 30cm (8 × 12in) yellow felt for the legs
See Chapter 3 for Basic Doll, excluding felt (above)
18 × 35cm (7 × 14in) green felt for the breeches
20 × 60cm (8 × 24in) dark blue felt for the coat
15 × 20cm (6 × 8in) black felt for shoes, eye and eye-patch
12 × 18cm (5 × 7in) silky fabric for the cummerbund
27cm (10½in) square of medium-weight cotton-type fabric for the headscarf
Cream braid, about 8-10mm (5/16-3/8in) wide, to trim coat; 40cm (½yd) full-width and 80cm (1yd) half-width (step 12)
18cm (7in) narrow round black elastic
Black 'chunky' thick-knit yarn for beard
Matching sewing threads
Clear adhesive
Stiff card

1. Make up the Basic Doll as directed in Chapter 3, using red felt for the body and arms, and yellow for the legs and soles.
2. Cut the breeches twice in green felt. Cut the coat front, back, sleeve, cuff and pocket flap twice each, in dark blue. Cut the cummerbund once in silky fabric. Cut the shoe upper four times, the sole twice, and the eye and patch once each, in black felt. Cut the nose once in flesh felt.
3. Join the inner leg seam of each breeches piece between A-B. Right sides together, join the two pieces together between C-A-C. Gather round the top edge, and round the bottom of each leg, as indicated.
4. Without turning to the right side, fit the breeches upside-down on the doll, so that the waist hangs down below the feet. Draw up the gathers tightly around the legs, just below knee level, and stitch securely to the leg, distributing the gathers evenly. Pull the breeches up, turning them to the right side, and draw up the top gathers evenly round the waist.
5. Right side inside, join the two long edges of the cummerbund. Turn to the right side and pin so that the seam is in the middle, level with the centre fold line on the pattern. Turn in the raw edges at each end and pin. Then gather each end, close to the edge, and draw up tightly.

6. Wrap the cummerbund round the waist, seam inside, over the top edge of the breeches, and join the two ends at the back, overlapping them as necessary.
7. Join the centre back seam of the coat. Then join the front pieces to the back at the shoulders.
8. Gather the top edge of each sleeve as indicated. Set the sleeves into the armholes, matching the side edges, notches and centre top of sleeve to the shoulder seam. Draw up the gathers to fit, then stitch into place, distributing the gathers evenly.
9. Join the sleeve and side seams of the coat. Press all the seams.
10. Join a cuff to the bottom of each sleeve, lower edges level and matching the notch to the seam; oversew (overcast) together, then turn to the right side.
    Turn the cuff up over the sleeve and oversew the side edges together.
11. Pin the pocket flaps to the coat as indicated, then appliqué along the top edge.
12. Glue wider braid along the centre front edges and around back of neck. Then cut the braid in half, or use narrower braid, and glue around the cuffs and pocket flaps as illustrated.
13. Fit the coat on the doll.
14. To make each shoe, join the centre back seam of two upper pieces. Then join the centre front seam, matching the double notches. Turn to the right side.
15. Fit the sole round the lower edge, matching the notches to the centre front and back seams, then oversew together.
16. Gather the top edge as indicated; fit shoe on the doll and draw up the gathers, catching the shoe securely at each side of the foot.
17. Cut a piece of stiff card 4cm (1½in) deep × about 18cm (7in) wide (see pattern) to make the beard; mark the centre section 13cm (5in) wide, as shown. Cut a 20cm (8in) length of yarn; place it along the top of your card, as indicated, extending at each end, and tape it to the card to hold it in place. Now wind yarn evenly round the card, keeping the strands very close together, beginning and ending at the marked lines.
    Using double matching thread, stitch along the top edge, catching the strands together and also taking in the horizontal strand; work back over your first line of stitches. Then slide the yarn carefully off the card.
18. Pin the loops round the lower half of the face as illustrated, the ends of the horizontal strand held at each side of the head.
19. Gather round the nose with tiny stitches close to the edge. Place a tiny ball of stuffing in the centre, then draw up the gathers tightly round it and secure the thread. Pin to the centre of the face, just above the beard.

20. Fold the patch in half, as indicated; place the elastic inside the fold, then glue the felt together below it, avoiding the elastic. Knot each end of the elastic and pin them to the head, positioning the patch as illustrated.

21. Pin the eye to the other side of the face.

22. Adjust the beard, nose, patch and eye if necessary; when you are satisfied with their positions, glue the beard, eye and patch to the face. Stitch the ends of the single strand of yarn, the knotted ends of the elastic, and the nose, securely into place.

Pirate and Scarecrow

23. Cut the edge of the headscarf with pinking shears or draw threads to neaten the raw edges. Then fold one corner under as in the diagram. Wrap the diagonal fold around the head as illustrated, pinning the ends of the fold to the back of the head. Stitch securely to hold in position, then pleat and fold the free fabric neatly in round the back of the head, catching the edges down; gather the remaining corner fabric together at the side of the head, as in the photograph.

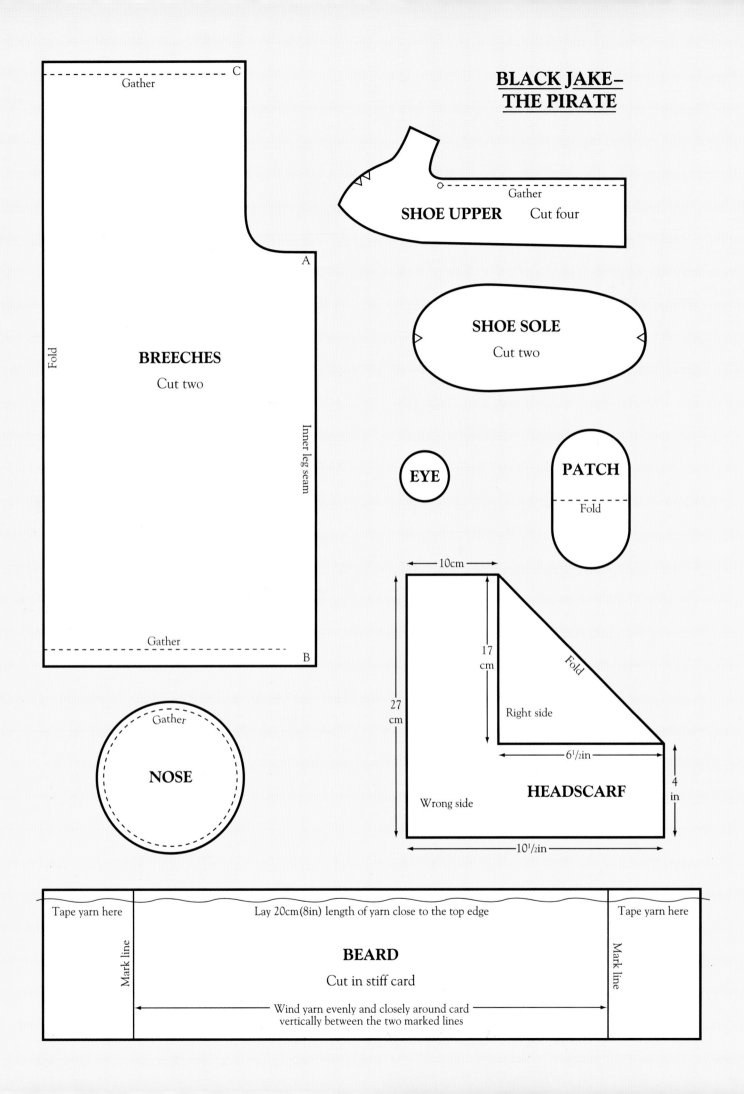

**BLACK JAKE–
THE PIRATE**

Gather — C

Fold

BREECHES

Cut two

Inner leg seam

Gather

A

B

SHOE UPPER Gather Cut four

SHOE SOLE

Cut two

EYE

PATCH

Fold

NOSE

Gather

←10cm→

27
cm

17
cm

Fold

Right side

6½in

4
in

Wrong side

HEADSCARF

10½in

Tape yarn here   Lay 20cm(8in) length of yarn close to the top edge   Tape yarn here

Mark line

BEARD

Cut in stiff card

Mark line

Wind yarn evenly and closely around card
vertically between the two marked lines

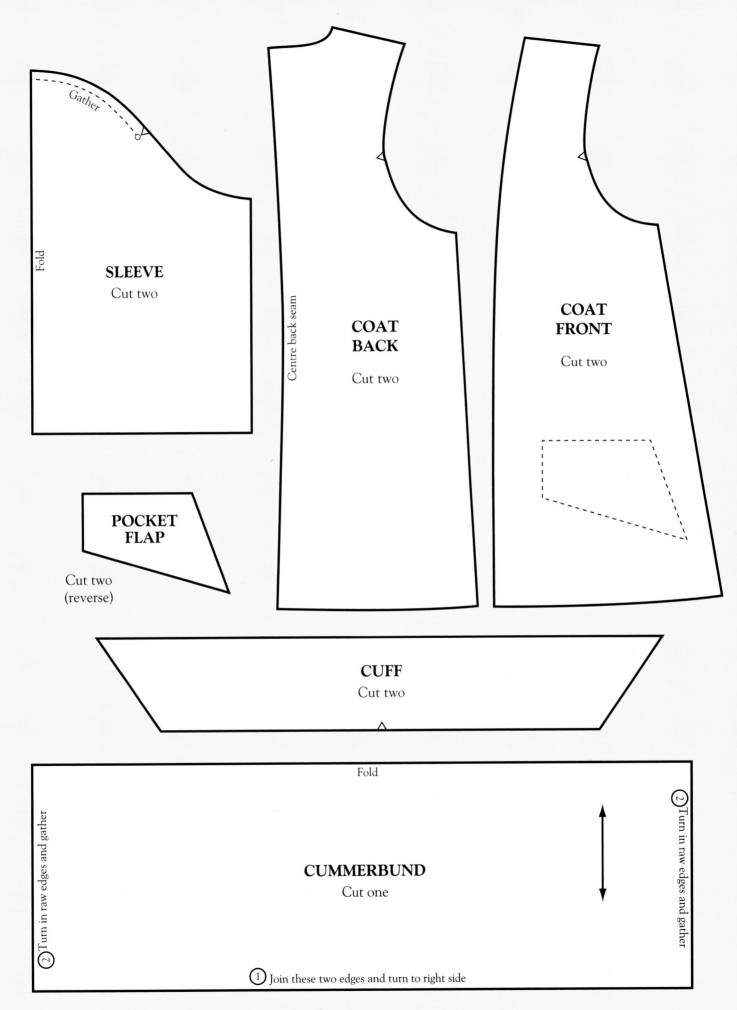

SLEEVE
Cut two

Gather

Fold

Centre back seam

COAT BACK
Cut two

COAT FRONT
Cut two

POCKET FLAP

Cut two
(reverse)

CUFF
Cut two

Fold

②Turn in raw edges and gather

②Turn in raw edges and gather

CUMMERBUND
Cut one

①Join these two edges and turn to right side

BLACK JAKE – THE PIRATE

CHAPTER 7

Amy-Louise, the Rag Doll

To end this section, here is Amy-Louise – the ultimate rag doll. She has all the essential elements of the traditional rag doll: simplicity and an old-fashioned charm. But these are coupled with the sophistication of an alluring hairstyle which emphasises her starry eyes, a fashion-conscious figure – and a wardrobe of feminine clothes to show it off.

Medium-weight cream poplin was used for the doll in the photograph, but any similar fabric, including calico, would do as well. A firmly woven, but fairly soft fabric will give better results, as any tendency to stiffness will prevent the gently rounded moulding of the head, body and limbs. A very thick 'chunky' knitting yarn is particularly effective for her hair. But if you can't find anything similar, use ordinary double-knit, increasing the number of strands accordingly.

Her slender neck is improved by some form of stiffening, but beware of using anything that might be dangerous if the doll is intended for a young child. A short length of split bamboo garden cane, well surrounded by stuffing, is ideal if the doll is for an older child or adult, but would not be suitable for a small child, or if you are selling your work. In this case, the kind of small plastic spatula that is supplied with certain adhesive makes a very good substitute, as there are no sharp ends that could penetrate the fabric. Position the flexible spreader end in the back of the neck and base of the head.

SEAM ALLOWANCE (FOR DOLL AND GARMENTS): *make 5mm (¹⁄₄in) seams, then trim edges (preferably with pinking shears), and clip curves. Press open. To join felt, oversew (overcast) the edges; approximately 1.5mm (¹⁄₁₆in) allowed. Press seams flat with your thumbnail.*

Amy-Louise is here wearing her flowered winter-dress, bonnet, cloak and muff. Also shown are her Victorian nightdress, matching petticoat, pantalettes and camisole, with two sets of slippers.

BASIC DOLL

MATERIALS

30cm (12in) cream medium-weight cotton-type fabric,
90cm (36in) wide (see above)
Polyester stuffing
Very thick ('chunky') knitting yarn for her hair, or
alternative (see above)
2 × 4cm (3/4 × 1½in) dark brown felt for the eyes
Pinky-red stranded embroidery cotton (floss)
Matching, and black and white, sewing threads
Stiffening for neck (optional: see above)
Stiff card
Clear adhesive

1. Cut the back once, following the pattern: then cut the pattern again for the front, but cut straight across the lower edge, as indicated. Cut the arm and leg four times each, and the sole twice (reverse arm and leg patterns if fabric is not reversible).

2. Mark darts on the *back* of the head, and notches and circles on the *front*; mark notches at the top of the arms and on the soles.

3. On the wrong side of the fabric, pin and stitch the darts round the back of the head. Gather round the front of the head, beginning and ending at the circles. Right sides together, pin the darts to correspond with the notches, then draw up the gathers to fit, distributing them evenly between the pins.

4. Join the front to the back all round the outer edge, leaving only the lower edge open. Trim seams and clip curves, taking special care round the neck to prevent the fabric pulling or fraying. Turn to the right side.

5. To make each leg, join two pieces along the front and back seams, leaving the upper and lower edges open. Fit the sole inside the lower edge, matching notches to seams, and stitch neatly into position. Trim and clip all seams, and turn to the right side.

6. To make each arm, join two pieces all round the outer edge, leaving open between the notches. Trim the seam, clipping carefully at the wrist, then turn to the right side.

7. Stuff the head very firmly, moulding it into shape with your hands (and inserting stiffening if wished); then the body, pushing the filling well up into the neck. Turn in and tack the raw lower edges, marking the centre of each with a pin.

Stuff the arms firmly, then turn in the raw edges (tack if necessary) and slip-stitch together. Stuff each leg, then gather across the top edge, placing the front and back seams together so that they meet at the centre.

8. Pin the lower edge of the front over the raw top edge of each leg (feet forward), then stitch securely. Now pin the lower edge of the back over the backs of the legs and stitch again, but this time insert more stuffing before you finish stitching, so that the base of the body is firmly filled.

9. Pin and then stitch the tops of the arms very securely to the shoulders, so that they move freely in all directions (use double thread for extra strength).

10. Wind very thick yarn thirty times around a 30cm (12in) deep card (more, if using a thinner yarn). Tie the loops tightly at each edge with single strands of yarn. Then slide the yarn off the card and tie the skein loosely round the centre with another strand.

Place the middle of the skein across the top of the head, overlapping the face so that the back of the skein is level with the seam; have the ends of the centre tie hanging down the back of the head and the knot visible at the top; pin the centre temporarily. Now take the sides of the skein round to the back and knot together the strands of yarn tying the loops. Using double matching thread, stitch the *knot* at the middle of the skein to the top of the head, at the point where the centre dart meets the seam; then stitch the tied ends securely together at the nape of the neck, catching any stray strands smoothly down and stitching the ends neatly to the back of the head.

Wind the yarn twenty-five times around the same card: prepare as before, but this time tie the middle of the skein *tightly*. Stitch the tied centre to the top of the head, close against the first skein. Then take the ends smoothly down and tuck them behind the ends of the first skein, stitching through to hold them in place. Draw any loose strands across to the centre back of the head and stitch them down neatly, catching in any stray ends too.

Wind the yarn again twenty-five times around the card, but this time cut the loops along one edge. Tie the resulting strands in a loose knot at the centre, then stitch this knot to the crown of the head, so that it forms a bun, with the ends hanging down at the back of the head: trim the cut ends neatly to length.

11. Cut the eye twice in felt. Embroider a white star in the centre of each, making four straight stitches with white sewing thread, used double. Pin to the face. Mark the position of the nose with a pin, level with the lower edge of the eyes. Mark the mouth with pins.

When you are satisfied with her expression, embroider the nose, making a straight stitch (about 4mm/⅛in long) with double black sewing thread. Embroider the mouth in stem (outline) stitch, using three strands of embroidery cotton.

Finally, glue the eyes into place.

AMY-LOUISE'S PETTICOAT, PANTALETTES AND CAMISOLE

First essential for any well-dressed rag doll is a dainty set of undies. Amy Louise's underpinnings are the epitome of Victorian modesty, and consist of a petticoat and pantalettes, both of which can be any length you wish, and a matching camisole top. All are lavishly trimmed with lace and ribbon, but here again, the choice is yours: length and decoration will be dictated by what she wears over them. The materials listed below make the set of underwear illustrated.

MATERIALS

45cm (½yd) lightweight cotton-type fabric, 90cm (36in) wide
3m (3⅜yd) lace, about 10mm (⅜in) deep
35cm (14in) satin ribbon, 3mm (⅛in) wide
70cm (¾yd) single-face satin ribbon, 7mm (¼in) wide
Narrow round elastic
2 snap fasteners
Matching sewing threads

1. Cut a piece of fabric for the petticoat 20 × 60cm (8 × 24in), as the diagram. Cut the camisole pattern once, and the pantalettes twice.
2. Join the inner leg seam of each pantalettes piece between A–B. Then, right sides together, join the two pieces between C–A–C.
3. Turn the top edge over, as indicated: turn the raw edge under and hem. Turn to the right side and thread elastic through, drawing it up to fit the waist.
4. Fit the pantalettes on the doll and turn up the leg hems to the required length: herringbone-stitch over the raw edges.
5. Stitch one row of lace overlapping the lower edge of each leg, then two more rows above, as illustrated.
   Trim with three butterfly bows at each side, made from 8cm (3in) of the wider ribbon; points b 2.5cm (1in) from a.
6. Join the side edges of the petticoat to form the centre back seam.
7. Turn the top edge over and make a hem as for the pantalettes (step 3), threading elastic through in the same way.
8. Fit the petticoat on the doll and turn up the hem to the required length; herringbone-stitch over the raw edge.
9. Stitch one row of lace overlapping the lower edge, then another row above.
   Trim with butterfly bows as the pantalettes (step 5).
10. Turn under the centre back edges of the camisole as indicated, and hem.
11. Make very narrow hems along the top and bottom edges.
12. Stitch a row of lace overlapping the top edge. Stitch another row a little lower, half-overlapping the first one.
13. Fit the camisole round the doll and mark the overlap. Stitch snap fasteners at O's.
14. To make each shoulder strap, join two 10cm (4in) pieces of lace by overlapping the straight edges to form a double-edged length about 1.5cm (⅝in) wide. Then stitch narrow ribbon along the centre.
   Fit the camisole on the doll again and pin the shoulder straps into position, slightly angled away from the centre. Stitch securely at front and back.
15. Trim with two butterfly bows as illustrated, made from 7cm (2¾in) lengths of narrow ribbon; points b 2cm (¾in) from a.

AMY-LOUISE'S VICTORIAN NIGHTDRESS

If roses, ribbons and ruffled lace can ensure sweet dreams, Amy-Louise's romantic nightgown must be the perfect choice. Choose a lightweight fabric in a pastel shade, with a delicate floral print; then echo the predominating colours of the pattern in the trimming.

MATERIALS

30cm (12in) lightweight cotton-type fabric, 115cm (45in) wide
1.8m (2yd) lace, 15mm (⅝in) deep
10cm (4in) single-face satin ribbon, 7mm wide, for the rose
25cm (10in) single-face satin ribbon, 7mm wide, for streamers
15cm (6in) matching bias binding
Narrow round elastic
2 snap fasteners
Matching sewing threads

1. Make a pattern for the skirt from a 30cm (12in) square of paper, following the diagram; trace the armhole pattern and use it as a template to draw and cut out the curved shape indicated on the diagram.
2. Cut the skirt and front yoke once each, and the back yoke and sleeve twice each.
3. Mark the top edge of the skirt *front* into four equal sections, then gather. Mark the top edge of each half of the skirt *back* at the centre; gather as before, but begin and end 2cm (¾in) from the side edges of the fabric.
4. Right sides together, pin the lower edge of the front yoke to the top edge of the skirt, matching side edges and marked points to notches: draw up the gathers to fit, distributing them evenly between the pins, and stitch together.

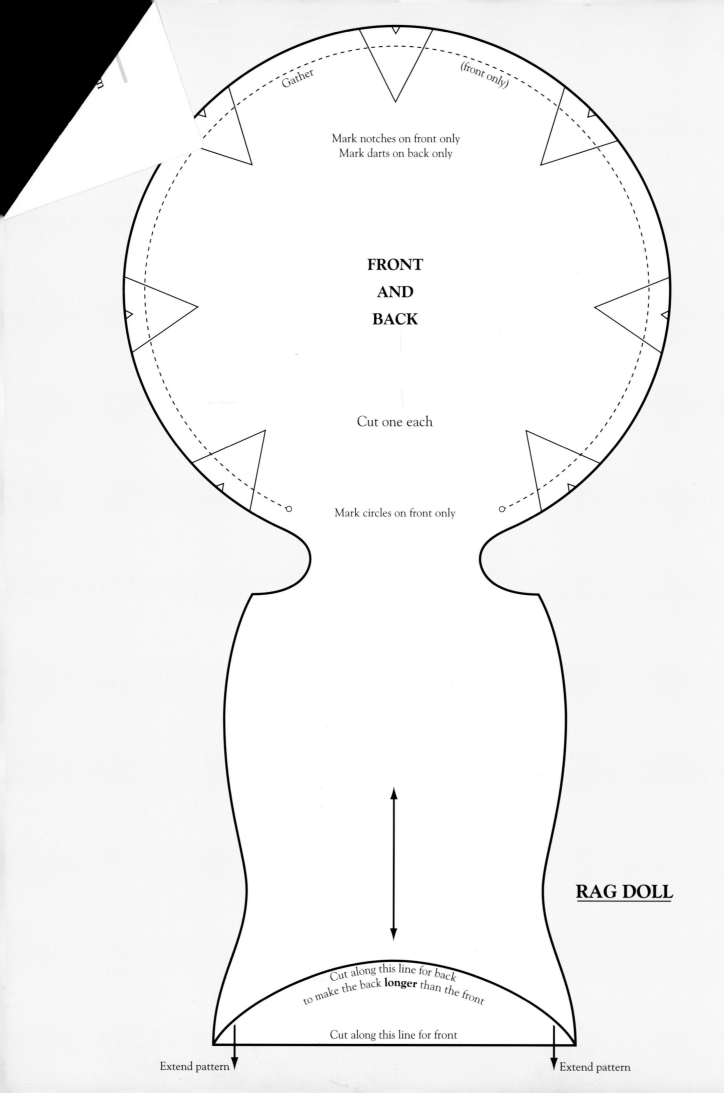

Gather   (front only)

Mark notches on front only
Mark darts on back only

FRONT

AND

BACK

Cut one each

Mark circles on front only

Cut along this line for back
to make the back **longer** than the front

Cut along this line for front

Extend pattern   Extend pattern

RAG DOLL

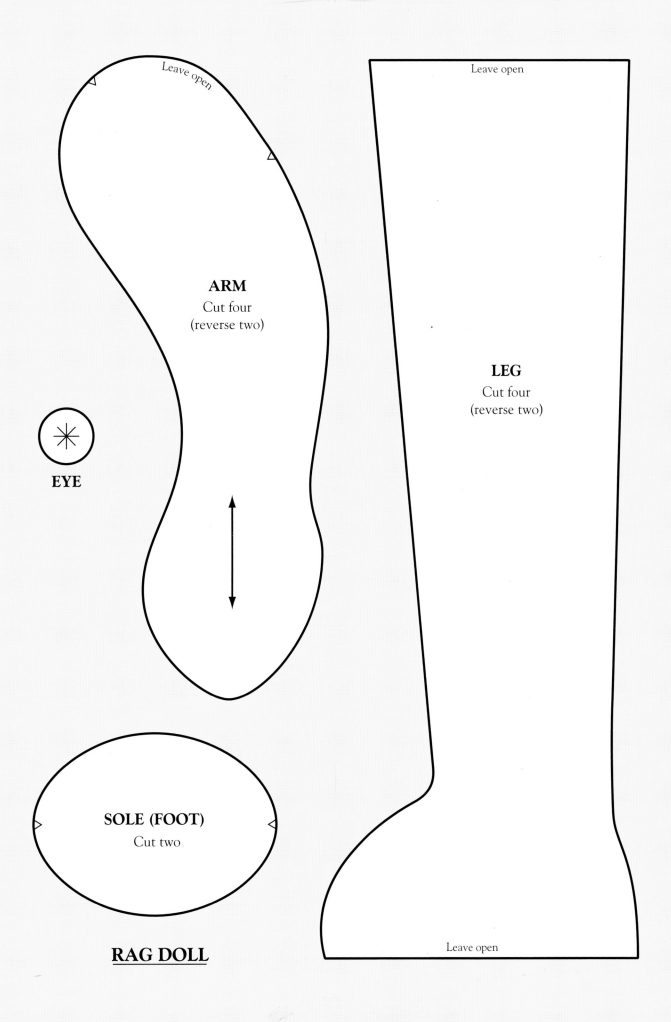

Leave open

ARM
Cut four
(reverse two)

Leave open

LEG
Cut four
(reverse two)

EYE

SOLE (FOOT)
Cut two

RAG DOLL

Leave open

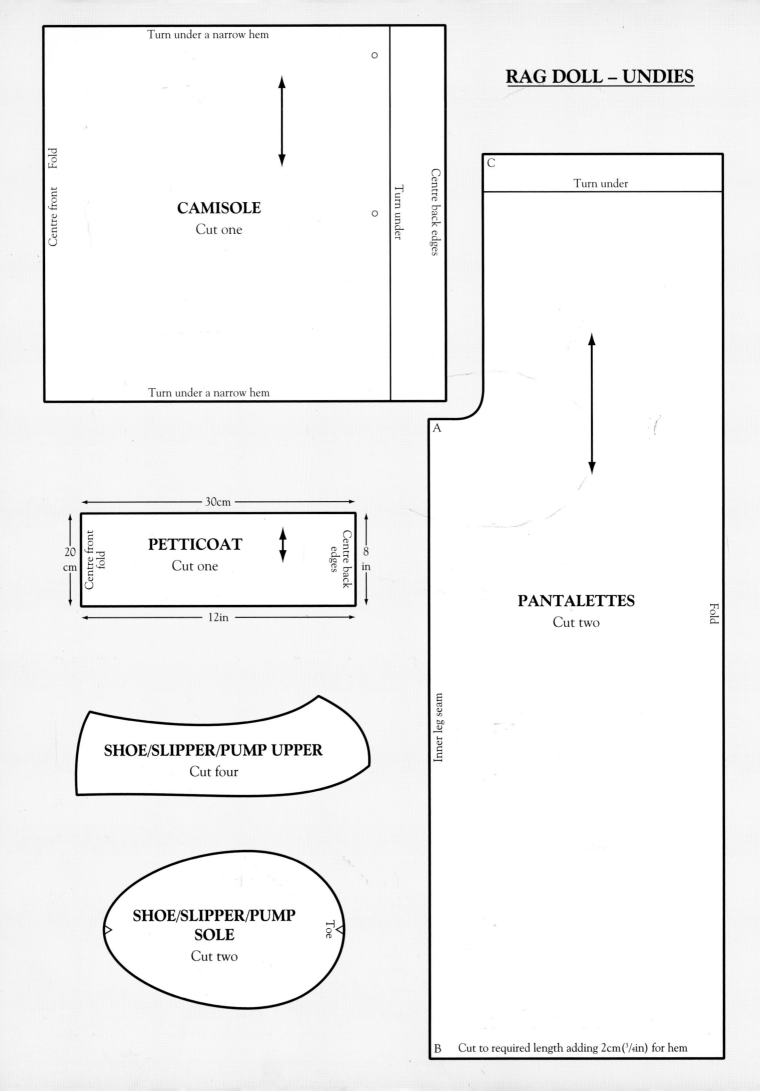

RAG DOLL – UNDIES

Turn under a narrow hem

Centre front Fold

o

o

Turn under

Centre back edges

CAMISOLE
Cut one

Turn under a narrow hem

C

Turn under

A

PANTALETTES
Cut two

Fold

Inner leg seam

B Cut to required length adding 2cm (³⁄₄in) for hem

30cm

20 cm

Centre front fold

PETTICOAT
Cut one

Centre back edges

8 in

12in

SHOE/SLIPPER/PUMP UPPER
Cut four

SHOE/SLIPPER/PUMP SOLE
Cut two

Toe

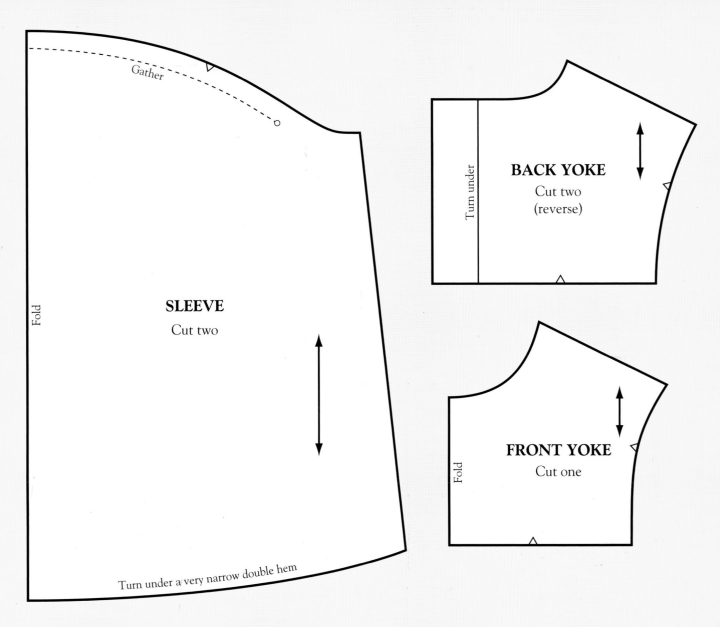

SLEEVE

Cut two

Gather

Fold

Turn under a very narrow double hem

BACK YOKE

Cut two
(reverse)

Turn under

FRONT YOKE

Cut one

Fold

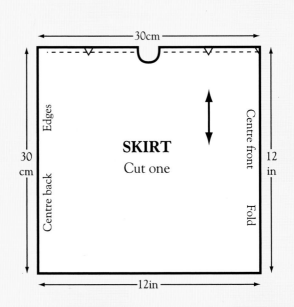

30cm

Edges

Centre back

SKIRT

Cut one

Centre front

Fold

12 in

30 cm

12in

RAG DOLL – NIGHTDRESS

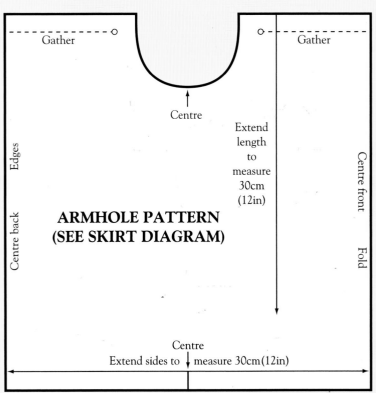

Gather

Centre

Gather

Edges

Centre back

Extend
length
to
measure
30cm
(12in)

Centre front

Fold

**ARMHOLE PATTERN
(SEE SKIRT DIAGRAM)**

Centre
Extend sides to measure 30cm(12in)

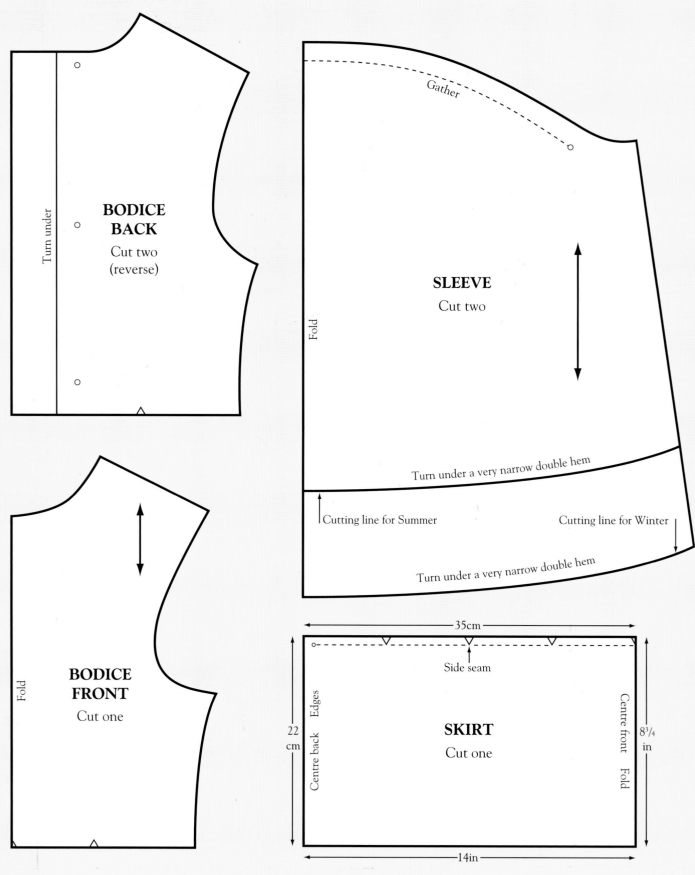

BODICE BACK

Cut two
(reverse)

Turn under

SLEEVE

Cut two

Gather

Fold

Turn under a very narrow double hem

Cutting line for Summer

Cutting line for Winter

Turn under a very narrow double hem

BODICE FRONT

Cut one

Fold

35cm

Side seam

Centre back   Edges

22 cm

SKIRT

Cut one

Centre front   Fold

8³/₄ in

14in

RAG DOLL – DRESS

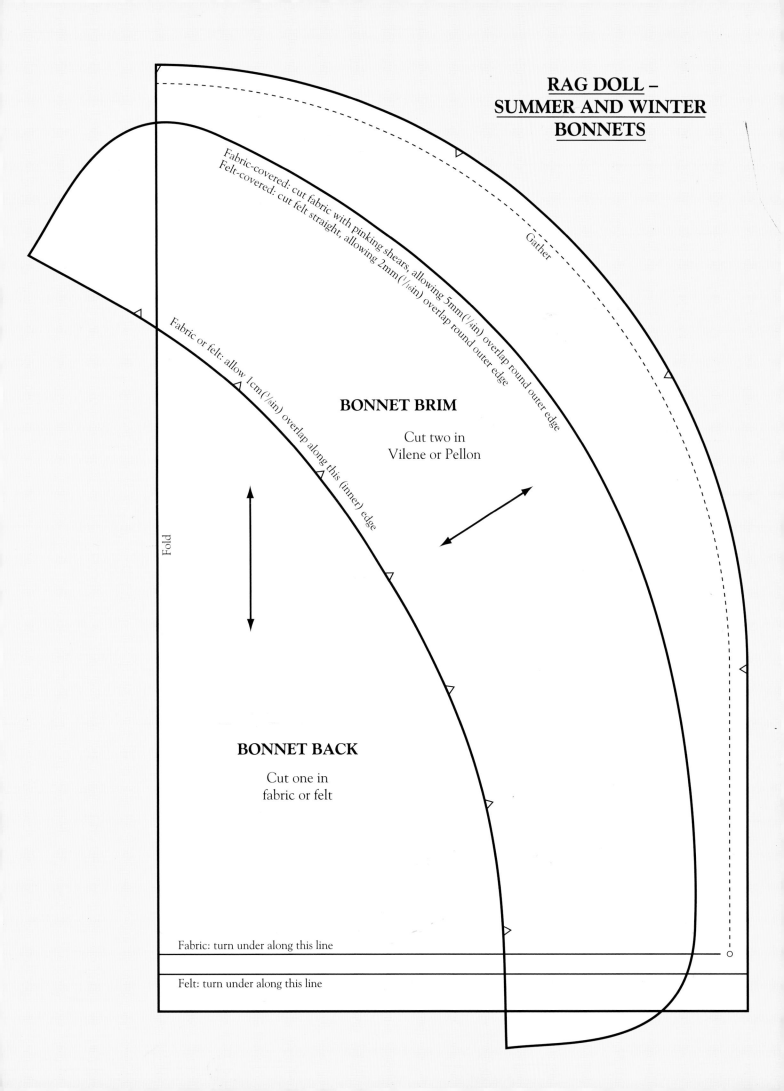

RAG DOLL –
SUMMER AND WINTER
BONNETS

Fabric-covered: cut fabric with pinking shears, allowing 5mm(⅛in) overlap round outer edge
Felt-covered: cut felt straight, allowing 2mm(¹⁄₁₆in) overlap round outer edge

Gather

BONNET BRIM

Cut two in
Vilene or Pellon

Fabric or felt: allow 1cm(⅜in) overlap along this (inner) edge

Fold

BONNET BACK

Cut one in
fabric or felt

Fabric: turn under along this line

Felt: turn under along this line

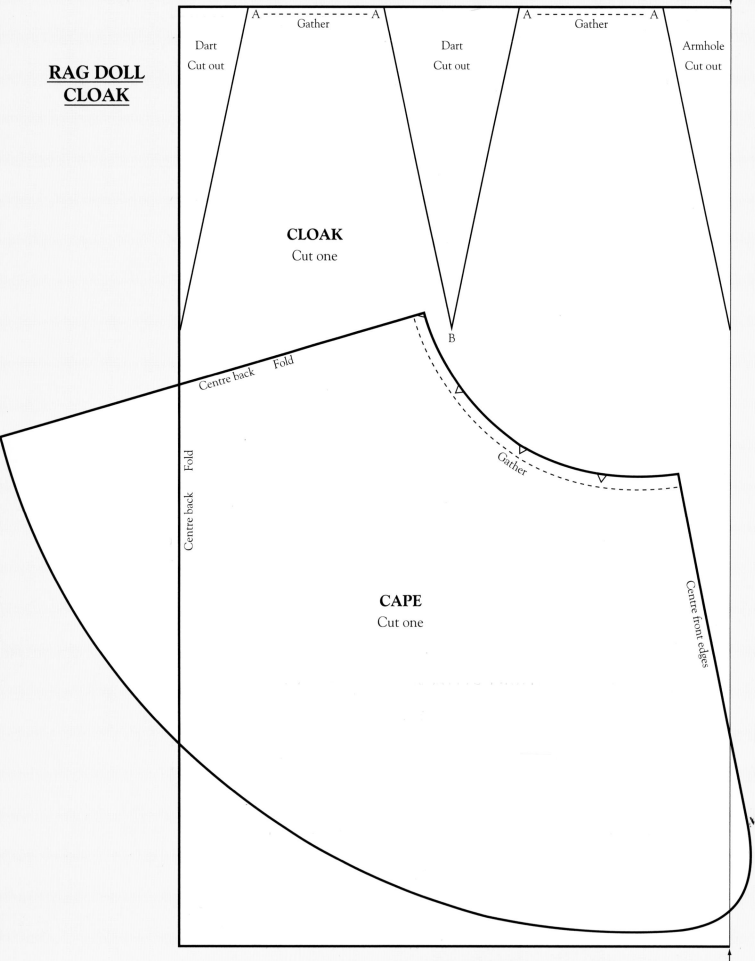

Join the two **RAG DOLL – CLOAK** pattern pieces together along this vertical line

A - - - - - - - - - A   A - - - - - - - - - A
Gather   Gather

Dart   Dart   Armhole
Cut out   Cut out   Cut out

**RAG DOLL
CLOAK**

CLOAK
Cut one

B

Centre back   Fold

Centre back   Fold

Gather

CAPE
Cut one

Centre front edges

Join the two **RAG DOLL–CLOAK** pattern pieces together along this vertical line

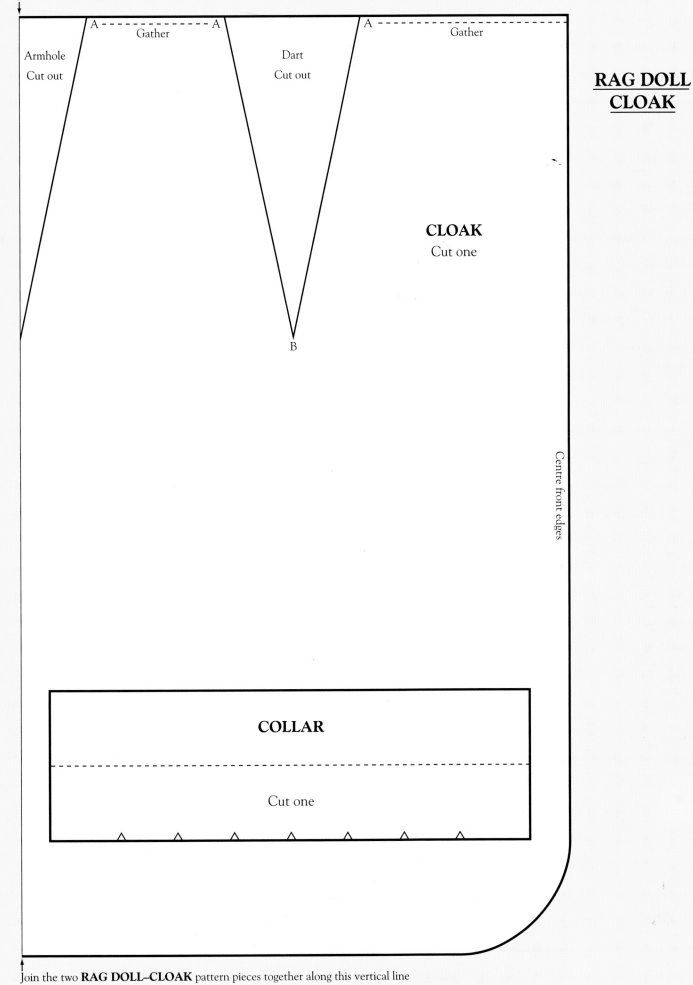

A - - - - - - - - - - - A   A - - - - - - - - - - -
Gather   Gather

Armhole
Cut out

Dart
Cut out

CLOAK
Cut one

B

Centre front edges

COLLAR

Cut one

**RAG DOLL
CLOAK**

Join the back yoke pieces to the skirt in the same way.

5. Join the shoulder seams of the yoke.

6. Join the side seam of each sleeve (below dot), then gather round the top, as indicated.

Set the sleeves into the armholes, matching the centre top to the shoulder seam, the sleeve seam to the centre of the armhole in the skirt, and the notches. Stitch into place, distributing the gathers evenly. Clip curves.

7. Make a very narrow double hem around the lower edge of each sleeve. Then turn to the right side and stitch lace so that it overlaps the hem.

8. Turn to the wrong side again, and herringbone-stitch elastic against the inner edge of each sleeve hem. Draw up to fit wrists and knot securely.

9. Join the side edges of the skirt to form the centre back seam, leaving 8cm (3in) open at the top.

10. Turn under the centre back edges of the yoke as indicated, and hem.

11. Bind the neck edge. Then stitch lace on top to form a stand-up collar.

12. Stitch snap fasteners inside the centre back opening, at top and bottom of the yoke.

13. Gather a 60cm (24in) length of lace. Pin evenly all round the outer edge of the yoke; draw up to fit, then stitch into place, distributing the gathers evenly between the pins.

14. Turn up a very narrow hem around the bottom of the skirt and herringbone-stitch over the raw edge.

Stitch lace on the right side, half overlapping the lower edge.

15. Make a ribbon rose and stitch at the centre of the lower edge of the yoke, as illustrated.

Fold the streamer ribbon slightly off-centre and stitch the fold under the lace below the rose.

AMY-LOUISE'S SLIPPERS –
SHOES OR PUMPS

This basic pattern makes smart walking shoes or dainty dancing pumps as well as slippers; it all depends on the style, colour and trimmings.

MATERIALS

A 9cm (3½in) square of felt for the uppers
8 × 10cm (3 × 4in) felt for the soles
OR a 15cm (6in) square of felt for uppers *and* soles
30cm (12in) single-face satin ribbon, 7mm (¼in) wide, for roses
20cm (8in) lace, about 10mm (⅜in) deep, for the rosettes
Matching sewing threads
Clear adhesive (optional)

1. Cut the upper four times and the sole twice, in the appropriate felts.

2. To make each slipper, oversew (overcast) two uppers together along the front and back seams.

3. Pin the lower edge to a sole, matching seams to notches, and oversew together.

4. Trim with a rosette made from 10cm (4in) lace, and a ribbon rose made from a 15cm (6in) length of ribbon. Stitch or glue the trimming over the front seam.

SHOES
Omit the lace rosette – and also the rose, if preferred. A butterfly bow made from 7mm (¼in) wide ribbon, makes an attractive alternative trimming.

PUMPS
Omit all trimmings. Stitch the centre of a 30cm (12in) length of 1.5mm (¹⁄₁₆in) wide ribbon inside the pump at the top of the back seam. Tie in a bow at the front, as illustrated on page 12 – or cross over the ankle at the front and knot the ends behind the leg.

AMY-LOUISE'S STRIPED
SUMMER DRESS

This versatile pattern adapts well for any season. Your choice of colour, fabric and trimmings will determine the finished effect: as seen from the photographs.

When choosing fabric for the winter dress, try to find something that gives an *impression* of warmth without excess thickness. Both of Amy-Louise's dresses are made of medium-weight cotton, but the brushed fabric, darker trimmings and cosy sleeves of the winter version contrast with the crisp fabric and fresh, light colours of her summer frock, making it look suitable for cold days.

For spring or autumn, make the pattern up as a blouse and skirt, using two different fabrics. Choose a light colour for the blouse and a dark plain or check for the skirt: then trim the neck of the blouse with a smart ribbon bow in the colour of the skirt.

MATERIALS

40cm (½yd) medium-weight fabric (see above), 90cm (36in) wide (70cm/¾yd if bonnet is required)
1.8m (2yd) double-edge lace, 15mm (⅝in) wide
20cm (8in) single-face satin ribbon, 15mm (⅝in) wide
15cm (6in) matching bias binding
3 snap fasteners
Matching sewing threads

1. Cut a strip of fabric 22 × 70cm (8¾ × 28in) for the skirt, as the diagram. Then cut the bodice front once,

Amy-Louise wearing her striped summer dress and bonnet.

and the bodice back and the sleeve twice each (note alternative cutting lines for sleeve).

2. Join the bodice front to the back pieces at the shoulders.

3. Gather round the top edge of each sleeve as indicated, then set into the armholes: pin, matching the side edges, and centre top of sleeve to the shoulder seam. Stitch into place, drawing up the gathers to fit and distributing them evenly. Clip the curve carefully.

4. Join the sleeve seams and side seams of the bodice.

5. Make a very narrow double hem along the bottom of each sleeve. Turn to the right side.

6. Stitch double-edge lace over the hem. Then stitch another row above, leaving about 1.5cm (^{5}/$_8$in) space between. (Winter version: see 6a below.)

7. Gather the top edge of the skirt, beginning and ending 2cm (^{3}/$_4$in) from the side edges. Mark the top edge equally into eight. Then, right sides together, pin to the lower edge of the bodice, matching side edges and marked points to notches and side seams.

Stitch into place, distributing the gathers evenly between the pins.

8. Join the side edges of the skirt to form the centre back seam, leaving 6cm (2^1/$_2$in) open at the top.

9. Turn under the centre back edges of the bodice as indicated, and hem.

10. Bind the neck edge neatly.
Stitch lace on top to form a stand-up collar.

11. Fit ribbon around lower edge of bodice and stitch the ends inside the centre back opening: catch lower edge close above skirt gathers.

12. Stitch snap fasteners inside centre back opening at 0's.

13. Fit dress on the doll and turn up hem to the required length.
Herringbone-stitch over the raw edge, then turn to the right side and sew a band of lace over the stitching line.

AMY-LOUISE'S FLOWERED WINTER DRESS

MATERIALS

As for the summer version, except for the lace: the winter dress is trimmed with 1.5m (1^3/$_4$yd) black lace, about 10mm (^{3}/$_8$in) deep.
You will also need narrow round elastic for the sleeves.

Follow the directions to make the summer dress, substituting the following step where indicated.

6a. Stitch one row of lace over the hem, overlapping the lower edge. Turn to the wrong side and herringbone-stitch elastic against the inner edge of each sleeve hem. Draw up to fit wrists and knot securely.

AMY-LOUISE'S SUMMER BONNET

Amy-Louise's face-flattering bonnet is both easy to make and wear. Although you can add ribbons at each side to tie in a pretty bow under her chin, the bonnet doesn't actually require any strings, as the elasticated back ensures that it fits closely to the head.

MATERIALS

30 × 65cm (12 × 26in) medium-weight cotton-type fabric
20 × 30cm (8 × 12in) heavyweight Vilene or Pellon interlining
30cm (12in) double-edge lace, 15mm (^{5}/$_8$in) wide (or as used on the dress)
Narrow round elastic
Matching sewing threads

1. Cut the brim twice in Vilene or Pellon, and the back once in fabric.

2. Tack each piece of Vilene or Pellon to the wrong side of the remaining fabric and cut round the *outer* edge with pinking shears, allowing about 5mm (^{1}/$_4$in) overlap; but allow a 1cm (^{3}/$_8$in) overlap round the inner curve. (Winter version: see 2a, page 91.)

3. Turn the narrower surplus neatly over the edge of the Vilene or Pellon and tack all the way round. Leave the wider surplus overlapping, but tack the interlining to the fabric close to the edge of the Vilene or Pellon. Press both pieces. (Winter version: see 3a, page 91.)

4. With wrong sides facing, tack the two pieces together; then oversew (overcast) neatly all round the outer edge. Tack the overlapping fabric round the inner curve. Press again.

5. Turn under a hem along the straight edge of the bonnet back, as indicated.

6. Gather all round the curved edge with a double thread.

7. Right sides together, pin the curved edge of the back to the inner edge of the brim, matching notches. Draw up the gathers to fit and stitch together, distributing them evenly between the pins.

8. Catch back the seam round the inner edge of the brim, so that it is held inside the bonnet.

9. Stitch lace round the inner edge of the brim.

10. Thread elastic through the hem at the back, then fit the bonnet on the doll and draw up the elastic so that it sits snugly in place. Knot both ends and stitch securely to the inside edge of the brim.

11 and 12. Winter version only.
Ties are not required, but if you wish to add strings for appearance, use 25-30cm (10-12in) ribbon (any width between 7mm/^{1}/$_4$in and 15mm/^{5}/$_8$in) at each side, stitching the top ends just inside the bonnet, behind the back corners of the brim.

AMY-LOUISE'S WINTER BONNET

MATERIALS

These are the same as for the summer bonnet, but substitute felt for fabric, and omit the lace. For the version illustrated you will also need:

15 × 30cm (6 × 12in) fabric to line the brim
45cm (½yd) braid, 7-10mm (¼-⅜in) wide
35cm (14in) ribbon, 9mm (⅜in) wide
Clear adhesive (optional)

Follow the directions to make the summer bonnet, using felt instead of fabric, and substituting the following steps where indicated. (Omit step 9 for the lined version.)

2a. For the lined brim, prepare only *one* piece of Vilene or Pellon as step 2 for the summer bonnet. Tack the second piece to the remaining felt; cut the inner edge as the first piece (1cm/⅜in overlap), but cut the *outer* edge straight, and leave only about 2mm (¹⁄₁₆in) overlap.
   For the all-felt version, prepare *both* pieces of Vilene or Pellon as described for the second piece above.
3a. Follow step 3 for the summer bonnet to prepare the brim lining, but tack all round the felt section, close to the edge of the Vilene or Pellon, without turning the surplus over.
11. Stitch or glue ribbon around inner edge of top brim, against the back gathers, turning the cut ends inside the bonnet.
12. Stitch or glue braid around the outer edge of the top brim.

AMY-LOUISE'S WINTER CLOAK

Snug and cosy on the coldest day, Amy-Louise's smart cloak matches her felt bonnet. Quick and easy to make because there are no sleeves, hems or turnings, and trimmed with fashionable braid.

MATERIALS

45cm (½yd) felt, 90cm (36in) wide
   (75cm/⅞yd if bonnet is required)
2.2m (2⅜yd) braid, 7-10mm (¼-⅜in) wide
50cm (½yd) ribbon, 9mm (⅜in) wide
Matching sewing threads
Clear adhesive (optional)

1. Cut the cloak, cape and collar once each, in felt.

2. Cut out the darts and armholes, on the cloak, as indicated.
3. On the wrong side, oversew (overcast) the edges of each dart between A–B.
4. Join the top of each armhole at points A.
   Reinforce the bottom point of the armhole with a few stitches.
5. Gather the top edge and draw up to measure 12cm (4¾in).
6. Gather the top edge of the cape and draw up to measure 12cm (4¾in).
7. With the wrong side of the cape to the right side of the cloak, top edges level and notches matched to the darts and armholes, oversew the two pieces together, distributing the gathers evenly.
8. Right sides together and matching notches, stitch the collar to the cape, on top of the gathers and overlapping equally at each end. Fold in half lengthways, as broken line, right side inside, and oversew the ends. Turn to the right side and slip-stitch the other long edge inside the cloak over the gathers and darts.
9. Stitch or glue braid all round the outer edges of both the cloak and cape, and also along the centre of the collar, turning the cut ends inside.
10. Cut the ribbon in half and stitch one tie at each side of the collar.

AMY-LOUISE'S COSY MUFF

Amy-Louise tucks her hands into a warmly lined muff which matches her cloak and bonnet; an essential accessory for winter weather.

MATERIALS

15 × 7cm (6 × 2¾in) felt
16 × 8cm (6½ × 3¼in) fabric for lining
30cm (12in) braid, 7-10mm (¼-⅜in) wide
15cm (6in) ribbon, 9mm (⅜in) wide
Matching sewing threads
Clear adhesive (optional)

1. Right sides together, join the felt and fabric along both long edges, stitching about 3mm (⅛in) from the edge of the felt and having the fabric overlapping equally all round. Turn to the right side.
2. Right sides together, oversew (overcast) the two short edges of the felt.
3. Turn in the raw edges of the fabric and slip-stitch together.
4. Turn to the outside and top-stitch each side to make a firm edge.
5. Stitch or glue braid along both edges.
6. Make the ribbon into a butterfly bow; points b 4.5cm (1¾in) from a. Stitch to centre of muff, as illustrated.

Dolls for Fun

CHAPTER 8

The Dumpy Mascot

Of all the basic figures in the book, you won't find one more basic than this! Merely a felt ball stitched to a weighted cylinder, the basic Dumpy (below left) couldn't be easier – or quicker. And yet, with only a little imagination and ingenuity, you can turn this simple shape into a host of colourful characters like Chula and Gipsy Rose (below).

The most exciting aspect of designing the 'Dumpies' in the following chapters is the fact that, unlike dolls intended for small children, you can use all the odd bits and bobs, buttons, beads and broken brooches that you have hoarded for just such a purpose – without worrying about the danger of such items in the hands of a child. Of course, if you are using the pattern as a toy for a small child, anything of this nature must still be avoided; look back to the first section for safe trimming ideas.

BASIC FIGURE

MATERIALS

17cm (7in) square of flesh-coloured felt, for whole figure
OR 8 × 18cm (3 × 7in) flesh felt, for head only
AND 6 × 18cm (2½ × 7in) coloured felt, for body
      (version A)
      6 × 16cm (2½ × 6¼in) coloured felt, for body
      (version B)
Polyester stuffing
Yarn (double-knit or thinner) or alternative, for hair
2 brown, black or coloured domed sequins, 5mm (³/₁₆in)
   diameter
Modelling clay
Kitchen foil
Medium-weight paper figure A: 3 × 50cm (1¼ × 20in)
   figure B: 3 × 40cm (1¼ x 16in)
Stiff card
Matching and black sewing threads
Pinky-red stranded embroidery cotton (floss) or sewing
   thread for mouth (optional)
Clear adhesive (optional)

See individual directions for specific characters for details of additional materials needed to dress the figures.

SEAMS:
Oversew (overcast) edges of felt to join; approximately 1.5mm (¹/₁₆in) is allowed. Oversew knitted edges also, using matching yarn or thread.

1. Cut the face, the body and the base once each, and the head section three times, in flesh felt. Cut the base again in stiff card, slightly smaller as broken line.
2. Join the short side edges of the body to form the centre back seam. Pin the lower edge to the base, matching notches, etc. Oversew (overcast) together all round and turn to the right side.
3. Using double thread, gather close to the top edge.
4. Fit the card base on top of the felt base.
5. Roll up the strip of paper, place it inside the body and allow it to open up so that it fits snugly against the sides and base.
6. Roll a walnut-sized ball of modelling clay, flatten it slightly and wrap it in foil; lower it into the body and press it down against the base.
7. Stuff the rest of the body firmly with polyester filling, then draw up the gathers tightly and secure.
8. Join two head pieces between A-B. Join on the other piece, but leave open between the notches. Then join the sides of the head to each side of the face, again matching points A and B.
9. Turn to the right side and stuff very firmly, pushing the filling well up into the top and bottom (points A

and B), and moulding to a smoothly rounded shape with the hands. Slip-stitch the opening neatly. Roll between your hands once more, if necessary moving the stuffing around inside with a darning needle.
10. Push a long darning needle straight through the head between points A and B; then push it down into position on top of the body.
   Ladder-stitch the head securely to the body.
11. For the hair, turn to the individual directions for the doll that you are making. But don't trim the hair until the hat or other head-covering is in place.
12. When the figure is dressed and the hair trimmed, pin the sequins to the face for the eyes. When you are satisfied with their position, stitch into place with black thread, making two tiny straight stitches between, one on top of the other, for the nose. Add eyebrows in the same way, if required, making a straight stitch in either double or single black thread.

   Embroider the mouth with either two strands of embroidery cotton (floss), or double sewing thread. Most of the dolls like Robin shown below have curved mouths embroidered in stem (outline) stitch; or they are formed by one horizontal straight stitch, or two straight stitches forming a V-shape, or a fly-stitch.

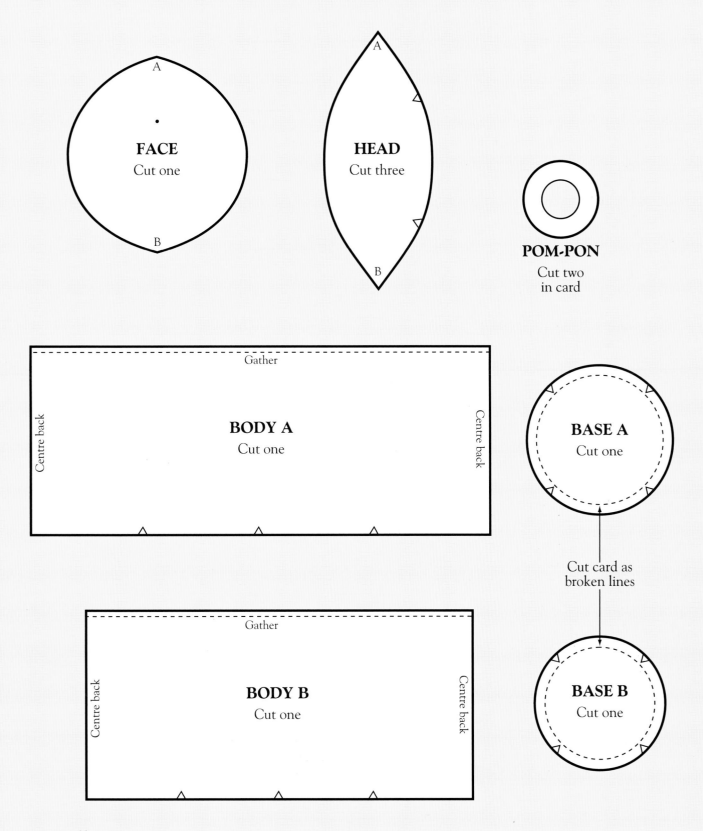

FACE
Cut one

HEAD
Cut three

POM-PON
Cut two
in card

BODY A
Cut one

Gather

Centre back

Centre back

BODY B
Cut one

Gather

Centre back

Centre back

BASE A
Cut one

Cut card as
broken lines

BASE B
Cut one

DUMPY MASCOTS: BASIC FIGURES

CHAPTER 9

Dumpy Knit-wits

This international collection of cosy kids demonstrates how very little it takes to turn the basic Dumpy figure into an amusing character. Fun to make and fun to own, they are quick, inexpensive and very saleable, too; making this is a specially profitable interpretation of the design if you are fund-raising.

BASIC KNIT-WIT BODY

First make the Basic Figure; version A (Chapter 8). Then sort through all your odd leftover bits of yarn, rejecting anything thicker than double-knit. The dolls in the photograph are wearing outfits knitted from Twilley's yarns, all roughly equivalent to double-knit in thickness.

However, you can use any size of needle and thickness of yarn that you wish; the secret is to knit a tension sample first. Bearing in mind that yarns heavier than double-knit will look too bulky, and that you will want a reasonably fine stitch on such a small scale, medium-

size needles are the most satisfactory (3mm/No 11/American size 2 were used for the examples).

Cast on 15 stitches and knit fifteen rows in stocking stitch (one row knit, one row purl). Cast off and press under a damp cloth. By placing your ruler horizontally, you can measure the number of stitches over 2cm (¾in): and by placing it vertically, you can count the rows. Then all you have to do is calculate the number of stitches needed to produce the width required – and the number of rows to make it the right length. The pieces themselves are so simple and straightforward

Thomas, Victoria and Robin

that you will find it easy to follow the measurements. Once you have knitted the plain stocking stitch version, you can if you wish, experiment with fancy stitches like moss, cable and lace effects. And as the examples show, colours too can be mixed and matched, creating a wonderful selection of very individual-looking dolls from one simple design.

Cast on the appropriate number of stitches to knit a piece approximately 12cm (4¾in) wide; try to choose a number that is divisible by four – then add one more (ie: 32 + 1 = 33).

1st row: Knit.
2nd row: K1; purl to last stitch; K1.
3rd and 4th rows: As 1st and 2nd.
5th row: Purl.

Continue in stocking stitch until the work measures 5cm (2in), ending with a purl row.

Decrease row: K1; (K2tog; K2) to end.

Continue in stocking stitch until the work measures 8cm (3-3¼in) from the commencement. Break off the yarn and slip it through the stitches, removing them from the needle.

Right side inside, and beginning at the bottom, join the side edges to form the centre back seam; stop at the decrease row, but don't finish off. Turn to the right side and fit over the body, lower edges level. Complete the back seam on the right side, then roll the top edge over and draw the stitches up tightly around the neck, finishing off securely.

Catch the lower edge to the base of the figure with matching yarn or thread. (This isn't essential, if you are in a hurry.)

THOMAS
all blue

For the hair, wind the yarn evenly round a 12.5cm (5in) deep card 20-30 times, according to thickness. Slide very carefully off the card and tie the centre tightly with a single strand. Holding the centre firmly, cut the loops at both ends. Spread glue over the top and sides of the head, then place the tied centre of the yarn over the crown of the head and spread the strands out evenly all round.

Follow the directions above to knit the body.

To make the hat, cast on the appropriate number of stitches to knit a piece approximately 14cm (5½in) wide; try to choose a number that is divisible by four or eight.

1st row: Knit.
2nd row: K1; purl to last stitch; K1.
Work seven more rows in stocking stitch.
10th row: Knit.

Continue in stocking stitch until the work measures 5.5cm (2⅛-2¼in).

Next row: K2tog to end.

Next row: K2tog; P2tog to last 2 stitches; K2tog.
Next row: K2tog to end (if your original number of stitches was divisible only by four, you will have an odd stitch left; in this case, K1).

Break off the yarn and slip it through the remaining stitches, removing them from the needle; draw up tightly and secure. Then, right side inside, join the side edges to form the centre back seam.

Fold the reverse stocking stitch section at the bottom inside the hat and catch the cast-on edge to the first row of the main stocking stitch section above (row 10). Turn to the right side.

Make a pompon using the pattern on page 13. Stitch to the centre top of the hat.

Fit the hat on the head and catch it lightly all round to hold it in position. Then trim the hair to length and return to Chapter 8, step 12, to add the features.

VICTORIA
mauve and white

For the hair, cut about twelve to fifteen 25cm (10in) lengths of double-knit yarn (more if using a thinner yarn, but have a number that is divisible by three). Tie tightly at the centre; then tie tightly again 4cm (1½in) each side of the centre. Divide the strands equally at each side and plait neatly into braids. Bind tightly with black thread and trim the cut ends neatly.

Stitch the centre to the centre top of the head (point A); then stitch the tie at each side over the side seam of the face. (If you prefer, the strands may be stitched to the centre and sides of the head before being plaited.)

Follow the directions above to knit the body, but change to contast colour on decrease row for collar.

Make the hat as directed for Thomas, but begin with contrast yarn and change to main colour on the 10th row.

Fit the hat on the head and catch it lightly all round to hold it in position. Then return to Chapter 8, step 12, to add the features.

CHULA
green and cerise

Follow the directions for Thomas' hair.

Follow the directions above to knit the body, but change to contrast colour on decrease row for collar.

Make the hat as directed for Thomas, but begin with contrast yarn and change to main colour on the 10th row. Omit the pompon.

Fit the hat on the head and catch it lightly all round to hold it in position. Then trim the hair to length and return to Chapter 8, step 12, to add the features.

ROBIN
all red

Follow the directions for Thomas' hair.

Follow the directions above to knit the body, but make and fit the pixie hood before completing the body.

To make the pixie hood, cast on the appropriate number of stitches to knit a piece approximately 12 cm (4¾in) wide.

1st row: Knit.

2nd row: K1; purl to last stitch; K1.

Work seven more rows in stocking stitch.

10th row: Knit.

Continue in stocking stitch until the work measures 8 cm (3-3¼in). Cast off.

Fold the reverse stocking stitch section at the bottom in half, turning it to the wrong side, and catch the cast-on edge to the first row of the main stocking stitch section (row 10). Fold the hood in half and join the cast-off edges to form the centre back seam. Gather the side edges, then fit the hood on the doll and draw up round the neck.

When the body is complete, trim the hair to length and return to Chapter 8, step 12, to add the features.

JONATHAN
blue and green

Follow the directions for Thomas' hair.

Follow the directions on page 96 to knit the body, but work the first four rows in the contrast colour, then change to your main colour. Return to contrast for the decrease row, and continue for the collar. Make and fit the pixie hood before completing the body.

Make the pixie hood as directed for Robin, but work

Jonathan and Conchita

the first nine rows in your contrast colour.

When the body is complete, trim the hair to length and return to Chapter 8, step 12, to add the features.

CONCHITA
red and yellow

For the hair, wind double-knit yarn fifteen times around a 12.5 cm (5in) deep card (more if using a thinner yarn). Tie tightly at each edge with a single strand, then slide the skein carefully off the card.

Using black thread, push your needle into the centre top of the head (point A): then bring it up 1.5 cm (⅝in) in front (dot on face pattern). Place the centre of the skein across the top of the face, between these two points, then stitch it into place, taking long stitches over it. Draw the sides of the skein down over the face as illustrated and take the ends round towards the back; knot the ties tightly at the nape of the neck and catch the knot securely to the head.

Follow the directions on page 96 to knit the body, but work the first four rows in the first colour. Change to your second colour for the next two rows, then back to the first colour for the next two rows. Continue to knit alternate stripes until the work measures 5 cm (2in), ending with a purl row in the first colour. Work the decrease row, then change to the second colour for the collar. Make and fit the bonnet before completing the body.

To make her bonnet, using the second colour, cast on the appropriate number of stitches to knit a piece approximately 12 cm (4¾in) wide; try to choose a number that is divisible by four or eight.

1st row: Knit.

2nd row: K1; purl to last stitch, K1.

Work seven more rows in stocking stitch.

10th row: Change to the first colour. Knit.

Continue to work in stocking stitch stripes as for the body until the work measures about 7 cm (2¾in), ending with a stripe in the second colour.

Change to the first colour for the next row and K2tog to the end.

Next row: K2tog; P2tog to last 2 stitches; K2tog.

Next row: K2tog to end (if your original number of stitches was divisible only by four, you will have an odd stitch left; in this case K1).

Break off the yarn and slip it through the remaining stitches, removing them from the needle; draw up tightly and secure, then join the side edges of the decrease rows and the last stripe. Fold the reverse stocking stitch section at the bottom in half, turning it inside, and catch the cast-on edge to the first row of the first stripe (row 10). Gather the side edges, then fit the bonnet on the doll and draw up round the neck.

When the body is complete, return to Chapter 8, step 12, to add the features.

ROSEBUD
pink and beige

For the hair, cut about thirty 20cm (8in) strands of double-knit yarn (more if using a thinner yarn); tie the centre loosely with a single strand. Glue the tied centre to the top of the head, then draw the strands down over each side of the face as illustrated and catch them tightly over the seam. Trim the cut ends neatly.

Follow the directions on page 96 to knit the body, but change to your contrast colour on the decrease row for the collar. Make and fit the bonnet before completing the body.

To make her bonnet, using the main colour, cast on the appropriate number of stitches to knit a piece approximately 12cm (4¾in) wide; try to choose a number that is divisible by four or eight.
1st row: Knit, increasing once in every stitch.
2nd row: K1; purl to last stitch; K1.
Work nine more rows in stocking stitch.
12th row: Change to contrast colour. K2tog to the end.
Continue in stocking stitch until the work measures 7.5cm (3in).
Next row: K2tog to end.
Next row: K2tog; P2tog to last 2 stitches; K2tog.
Next row: K2tog to end (if your original number of stitches was divisible only by four, you will have an odd stitch left; in this case, K1).

Break off the yarn and slip it through the remaining stitches, removing them from the needle. Draw up tightly and secure; then join the side edges for 1.5cm (⅝in).

Fold the reverse stocking stitch section in half, turning it inside the bonnet, and catch the cast-on edge to the first (decrease) row of the contrast section (row 12) Gather the side edges, then fit the bonnet on the doll and draw up round the neck. Finally, gather round the inner edge of the brim (cast-on row) and draw up to fit neatly round the head.

When the body is complete, return to Chapter 8, step 12, to add the features.

MAGGIE
all lilac

Follow the directions for Victoria's hair.

Follow the directions on page 96 to knit the body.

To make her hat, cast on the appropriate number of stitches to knit a piece approximately 14cm (5½in) wide; try to choose a number that is divisible by four or eight.
1st row: Knit, increasing once in every stitch.
2nd row: K1; purl to last stitch; K1.
Work seven more rows in stocking stitch.
10th row: K2tog to end.
Continue in stocking stitch until the work measures 6cm (3⅜in), ending with a purl row.
Next row: K2tog to end.
Next row: K2tog; P2tog to last 2 stitches; K2tog.
Next row: K2tog to end (if your original number of stitches was divisible only by four, you will have an odd stitch left; in this case, K1).

Break off the yarn and slip it through the remaining stitches, removing them from the needle; draw up tightly and secure. Then, right side inside, join the side edges to form the centre back seam.

Fold the reverse stocking stitch section inside the hat and catch the cast-on edge to the first row of the main stocking stitch section (row 10). Turn to the right side.

Fit the hat on the head and catch it lightly all round to hold it in position. Then return to Chapter 8, step 12, to add the features.

Maggie, Rosebud and Chula

CHAPTER 10

Dumpies for Luck

Everyone wants to escape danger and avoid trouble – whilst hoping to enjoy the good things of life too. And here is a comprehensive selection of mascots, symbolising all you could possibly need to keep you safe, happy, healthy and prosperous – or just to offer assistance with the job in hand. A little bit of Dumpy luck is yours for the making.

The basic figure is the same as that used for the knit-wits – except that it is a little slimmer. Most of the bodies are made in coloured felt to form the basis of the clothing. The collection of characters which follow are only a beginning, just to give you some idea of the scope – and to show you how to handle the basic concept of the design. They should set your imagination working overtime; so now start planning your own creations!

SEAMS: Oversew edges of felt to join (approximately 1.5mm/(¹/₁₆in is allowed). Make tiny seams on fabric: about 3mm (¹/₈in). Try to cut fabric straight along a thread, and avoid turning up hems where possible; if a hem is necessary, herringbone-stitch over the raw edge.

Harriet the Graduate and (opposite) Gipsy Rose, Garden Gnome, Little Leprechaun and Jester Merrythought.

GIPSY ROSE

Cross her palm with silver and she'll look into the future for you. Busy patterns in vibrant colours on black or white grounds emphasise her black hair and sparkling black eyes. The secret of success is to choose closely woven medium- or lightweight cotton-type fabrics, and to cut carefully along the straight, following the woven thread.

MATERIALS

See Chapter 8 for Basic Figure
3 × 15cm (1¼ × 6in) patterned white fabric for the petticoat
6 × 20cm (2⅜ × 8in) patterned black fabric for the dress
10cm (4in) square of toning fabric for her shawl
3.5 × 4cm (1⅜ × 1⅝in) white fabric for her apron
14cm (5½in) square of patterned fabric for the headscarf
15cm (6in) narrow white lace for petticoat
20cm (8in) narrow black lace for dress
Tiny beads, diamanté (rhinestone) etc, for necklace, earrings and brooch
Matching sewing threads

1. Make the basic figure, version B (Chapter 8), in flesh felt.
2. Cut out the petticoat and join the centre back seam. Turn to the right side. Stitch lace to overlap the lower edge. Turn the top edge under and gather close to the fold. Fit the petticoat on the figure and draw up the gathers at waist level; distribute them evenly and catch into place so that the lower edge of the lace is level with the base of the figure.
3. Cut out the dress and join the centre back seam.

Turn to the right side. Gather round at waist level, as indicated, but do not draw up. Turn the top edge under and gather close to the fold.
4. Fit the dress on the figure and draw up the gathers evenly round the neck. Now draw up the waist gathers. Pin lace around the bottom of the skirt so that it is level with the base of the figure, then stitch it into place over the raw edge.
5. Cut out the apron, turn the top edge under and gather close to the fold. Draw up slightly and stitch the apron to the centre front of the dress over the waist gathers.
6. Follow the directions for Conchita's hair (see Chapter 9).
7. Cut a 10cm (4in) square of fabric for the shawl and draw threads all round to form a 5mm (¼in) fringe. Fold diagonally and drape round the figure as illustrated, catching the crossed corners at the front over the apron.
8. Cut a 14cm (5½in) square of fabric for the headscarf and draw threads all round to form a narrow fringe. Fold diagonally and drape round the head as illustrated, catching the corners at the nape of the neck and folding in the straight edges above before allowing the scarf to fall down over the back of the head. Catch securely into place at all these points.
9. Follow the directions in Chapter 8 for the features (step 12), adding short eyebrows in double black thread.
10. Stitch on tiny beads and diamanté for necklace, earrings and brooch, following the illustration for guidance.

JESTER MERRYTHOUGHT

With traditional cap and bells and that cheery grin, the jester is a centuries-old symbol of fun and merriment. Choose your own contrasting satin ribbons, or follow the colour scheme suggested in the photograph.

MATERIALS

See Chapter 8 for Basic Figure
25cm (10in) square of bright green felt for body and cap
20cm (8in) single-face satin ribbon, 6mm (¼in) wide, in *each* of three colours PLUS 30cm (12in) in another colour
20cm (8in) satin ribbon, 1.5mm (1/16in) wide, in *each* of the first three colours above

5 silver or gold beads, approximately 5mm (¼in) diameter
Cotton wool (absorbent cotton)
Thin card
Paper clips
Matching sewing threads
Glue stick (or clear adhesive)

1. Make the basic figure, version B (Chapter 8), using green felt for the body and base.
2. Cut the cap front in thin card, using the pattern as a template. Spread glue over the front of the card, then press it down onto green felt. When it is dry, cut the felt very carefully, level with the edge of the card.
3. Cut the hood once in green felt. Cut the cap back

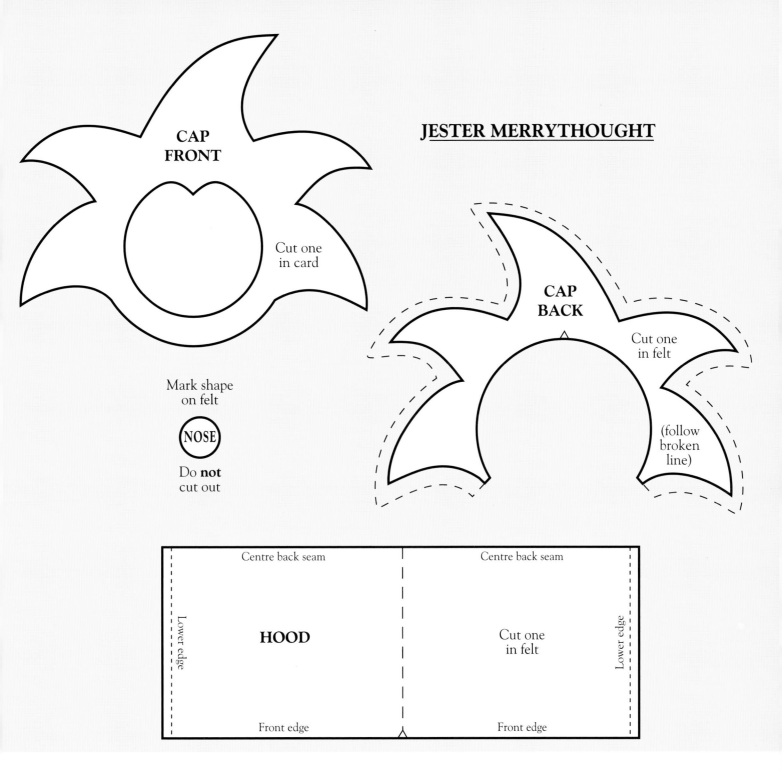

JESTER MERRYTHOUGHT

CAP FRONT

Cut one
in card

Mark shape
on felt

NOSE

Do **not**
cut out

CAP BACK

Cut one
in felt

(follow
broken
line)

Centre back seam

Centre back seam

Lower edge

HOOD

Cut one
in felt

Lower edge

Front edge

Front edge

once also, but allow extra all round the *outer* edges, as indicated by the broken line.

4. Right sides together, join the front edge of the hood to the inner edge of the cap back, matching centre notches.

5. Right side inside, fold the hood as the broken line and join the centre back seam. Turn to the right side. Fold the point down over the back seam and catch into place from the inside.

6. Using paper clips, fix the cap back behind the front, allowing the back to overlap all round. Then, one pointed section at a time, glue the front to the back. When dry, cut the overlapping felt level with the card.

7. Cut about fifteen 10cm (4in) lengths of yarn (according to thickness), for the hair. Tie the centre tightly, then fold in half and stitch the fold to the centre top of the head, so that all the cut ends overlap the forehead. Trim straight across, then fit the cap over the head to check hair length and adjust as necessary.

8. Make the nose as follows. Mark the nose circle on a piece of flesh felt, then gather round the marked line with very tiny stitches. Trim away the outer felt, as close to the stitches as possible. Roll a minute piece of cotton wool into a ball and, partly drawing up the gathers, place it inside the nose. Draw up tightly and secure, catching the edges of the felt together at the back.

9. With the cap temporarily in place again, pin the nose to the centre of the face. Then pin the sequin eyes into place. Finally, mark the mouth with pins.

When you are satisfied with the position of the features, carefully remove the cap and stitch the nose and eyes into place. Then embroider the curved mouth in stem (outline) stitch, using two strands of embroidery cotton or double thread.

10. Cut four 4cm (1½in) lengths of 6mm (¼in) wide ribbon, one in each colour. Cut one end of one piece to a point, then fold under 5mm (¼in) at the other end, and glue it to the top of the body, with the fold close under the head. Repeat with the other three lengths of ribbon, gluing them side-by-side. Glue more ribbons all round the body, following the same order.

11. Glue 6mm (¼in) ribbon around the base. Then plait the narrow ribbons to make braid and glue on top of the wider ribbon.

12. Stitch a bead to each point of the cap.

13. Gather the lower edge of the hood, then fit the cap on the figure and draw up the gathers tightly round the neck.

GARDEN GNOME

Every horticulturist needs a garden gnome to encourage the seeds to grow, as well as to chase away all those nasty slugs that invade the plot.

- MATERIALS

See Chapter 8 for Basic Figure
20cm (8in) square of scarlet felt for body and cap
2 × 3cm (¾ × 1¼in) green felt for apron
Scrap of pink felt for nose
3.5 × 10.5cm (1⅜ × 4⅛in) check cotton-type fabric for shirt
5.5cm (2¼in) spotted blue ribbon, 2.5cm (1in) wide, for scarf
12cm (4¾in) black ribbon, 9mm (⅜in) wide, for belt
Cotton wool (absorbent cotton)
Scraps of stiff paper and kitchen foil or silver foil paper for buckle
Wooden cocktail stick or matchstick, and wooden bead, for pipe
Brown felt pen, paint or ink to colour stem of pipe
Pipe cleaner (or chenille stem), 16.5cm (6½in) long
Adhesive tape and pencil (to make beard)
Matching sewing threads

1. Make the basic figure, version B (Chapter 8), using red felt for the body and base, *but* before making up the body, pin the check fabric to the felt, top and side edges level; tack the outer edges of the fabric, and stitch the lower edge.

2. Follow the directions for Thomas' hair (Chapter 9), using grey yarn.

3. Using the same grey yarn, make a 5cm (2in) length of curly beard (see Hairstyling, p10).

4. Wrong side inside, fold the corners of the spotted ribbon under as figure 1 and catch together as indicated by the x's on figure 2. Then gather the centre and draw up tightly. Stitch scarf under his chin, as illustrated.

5. Cut the apron in green felt and glue the top edge to the centre front of the body, against the lower edge of the shirt.

6. Glue black ribbon lightly round the body, over the edge of the shirt, join at back.

7. Cut the buckle in stiff paper and glue it to the back of the foil. Cut the foil as indicated in figure 3, making a cross in the centre: then fold the overlapping foil neatly over the outer and inner edges, and round to the back. Glue the buckle to the figure, over the ribbon.

8. Join the straight edges of the cap to form the centre back seam. Turn to the right side. Fit a pipe cleaner inside and push it right up into the point; catch the cleaner over the seam at the base of the cap, then bend the surplus back inside and catch the cleaner along the length of the seam.

9. Fit the cap on the head, and when you are satisfied with the position, stitch it all round the lower edge. Then trim the hair to length (see photograph).

10. Glue the beard round his face, as illustrated.

11. Cut the nose in pink felt and make as directed for the Jester (step 8).

Pin the eyes and nose to the face, check the expression and then stitch into place.

12. Cut the sharp pointed tip off one end of the cocktail stick, then shave the blunted point flat on one side. Cut the stick 2cm (¾in) from the point, and colour brown. Glue the bead onto the shaved end. When dry, glue the top end into the beard.

GIPSY ROSE

Turn under

Neck gathers

GIPSY **DRESS**

Fold

Centre front

Waist gathers

Centre back edges

Cut one

Turn under

Waist gathers

Centre front Fold

GIPSY **PETTICOAT**

Cut one

Centre back edges

Turn under

Gather

GIPSY **APRON**

Cut one

GIPSY ROSE

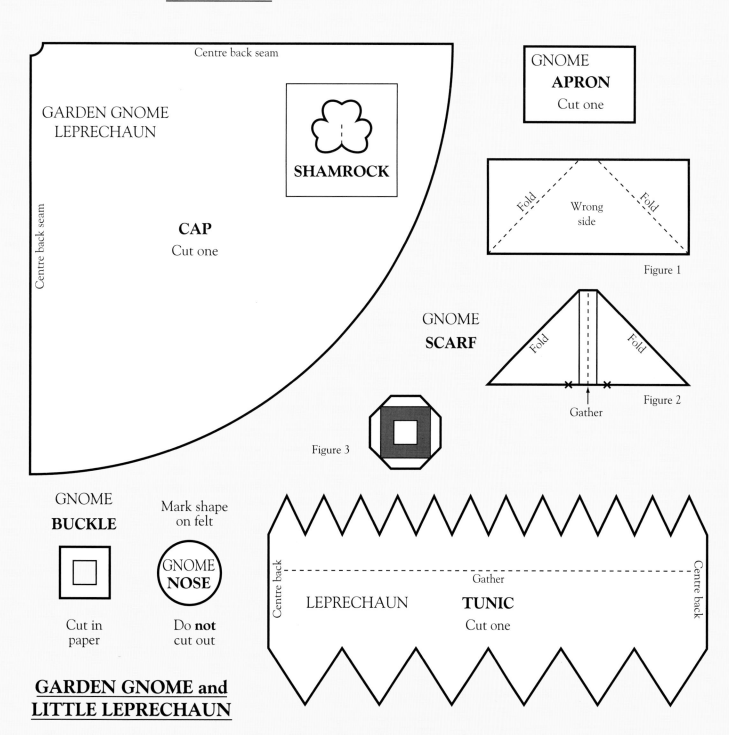

Centre back seam

GARDEN GNOME LEPRECHAUN

SHAMROCK

Centre back seam

CAP

Cut one

GNOME **APRON** Cut one

Fold Fold

Wrong side

Figure 1

GNOME **SCARF**

Fold Fold

Gather

Figure 2

Figure 3

GNOME **BUCKLE**

Cut in paper

GNOME **NOSE**

Mark shape on felt

Do **not** cut out

Centre back

Gather

LEPRECHAUN **TUNIC**

Cut one

Centre back

GARDEN GNOME and LITTLE LEPRECHAUN

LITTLE LEPRECHAUN

If you're Irish, you'll know how useful it is to have Paddy, the little leprechaun, on your side. His traditional green outfit symbolises the lush green grass and clear fresh air of the Emerald Isle.

MATERIALS

See Chapter 8 for Basic Figure
20cm (8in) square of deep emerald felt for body and cap
7 x 13cm (2¾ × 5¼in) mid-emerald felt for tunic
60cm (¾yd) satin ribbon, 1.5mm (¹⁄₁₆in) wide, *each* in light green, mid-emerald and deep emerald
3 green wooden beads, not more than 10mm (³⁄₈in) diameter
Small silver bell
Scrap of green paper and 5cm (2in) green stem wire, for shamrock
Pipe cleaner (or chenille stem), 16.5cm (6½in) long
Matching sewing threads

1. Make the basic figure, version B (Chapter 8), using green felt for the body and base.

2. Follow the directions for Thomas' hair (Chapter 9). (A bouclé-type yarn was used in the example shown.)
3. Make and fit his cap as directed for the Garden Gnome (steps 8 and 9), *but* before beginning step 9, stitch the three beads at equal intervals down the centre front, and the bell to the point of the cap.
4. Cut the tunic in mid-emerald felt and mark the broken line. Join the side edges to form the centre back seam. Gather along the marked line, leaving the thread on the right side. Turn the tunic to the right side and fit on the figure; draw up tightly round the neck, turning the collar down as illustrated.
5. Plait the ribbons to make braid and glue two rows round the lower edge of the cap. Glue the remainder down the centre front of the tunic, catching the braid at the bottom and allowing the cut ends to unravel.
6. Trim the hair to length, then follow the directions in Chapter 8 (step 12) for the features.
7. Cut the shamrock in green paper and glue it to the end of the stem wire. Glue the stalk inside the tunic, as illustrated.

BROTHER FRANCIS

A friendly friar to bless you every morning and keep you company as you travel life's stony path. Quick, easy and cheap to make, he's dedicated to helping nimble-fingered fundraisers support their favourite good causes.

MATERIALS

See Chapter 8 for Basic Figure (use beige felt for body and base)
18cm (7in) square of mid-brown felt for habit, etc
90cm (1yd) matching satin ribbon, 1.5mm (¹⁄₁₆in) wide, for belt
Cotton wool (absorbent cotton)
Adhesive tape and pencil (to make tonsured hair)
Matching sewing threads

1. Make the basic figure, version B (Chapter 8), using beige felt for the body and base.
2. For his tonsure, make a 15cm (6in) length of curly beard. When it is ready, cut carefully along it, to form a fringe; run a little glue inside, along the central strand, then pinch the two layers of fringe to hold them together. Glue the tonsure round the head as illustrated, and trim the cut ends quite severely, following the illustration for guidance.

3. Cut the habit, cowl and hood once each in brown felt.
4. Gather the top edge of the habit, then draw up round his neck, top corners meeting under the chin.
5. Gather the top edge of the cowl, as indicated, and draw up round the neck, over his habit, top corners meeting at centre back; slip-stitch the straight edges together.
6. Join the centre back seam of the hood and turn to the right side. Turn the point down 2cm (¾in) and catch over the seam from inside. Gather round the lower edge, then fit over the head and draw up round the neck, the front corners positioned at each side of the face, level with the seam.
7. Plait the ribbon to make a braid belt. Then fit round the body as illustrated, catching together at the front. Bind the ends tightly with thread just above the point where you plan to cut them. Trim neatly.
8. Follow the directions for the Jester's nose (step 8) (p103) and pin to the centre of the face. Then pin the sequin eyes into place and mark the mouth with pins.

When you are satisfied, stitch the nose and eyes into place, then embroider the curved mouth in stem (outline) stitch, using two strands of embroidery cotton or double thread. Complete with short straight-stitch eyebrows in double black thread.

SISTER SERAPHINA

With her serene smile and rosary at the ready, the little nun is only too happy to pray for your welfare and safety. Another inexpensive design for potential fund-raisers.

MATERIALS

See Chapter 8 for Basic Figure
25cm (10in) square of black felt for body, habit and veil
10cm (4in) square of white felt for cowl, coif and headband
5cm (2in) length of tiny beads
Matching sewing threads

1. Make the basic figure, version B (Chapter 8), using black felt for the body and base.
2. Cut the habit and veil once each in black felt. Cut the cowl, coif and headband once each in white.
3. Gather the top edge of the habit, then draw up round her neck, top corners meeting at centre back. Slip-stitch the straight edges to form centre back seam.
4. Gather the top edge of the cowl, as indicated on the pattern, and draw up round the neck, over her habit, top corners meeting at centre back; slip-stitch the straight edges together.
5. Gather the lower edge of the coif, then fit it smoothly round the lower part of her face, pinning the top corners over the seam at each side of the face. Now pin the headband smoothly round the top of her face, the lower corners over the top corners of the coif. Draw up the coif gathers to fit, and stitch the other outer edges of both the coif and headband to the head.
6. Follow the directions in Chapter 8 for the features (step 12), adding short straight-stitch eyebrows in double black thread.
7. Drape the veil over her head, folding in the straight edges at each side as indicated on the pattern; pin the folded sides, adjusting until you are satisfied. Then remove the veil and stitch the folds from inside, to hold them in position. Catch the lower edge together, matching the notches.

Drape the veil over the head again and catch into place at each side. Then catch the joined lower edge over the centre back seam of the habit; finally, fold the centre back of the veil down, and catch this on top.
8. Thread the beads to make her rosary, and stitch to the front of her habit, as illustrated.

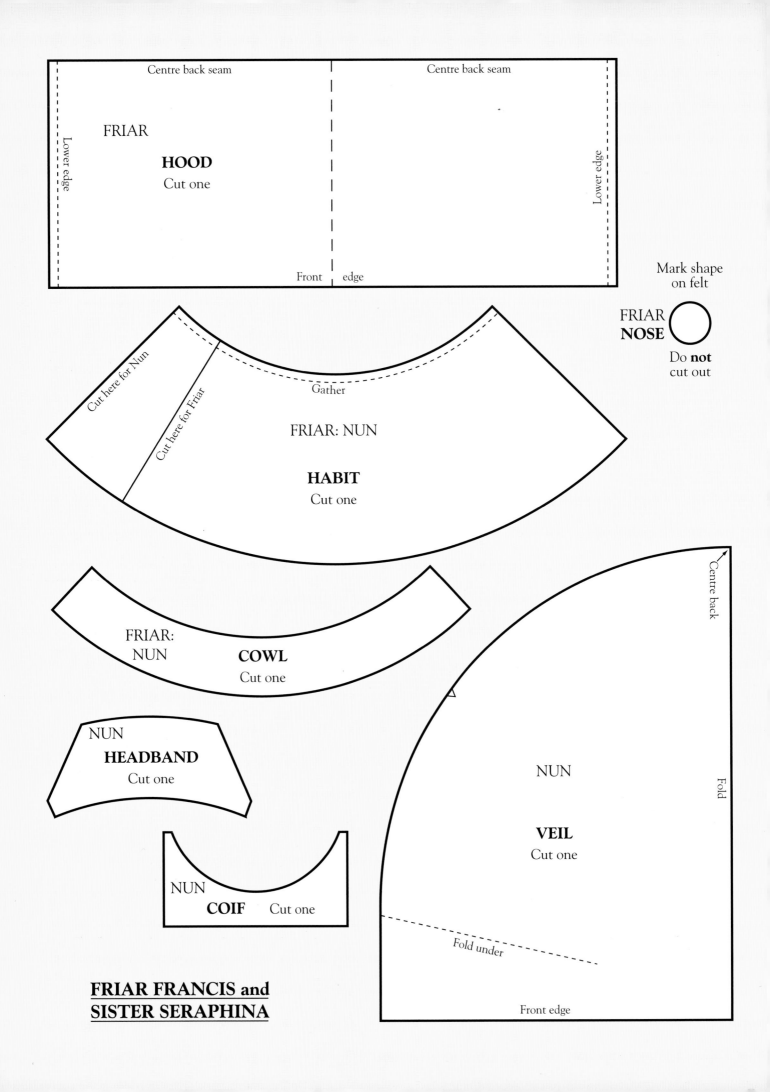

Centre back seam   Centre back seam

FRIAR

HOOD
Cut one

Lower edge   Lower edge

Front   edge

Mark shape
on felt

FRIAR
NOSE

Do **not**
cut out

Cut here for Nun

Cut here for Friar

Gather

FRIAR: NUN

HABIT
Cut one

Centre back

FRIAR:
NUN   **COWL**
             Cut one

NUN
HEADBAND
Cut one

NUN

VEIL
Cut one

Fold

NUN
COIF   Cut one

Fold under

**FRIAR FRANCIS and
SISTER SERAPHINA**

Front edge

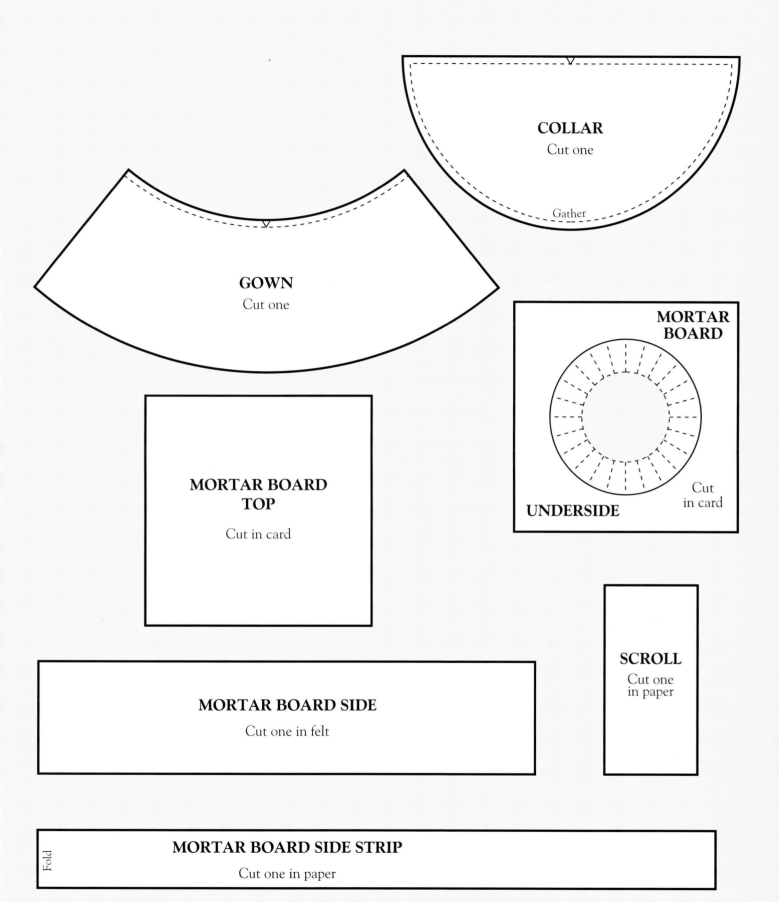

COLLAR
Cut one

Gather

GOWN
Cut one

MORTAR BOARD

UNDERSIDE

Cut
in card

**MORTAR BOARD
TOP**

Cut in card

SCROLL
Cut one
in paper

MORTAR BOARD SIDE

Cut one in felt

Fold

MORTAR BOARD SIDE STRIP

Cut one in paper

HARRIET THE GRADUATE

HARRIET THE GRADUATE

The successful graduate shown here is a beautiful blonde; but for a brainy young man, follow the directions for Thomas' hair (Chapter 9).

MATERIALS

See Chapter 8 for Basic Figure
25cm (10in) square of black felt for body, gown, collar and mortar board
50cm (20in) black satin ribbon, 1.5mm (¹/₁₆in) wide, for tassel (or alternative; see step 9)
10cm (4in) scarlet satin ribbon, 1.5mm (¹/₁₆in) wide
Thin card
Medium-weight paper
Black permanent marker or ink
Elastic band
Glue stick (optional)
Adhesive tape

1. Make the basic figure, version B (Chapter 8), using black felt for the body and base.
2. Cut the gown and collar in black felt (leaving sufficient for the three mortar board pieces).

Right sides together, join the straight edge of the collar to the top curved edge of the gown, centres matched and easing gently to fit. Turn to the right side and gather through the double thickness, close against the seam.

Using a separate thread, gather the curved edge of the collar.

Fit the gown on the figure and draw up the first thread round the neck, top corners meeting under her chin. Then draw up the collar, tucking the gathers underneath and arranging the collar neatly round the neck.

3. For her hair, wind double-knit yarn fifteen times around a 13cm (5in) deep card; slide carefully off the card and tie tightly with a single strand 3.5cm (1³/₈in) from one end; cut the loops at the other end. Stitch the tied section to the top of the head (point A), so that the loops fall over the forehead and the cut ends cover the back of the head.

Wind the yarn fifteen times around a 20cm (8in) deep card; slide off and tie *loosely* at the *centre*; then cut the loops at both ends. Stitch to the top of the head, across the first piece, to hang down equally on each side.

Smooth the hair down and fix an elastic band tightly round the neck to enable you to trim the ends neatly.
4. Follow the directions in Chapter 8 (step 12) for the features. (Blue sequins were used for the figure shown.)
5. Cut the mortar board top and underside (ignoring broken lines) once each in thin card; cut the side strip in paper.

Roll up the side strip and place it inside the central hole of the underside; allow it to open out so that it fits snugly against the sides, then remove it and tape the join.
6. Stick the underside to felt; trim the felt level with the outer edge of the card, but cut a smaller circle in the centre, as the broken line. Then cut the surplus felt into tiny tabs, as indicated.

Run a trail of glue inside the side strip circle, covering the upper half of the paper. Place the underside on top, felt side down, and press the tabs down inside the circle.
7. Cut the side pattern in felt and use it to cover the side strip; have the top edge against the underside and glue the overlap below up inside the circle.
8. Stick the top card to felt and cut out, leaving a 5mm (¹/₄in) surplus all round.

Glue on top of the underside, edges of card level, then trim each side neatly. Blacken the cut edges of the card with marker or ink.
9. To make the tassel, cut 10cm (4in) off the black ribbon. Cut the remainder into eight equal lengths. Tie the centre of the bunch tightly with the 10cm (4in) ribbon about 2.5cm (1in) from one end. Fold in half, including the shorter end of the tie in the bunch. Bind tightly with black thread close under the fold. Trim the cut ends neatly to length.

Make a small hole in the centre of the mortar board top and insert the other end of the tassel tie; knot the end inside to hold it in place.
10. Glue the mortar board very firmly to the head.
11. Cut the scroll in white paper and roll up around a knitting needle or similar object. Then tie the centre with red ribbon. Trim the ends and glue to hang as shown. Then glue one end of the scroll to the body and inside the gown, as illustrated.

CHAPTER 11

Fun with Animation

Animate a figure and you bring it to life. An impression of movement can emphasise character by suggesting youth or age, humour or wickedness, romance or adventure – and it is essential if you wish to create a dramatic situation. A stiff, straight figure robs a doll of its inherent charm – which is why so many fail to capture that elusive element that makes a doll irresistible.

If you want a figure that can literally bend over backwards to prove its agility, the versatile tubing doll has to be the answer. Made in minutes, it often needs only a few small additions to turn it into a recognisable character. Then all you have to do is experiment until you find the most effective bending of body and limbs.

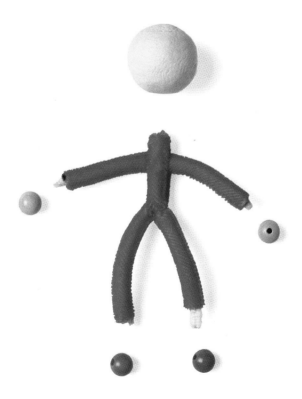

BASIC FIGURE

Velvet tubing, made by Offray, the ribbon people, shapes the figure – and can represent its clothing, too. The inner 'skeleton' is pipe cleaners or chenille stems, and the hands and feet are wooden beads. The turned paper craft ball that forms the head comes in a range of sizes, and is available in a pink flesh tint or plain white.

An inexpensive alternative to purchased velvet tubing is to 'knit' your own tubes, using up leftover oddments of yarn. Our grandmothers used to hammer staples into old-fashioned wooden cotton reels to do 'French knitting': long narrow tubes that would have been ideal for this figure. Unfortunately, plastic reels prevent us following their example, but now you can buy an ingenious little machine that does the job even better (see Acknowledgements). Feed in the yarn, turn the handle, and it produces knitted tubing so neat that Granny would be green with envy!

The wooden beads can be purchased plain or coloured, in packets or on a string. Natural beads are usually best for hands – and the same beads can be coloured with a felt pen or marker to make feet.

MATERIALS

25cm (10in) Offray velvet tubing (or alternative: see above)
OR 14cm (5¹⁄₂in) for the body and arms
10cm (4in) for the legs
2 pipe cleaners or chenille stems
Turned paper, or alternative, craft ball, 3cm (1¹⁄₄in) diameter, flesh-tinted, if possible, for the head
2 natural wood beads, 1cm (³⁄₈in) diameter, for hands
2 coloured wood beads, 1cm (³⁄₈in) diameter, for feet
Twilley's stranded embroidery wool, or knitting yarn, for hair (see individual directions for specific details)
Flesh-coloured poster paint (if the ball is not coloured)
Sepia (or black) watercolour pencil or ball-point pen or ink, to draw features
Matching sewing thread
Clear adhesive

1. Cut the pipe cleaners (or chenille stems), and the velvet tubing, as follows:

	Pipe Cleaners	*Velvet Tubing*
Arms:	9cm (3¹⁄₂in)	8cm (3¹⁄₈in)
Body:	7cm (2³⁄₄in) *	6cm (2³⁄₈in)
Legs:	11cm (4¹⁄₄in)	10cm (4in)

*Use remainder of above cleaner

2. Push the pieces of pipe cleaner through the tubing so that they protrude equally at each end; hold the inner cord to prevent it slipping, but if you accidentally lose the end, pull it right out and discard it.

3. Following the diagram, bend the body in half and glue the arms between (mark the centre of the arms beforehand, to ensure they are exactly equal).
4. Bend the legs as indicated. Then stitch the body and legs securely together.
5. Glue the appropriate beads onto the ends of the pipe cleaners for the hands and feet.
6. Paint the ball if necessary, then examine it to choose the best surface for the face; indicate this with a pencil arrow on top of the head. Glue the head onto the ends of the body pipe cleaner (unless otherwise directed; you may need to delay this until the figure is dressed).
7. Follow the individual instructions for the hairstyle (referring to Hairstyling if necessary).

When you reach the final stage of trimming the wool to length, wrap a face tissue or paper towel around the figure, to protect the garments. If any bits *do* fall onto the velvet or felt, brush them off with a stiff paintbrush, or remove with adhesive tape.
8. When the figure is completely dressed and the hairstyle is finished, mark round dots for the eyes and a very short line for the nose; draw longer lines or curves for eyebrows, and a curve for the mouth, if required; although black is very satisfactory, dark brown or sepia (as illustrated) gives a slightly softer effect, and may be preferred.

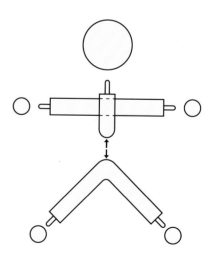

CHAPTER 12

Mobile Mascots

T*he simple animated figure introduced in the previous chapter is a basic design with enormous potential. Made in minutes, it offers limitless scope for development. The designs in this chapter deliberately emphasise the animation by arranging two dolls together in a moving situation.*

SPORTING DOUBLE

When you feel deeply about something, it's important to get your message across as strongly as possible. These two fans (page 113) have decided that a banner headline is the answer. So quick and easy to make – and the message can be as personal as you wish.

Make two basic figures, as directed in Chapter 11, using emerald velvet tubing for one, and scarlet for the other.

ADDITIONAL MATERIALS

Small amounts of green and red knitting yarn (see step 2)
Seven 76cm (30in) strands Twilley's stranded embroidery wool for EACH: shade 55 (emerald figure) and shade 49 (scarlet figure), OR fine knitting yarn
2 wooden cocktail sticks
Medium-weight paper for banner
Black felt-tip pen, marker or ink
Small curtain ring
Matching and black sewing threads

1. For the hair, cut forty-eight 9.5cm (3³/4in) strands of wool and tie them tightly at the centre with a single strand.

Pin the tied centre to the crown of the head, then spread the strands out evenly all round the head and glue into place. Do not trim until the hat is in place.

2. You can use any weight of yarn and size of needles to knit the hat and scarf, although the same considerations apply as to the Dumpy Knit-wits (Chapter 9). The examples illustrated are made with double-knit yarn on 3mm/No 11/American size 2 needles; the figures in brackets indicate the number of stitches used in each case.

3. To make the hat, cast on sufficient stitches to make a piece about 10cm (4in) wide, the number of stitches being divisible by four (28).

First row: Knit
Second row: K1; purl to last stitch; K1
Repeat these two rows until the work measures 2.5cm (1in).
Next row: Knit 2 together to end.
Next row: As second row.
Next row: Knit 2 together to end.

Break off the yarn and slip the end through the remaining stitches; draw up tightly. With right side inside, join the side edges to form the centre back seam. Turn to the right side and fit on the figure, stitching the lower edge to the head to hold it in position.

For the brim, cast on sufficient stitches to make a piece about 1.5cm (⁵/8in) wide (4). Knit a strip long enough to fit snugly around the head over the lower edge of the hat (about 11-12cm/4¹/2in). Cast off and join the short ends, then fit over the head and glue into position, join at back.

Trim the hair neatly to length.

4. To make the scarf, knit a strip in exactly the same way as the hat brim, but cast off when it is 15cm (6in) long.

Darn in and trim off the ends of yarn, then wind the scarf around the neck as illustrated, catching into place with matching thread and gluing to centre front of body.

5. Catch the two figures together with matching thread, as shown.

6. Fix the cocktail sticks in their raised outer hands, as illustrated.

7. Cut the banner 2.5cm (1in) deep × about 12cm (4³/4in) wide, adding about 1.5cm (¹/2in) at each side to fix to the cocktail sticks.

Write your message boldly, then glue the side edges around the sticks.

8. Suspend with a length of black thread fixed between the tops of their heads, slipping a curtain ring onto the thread as you do so.

DUET ON A BROOMSTICK

There's magic in the air when two witches share the same broomstick, making sure that their spells work twice as well. The dress and cloak are very useful basic patterns, which can be adapted to create a wide variety of characters.

Make two basic figures, as directed in Chapter 11, using black velvet tubing.

ADDITIONAL MATERIALS

25cm (10in) square of black felt
10 × 15cm (4 × 6in) lilac felt for first dress
10 × 15cm (4 × 6in) mauve felt for second dress
Nine 76cm (30in) strands Twilley's stranded embroidery wool EACH, shades 3 and 4, for hair, OR fine knitting yarn
20cm (8in) length of wooden dowelling, 5mm (³/₁₆in) diameter
Garden raffia
Medium-weight paper
Small curtain ring
Matching sewing threads

1. To make each witch, cut the dress in lilac or mauve, making slits for the armholes, as indicated.

Join the centre back seam and turn to the right side. Fit the dress on the doll and gather the top edge; draw it up closely around the neck and secure.
2. Cut the cloak in black felt. Gather the top edge and draw up around the neck, corners meeting under the chin.
3. For the hair, cut forty-eight 12.5cm (5in) strands of wool and tie them loosely at the centre with a single strand.

Glue the tied centre to the top of the head, then bring the strands smoothly down and glue to cover the sides and back of the head evenly.

Trim the cut ends to length.
4. Trace the hat crown and brim (ignore broken lines) onto paper and cut out. Glue the larger section of the crown to black felt, leaving the overlap clear; trim level with the edge of the paper. Then curve round to form a cone and glue the overlap inside, lower edges level.

Glue the top of the brim to black felt and trim level with the inner and outer edges of the paper. Cover the underside and trim the outer edge level; but cut away a smaller circle at the centre, then snip the surplus into tiny tabs, as indicated by the broken lines.

Spread glue on the underside of the tabs, then press down firmly on the witch's head. Run a trail of glue just inside the crown and press it firmly down over the brim.
5. Cut a bunch of raffia strands about 9cm (3¹/₂in) long. Spread glue liberally over about 2cm (³/₄in) at one end of the dowelling, then arrange the strands around it and bind them tightly with a single strand of raffia.
6. Cut small slits at back and front of dresses, then slide the witches onto the broomstick in sitting positions, following the illustration for guidance. Stitch and glue to hold in place, then suspend with a length of black thread fixed between the points of their hats, slipping a curtain ring onto the thread as you do so.

PARTNERS IN CRIME

Make two basic figures, as directed in Chapter 11, using black velvet tubing.

ADDITIONAL MATERIALS

10cm (4in) square of beige felt for first cap
10cm (4in) square of pale grey felt for second cap
8 × 6cm (3 × 2½in) mid-grey felt for swag bags
3cm (1¼in) square of black felt for masks
Seven 76cm (30in) strands Twilley's stranded embroidery
    wool EACH, shades 53 and 97, for hair, OR fine knitting
    yarn
Dark grey knitting yarn for jumpers (see step 2)
Cotton wool (absorbent cotton)
70cm (¾yd) medium thickness piping cord
Matching sewing threads

1. For the hair, follow the directions for the 'Sporting Double' figures, step 1.
2. You can use any weight of yarn and size of needles to knit their jumpers, although anything thicker than double-knit will be too bulky. Those illustrated are knitted with twelve stitches on fine needles (2¼/No 13/American size 00), using a thin 3-ply yarn. The slinky result is quite effective for this particular subject. But if you prefer to use a thicker yarn, refer back to the Dumpy Knit-wits (Chapter 9).
3. For the front, cast on sufficient stitches to make a piece 3cm (1¼in) wide.

> First row: Knit
> Second row: K1; purl to last stitch; K1
> Repeat these two rows until the work measures 3cm (1¼in), ending with a knit row.
> Next row: Knit.
> Next row: K1; purl to last stitch; K1.
> Continue until the work measures 5cm (2in) from the beginning.
> Cast off.
> Make a second piece in exactly the same way for the back.

4. On each piece, fold the top half of the reverse stocking stitch section under, to form the collar; catch the cast-off edge to the top row of the main stocking stitch section.
    Right sides together, join the front and back at each side, but leave 1cm (⅜in) open below the collar for the armholes. Turn to the right side and fit on the doll.
5. To make the cap, cut the top and underside once each, in felt. Trace the peak and cut it out, then stick the tracing to felt, and cut the felt level. Stick the other side of the paper to felt, and cut level again.
    Oversew (overcast) the top and underside together all round the outer edges. Turn to the right side and glue the inner edge of the peak to the underside, cut edges level.
    Glue the cap to the head and trim the hair to length.
6. To make their masks, trace the pattern and cut it out, then stick the tracing to black felt and cut the felt level with the paper.
    Punch holes for the eyes before gluing to the face.
7. Cut the swag bags in felt and fold in half as the broken line. Join the side edges of each, then turn to the right side and two-thirds fill with cotton wool. Gather the top edge and draw up tightly, then stitch to the figure's wrist and shoulder, as illustrated.
8. Fold over and knot the top of the piping cord to form a loop. Then fix the figures in climbing positions, following the illustration for guidance; catch into place with matching thread.

KNIT 2 TOGETHER

'Will she *ever* stop knitting?' wonders Grandad, as Grandma begins yet another row. He'll be able to wrap that scarf around his feet and head, as well as his neck, by the time it's finished. The perfect gift for an intrepid knitter! (See also page 7.)

Make two basic figures, as directed in Chapter 11, using green velvet tubing for Grandad, and scarlet for Grandma's body and arms, with black for her legs.

ADDITIONAL MATERIALS

7 × 9cm (2¾ × 3½in) scarlet felt, for her dress
20cm (8in) cream lace, 10mm (⅜in) deep, for her collar and cuffs
10cm (4in) black lace, 10mm (⅜in) deep, to trim her hem
Three 76cm (30in) strands Twilley's stranded embroidery wool, shade 3, for his hair etc, OR fine knitting yarn
Fluffy white yarn (double-knit or thinner), for her hair
Fine (3- or 4-ply) bright multi-coloured knitting yarn, for the scarf
Small skein of thicker yarn in contrasting colour, for 'seat'
2 jewellery jump rings for her spectacles
2 wooden cocktail sticks for knitting needles
2 coloured wooden beads, 5mm (³⁄₁₆in) diameter, for needles
1 natural wooden bead, 5mm (³⁄₁₆in) diameter, for his nose
2 tiny pearl beads for her earrings
Small curtain ring
Matching and black sewing threads

1. Using fine knitting needles (2¼mm/No 13/ American size 0) and one strand of grey embroidery wool (or fine knitting yarn), cast on sufficient stitches (about 20) to work a piece 6cm (2½in) wide; work in stocking stitch for 1cm (⅜in) – about five rows. Do not cast off, but draw the yarn through the stitches, slipping them off the needle as you do so. Then darn the ends in neatly. Glue the strip around his head, as illustrated, reverse side of work outwards.
2. To make his moustache, wind a strand of wool around a pencil ten times; slide off the pencil, slip a length of yarn through the centre and tie the loops tightly, then fold the tied point, pinching it together, and cut the loops.
   Glue to the face, then trim neatly.
3. Glue the nose bead on top of his moustache.
4. Mark the eyes, then glue 1cm (⅜in) lengths of wool above, for his eyebrows.
5. For her hair, wind the yarn about twenty times

around a 10cm (4in) deep card. Tie tightly at each edge with a single strand before removing from the card, then tie the centre loosely with white thread.

Glue the centre of the skein to the top of her head, then spread glue over the rest of the head and take the sides of the skein down and round to the back, knotting the ties together at the nape of the neck; arrange the strands evenly to cover the head, and trim ends neatly.
6. Cut her dress in felt, making slits for the armholes, as indicated.
   Join the centre back seam and turn to the right side. Stitch black lace around the hemline.
   Fit the dress on the doll and gather the top edge, drawing it up closely around the neck, and secure.
7. Gather 6cm (2½in) cream lace along the *centre* and draw it up around her neck to form a collar, join at the back.
   Fold the same lace in half lengthways and stitch around her wrists to form cuffs.
8. Glue pearl bead earrings at each side of her face.
9. Glue the jump rings into position for her spectacles, then mark features.
10. Make their 'seat' by winding the thicker yarn into a neat skein about 11-12cm (4¼-4¾in) long. Arrange the figures in sitting positions on the seat, following the photograph for guidance, and catch them securely to the skein of yarn at back and front.
11. Using the same needles as before and yellow yarn, cast on sufficient stitches (about 6) to knit a piece approximately 1.5cm (⅝in) wide. Work in garter stitch until the scarf is approaching the required length (about 35-40cm/14-16in).
12. Wrap the end of the scarf around his neck, as illustrated, then take it down behind the seat and bring the other end up at the front, arranging it to sit neatly in her lap; make it a little longer, if necessary.
13. Make her knitting needles from 4cm (1½in) lengths of cocktail stick, with coloured beads fixed on the cut ends. Slip the stitches off your own needles onto these, then glue them to her hands. Cut the yarn, leaving enough to wind into a small ball to hang down below, as illustrated: catch the strand to the ball to prevent it unwinding.
14. Catch or glue the scarf to hold it in position, wherever necessary.
15. Suspend the figures with black thread taken through the tops of their heads, slipping a curtain ring onto the thread as you fix it.

TWO MUCH IN LOVE

Make two basic figures, as directed in Chapter 11, using emerald velvet tubing for the elf, and white for the fairy's body and arms, with black for her legs.

ADDITIONAL MATERIALS

10cm (4in) square of emerald felt
70cm (¾yd) white lace, 20mm (¾in) deep
10cm (4in) blue lace, 10mm (⅜in) deep
Tiny pearl beads
Mother-of-pearl flower sequin (optional)
Tiny forget-me-not blue artificial flower-heads
Nine 76cm (30in) strands Twilley's stranded embroidery wool, shade 81, for her hair, and seven strands of the same wool, shade 102, for his hair, OR fine knitting yarn
Cotton wool (absorbent cotton)
Stiff card (artists' mounting board)
Gold foil gift-wrap paper (Hallmark)
Small curtain ring
Matching and sewing black threads
Glue stick

1. Cut the white lace into four equal lengths; overlap and glue the cut ends of each strip to form four circles. Gather the straight edge of one circle and draw it up tightly around the fairy's waist, spreading the gathers out evenly. Gather another circle and draw it up close underneath the first one. Repeat with the remaining two circles.
2. Make the blue lace into a collar around her neck in the same way.

3. For her hair, follow the directions for the 'Duet on a Broomstick' witches, step 3.
4. Glue a circlet of pearls to the top of her head, as illustrated, with a flower sequin at centre front, over the join.
   Decorate the sequin and hair with flower-heads and single pearls.
5. Glue a flower-head to each shoe.
6. Cut the hat pattern four times, the stalk once, and the leaf six times, all in green felt.
7. Glue the leaves neatly around the elf's neck.
8. For his hair, follow the directions for the 'Sporting Double' figures, step 1.
9. To make his hat, join two pieces together between A-B. Repeat with the other two pieces. Then join the two halves, matching points B-A-B. Turn to the right side.
   To make the stalk, roll the felt up and slip-stitch the join, then stitch one end to the crown of the hat (point A). Cut the other end at an angle, as illustrated.
   Pad the inside with cotton wool, then fit the hat on the head and stitch (or glue) it securely. Then trim the hair to length.
10. Cut the moon in stiff card and cover both sides smoothly with gold foil paper.
11. Arrange the figures as illustrated and, when you are satisfied, stitch them into position.
12. To hang, slip the curtain ring onto a length of black thread, and then fix it between the top of her head and the top point of the moon.

PERFORMING PAIR

Satin ribbon makes a wonderful clown costume – and you don't even need a pattern.

Make two basic figures as directed in Chapter 11, but *don't* glue the arms between the body; use white balls for the heads (fix them later), and match the colour of the feet to the costume.

ADDITIONAL MATERIALS
(for each clown)

90cm (1yd) single-face satin ribbon, 23mm (1in) wide, for the costume

50cm (exact) (⅝yd) single-face satin ribbon, 9mm (⅜in) wide, for frills etc

Brightly coloured double-knit yarn for hair

Red wooden ball, 5-7mm (¼in) diameter, for nose

Thin white paper

Lead pencil or black ink

Matching and black sewing threads

Glue stick (optional)

For the trapeze

3m (3yd) satin ribbon, 1.5mm (1/16in) wide

Balsa wood: 12.5cm (5in) long × 5mm (¼in) wide × 3mm (⅛in) thick

Curtain ring

Thin pins (lace or dressmaker)

1. Cut six 10cm (4in) lengths of the 23mm (1in) ribbon: two for the sleeves and four for the body and legs. Cut a 20cm (8in) length of the same ribbon for the collar.

2. Right sides together, join the two sleeve pieces by stitching close against the woven edges.

Turn to the right side. At one end turn the cut edge inside and gather very close to the fold. Push the arms through the tube and draw up the gathers tightly around one wrist. Turn under and gather the other end in the same way, and draw it up around the other wrist.

3. Fit the arms between the body (centre carefully), then bind them tightly into place with thread, so that the sleeves are gathered in at the shoulders.

4. Right sides together, join two pieces of ribbon for each side of the body and a leg, as figure 2; first join each side between B-C, leaving 3cm (1¼in) open at the top, and then between E-F, leaving the upper 5cm (2in) open.

Now join the two halves together between D-E, to form the centre back and front seams. Turn to the right side.

Turn the cut edge of each leg inside and gather, as for the sleeves. Then fit on the body and draw up the gathers tightly around the ankles.

Finally, turn the top edges (A-D-A) under at back and front and gather along both edges, then draw up around the neck, stitching to hold in position.

5. Overlap and glue the cut ends of the collar to form a circle, then gather close to one long edge. Draw up around the neck and stitch securely into place.

6. Make the wrist and ankle frills in the same way, from 10cm (4in) lengths of 9mm (⅜in) ribbon, and draw up tightly against the gathered sleeves and ankles.

7. Make two rosettes in the same way from 5cm (2in) lengths of the same ribbon, but this time gather along the *centre* of the ribbon, and draw up as tightly as possible.

Stitch one rosette to the front of the costume and reserve the other for his hat.

8. Glue the head firmly into position.

9. For the hair, cut 15-20 strands of double-knit yarn, 10cm (4in) long; tie the centre with a single strand. Then pin (or glue) the tied centre to the top of the head, and glue the strands smoothly down to cover the sides and back of the head. Trim the ends to length.

10. Trace the face onto thin white paper, making a strong outline. Cut it out, as the broken line, snipping between the eyes and mouth.

Stick the paper face to the head, then glue the nose in the centre, pushing it firmly against the ball.

11. Trace the hat onto thin paper and cut it out. Then stick it to the wrong side of the wide ribbon; cut ribbon level with paper. Curve round and glue the overlap. Glue on top of the head.

Glue the second rosette to the point of the hat.

12. Plait the very narrow ribbon to make braid.

13. Glue braid along one *narrow* edge of the balsa wood (this will be the front). Then sit and stand the figures on top, pinning them into position.

Beginning at the centre, glue one end of the braid underneath the balsa strip, then bring it over the end and up the side, pinning a clown's hand to it as illustrated; take it over the top, threading on the curtain ring, then pin the other clown's hand, and take the braid over the opposite end of the balsa wood, gluing it underneath the remaining half so that it joins at the centre. Pin the braid at both ends to hold securely.

14. Fix a black thread to the sleeve of the upper clown, take it up through the curtain ring and down to finish on the clown's sleeve again. Stitch the thread and braid together against the ring so that the bar is horizontal.

PERFORMING PAIR

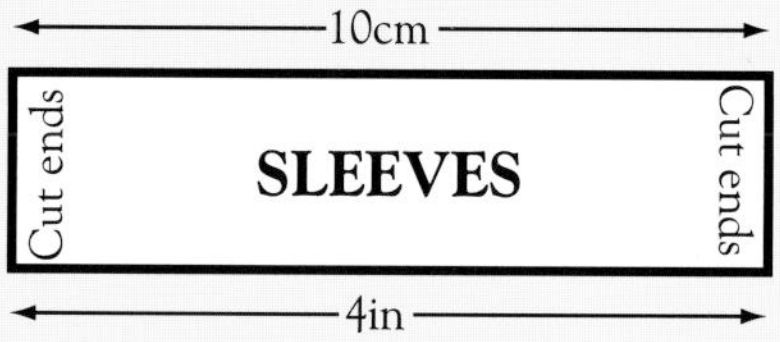

Snip ← → Snip

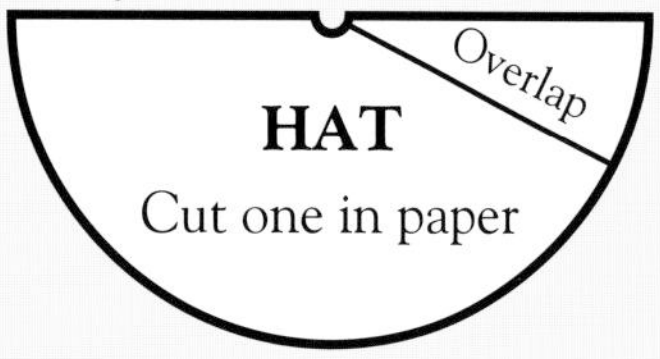

HAT
Cut one in paper

Overlap

10cm

Cut ends   **SLEEVES**   Cut ends   Figure 1

4in

A D   D A

3 cm   **BODY**   **BODY**   1¼ in

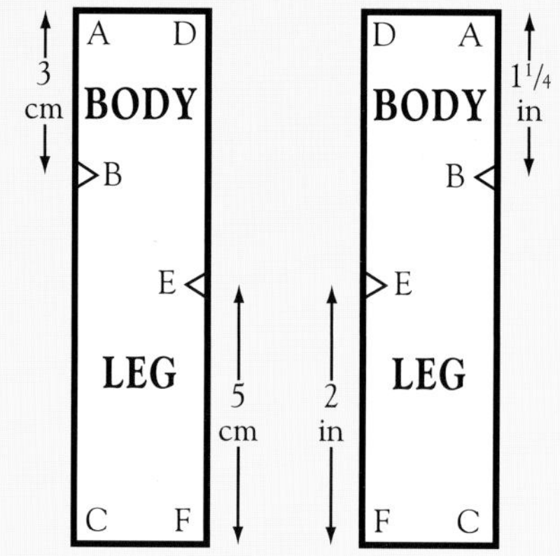

B   B

E   E

LEG   5 cm   2 in   **LEG**   Figure 2

C F   F C

A

HAT
Cut four

B   B

TWO MUCH IN LOVE

LEAF

Cut six

HAT STALK
Cut one

MOON

Cut one in card

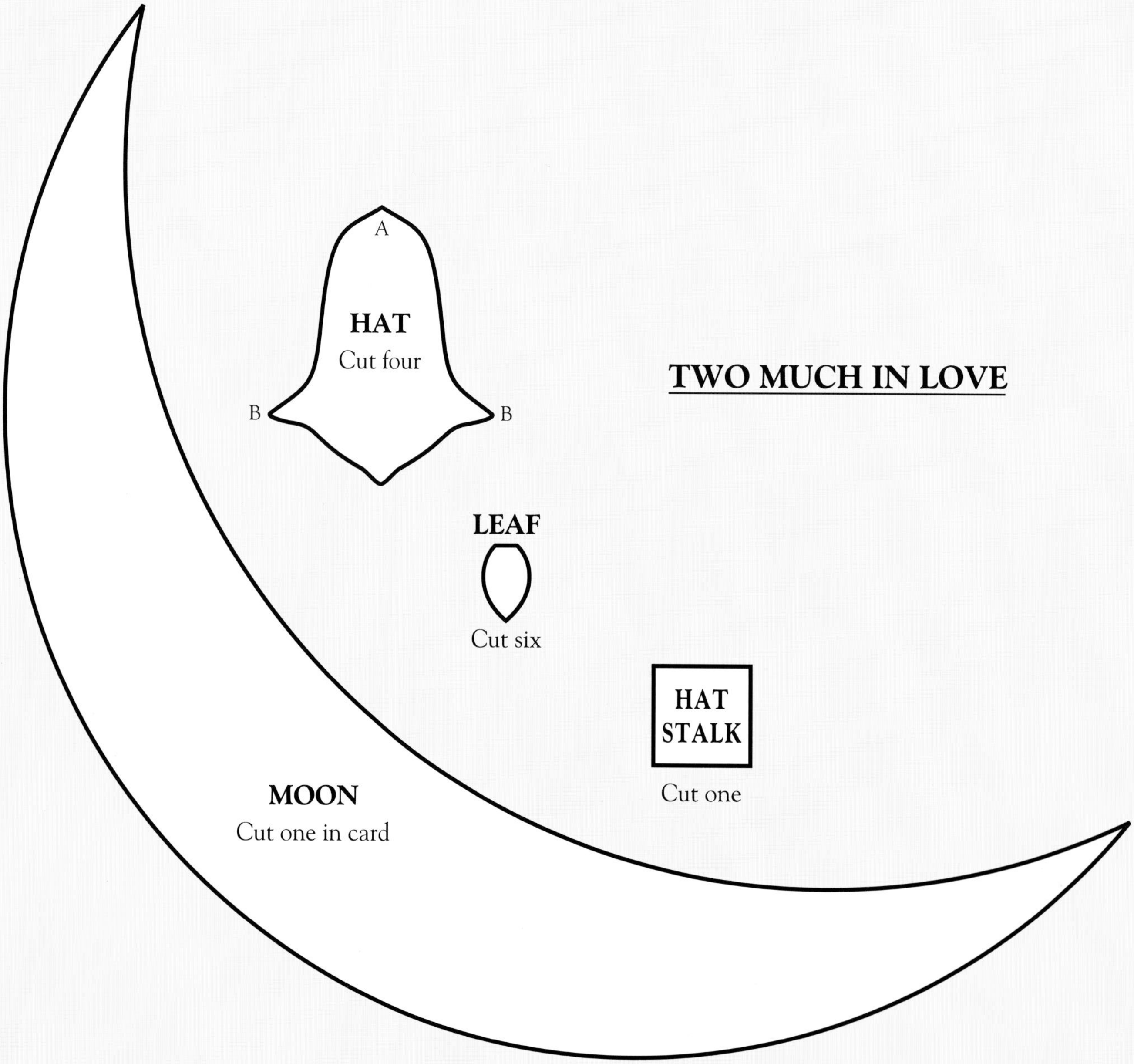

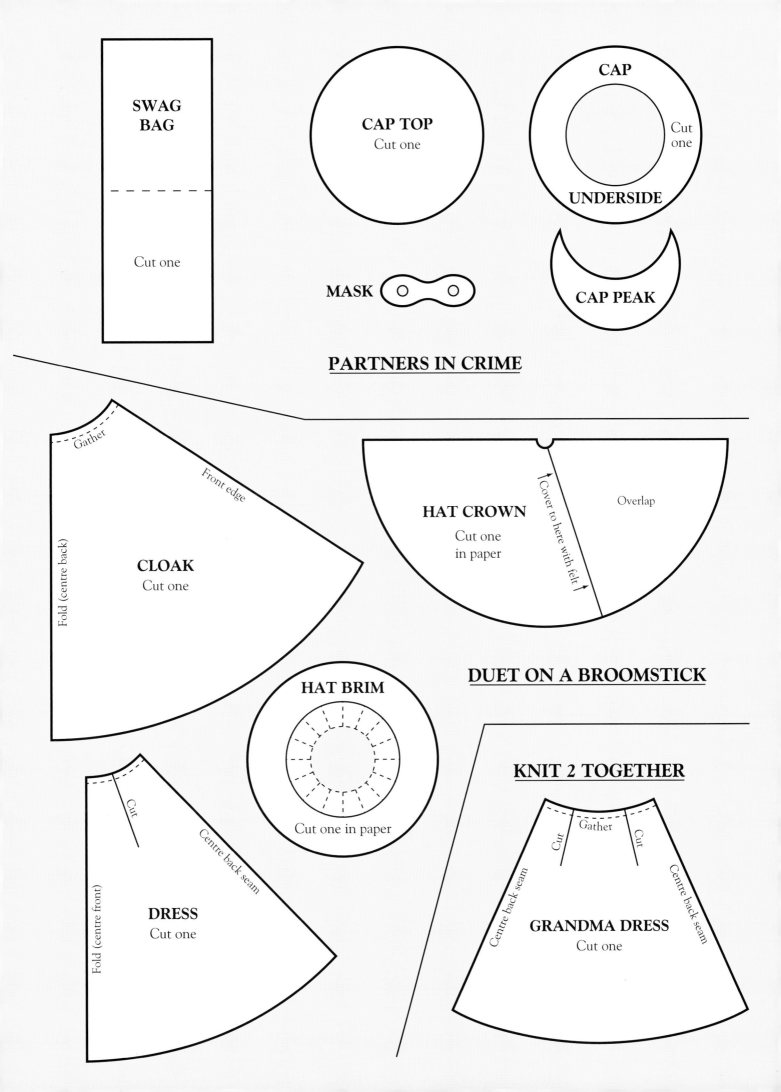

SWAG BAG

Cut one

CAP TOP

Cut one

CAP

Cut one

UNDERSIDE

MASK

CAP PEAK

PARTNERS IN CRIME

Gather

Front edge

Fold (centre back)

CLOAK

Cut one

Cover to here with felt

Overlap

HAT CROWN

Cut one
in paper

DUET ON A BROOMSTICK

HAT BRIM

Cut one in paper

Cut

Centre back seam

Fold (centre front)

DRESS

Cut one

KNIT 2 TOGETHER

Gather

Cut

Cut

Centre back seam

Centre back seam

GRANDMA DRESS

Cut one

Dolls for Decoration

CHAPTER 13

Sweet Lavender Ladies

The basic concept of the Dumpy figure (Chapter 8) is nothing more than a straight cylinder with a round ball on top. But Chapters 9 and 10 demonstrate how it requires only a little imagination to turn something so simple into an amusing character. So it's worth taking a second look at this useful shape to see how much more potential it offers for further development in other directions.

The three little scented dolls in the photograph are made on exactly the same principle as the Dumpies; only the measurements and materials have changed. They effectively demonstrate how easy – and exciting – it is to adapt a basic idea to suit yourself; in this case, transforming a fun figure into a sophisticated dressing- table decoration.

Instead of felt, the body cylinder is made from fabric – forming the dress. And the head is a turned paper ball, as used for the tubing figure in Chapter 11. All three dolls are basically the same design, but interpreted in various ways, with contrasting colour schemes and a generous assortment of trimmings creating completely different effects. Study the photograph carefully and you will see that, apart from their hats, the method for each doll is exactly the same.

SEAMS: *approximately 3mm (¹/₈in) is allowed for turnings.*

SWEET LAVENDER LADIES

MATERIALS (for each doll)

13 × 18cm (5 × 7in) medium-weight, plain or printed, cotton-type fabric for body/dress

Matching or toning fabric for cape; see step 1 pattern

Polyester stuffing

Dried lavender (or fine pot-pourri)

Turned paper, or alternative, craft ball, 3cm (1¼in) diameter, flesh-tinted, if possible, for the head

5cm (2in) pipe cleaner or chenille stem

Nine 76cm (30in) strands Twilley's stranded embroidery wool, for hair, or fine knitting yarn

Lace, ribbons and braid: to trim, and for hats (see directions: steps 5, 9, 10 and 11)

2 tiny pearl beads for earrings

Tiny dried or artificial flowers for bouquets

Scraps of stiff and thin card

Flesh-coloured poster paint (if the ball is not coloured)

Sepia (or black) watercolour pencil or ball-point pen or ink, to draw features

Matching sewing threads

Clear adhesive

1. Cut the body and base, and the cape of your choice, in the appropriate fabrics. Cut the base again, slightly smaller, in stiff card.

2. Right sides together, stitch the lower edge of the body around the base. Then join the side edges to form the centre back seam. Turn to the right side.

Turn the top edge under and gather. Gather again 2.5cm (1in) below. Don't draw up.

3. Push the card base down into the bottom of the body. Two-thirds fill with lavender, then complete with polyester stuffing.

4. Draw up the top gathers tightly, then the waist gathers.

5. Glue 10cm (4in) satin ribbon, 3mm (⅛in) wide, around waist; trim and join at the back.

6. Paint the ball if necessary, then examine it to choose the best surface for the face; indicate this with a pencil arrow on top of the head.

7. Bend the pipe cleaner in half and push it into the ball. Insert and glue it into the top of the body.

8. Wind eight strands of wool around a 10cm (4in) deep card. Tie the loops tightly at each end, then slip off and tie the centre more loosely.

Glue the centre of the skein to the top of the head, then take the ends down over each side and round to the back, gluing to hold in place; knot the ties at the nape of the neck and tuck in or trim the loose ends neatly.

9. Glue 12cm (5in) lengths of lace, plaited ribbon or braid around the hem etc, following the photograph for guidance.

10. Turn the top edge of the cape under, and gather. Glue narrow braid, lace or other trimming all round over the cut edge.

Draw up around the neck. Gather 15-20cm (6-8in) lace around the neck to form a collar.

11. Let your imagination run riot and design your own millinery!

In the photograph, the lilac doll has a rosette of 10mm (⅜in) wide lace with an 8mm (½in) hole in the centre, pinned (or glued) to the top of her head. Over this is a similar rosette of navy blue lace, with satin roses nestling on top, made from 6mm (¼in) wide ribbon. The roses pick up the colours of the dress, whilst streamers of the same ribbon match her cape.

The green doll has a similar rosette pinned to the top of her head. Her wide-brimmed hat is made from plaited ribbon coiled round and stitched to form the required shape; the crown (glued to a circle of thin card) is 2.5cm (1in) in diameter, and the brim 5cm (2in).

The brown doll has 15cm (6in) feather-edge satin ribbon, 10mm (⅜in) wide, folded in half and pinned to the top of her head to form streamers at the back. On top a lace rosette is trimmed with roses and a ribbon bow.

12. Mark round dots for the eyes and a tiny line for the nose.

13. Glue pearl bead earrings at each side of the face.

14. Glue a spray of dried flowers to the skirt, as illustrated.

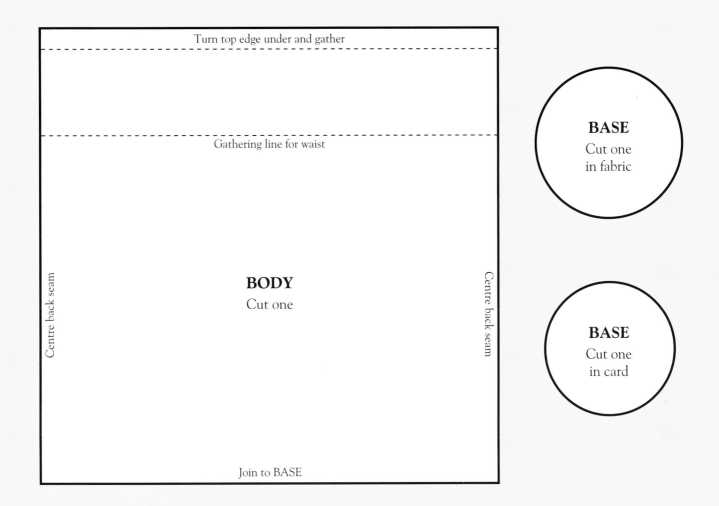

Turn top edge under and gather

Gathering line for waist

Centre back seam

BODY
Cut one

Centre back seam

Join to BASE

BASE
Cut one
in fabric

BASE
Cut one
in card

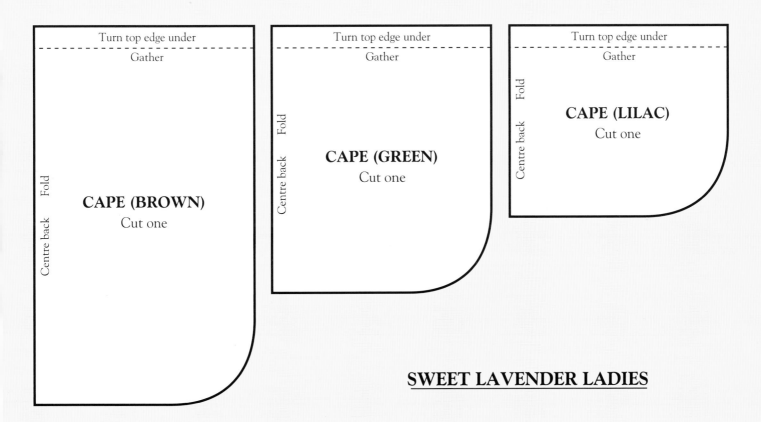

Turn top edge under

Gather

Centre back   Fold

CAPE (BROWN)
Cut one

Turn top edge under

Gather

Centre back   Fold

CAPE (GREEN)
Cut one

Turn top edge under

Gather

Centre back   Fold

CAPE (LILAC)
Cut one

SWEET LAVENDER LADIES

Fashion and Costume Basic Doll

The little lavender ladies demonstrate how it is possible to depict an elegant human form very simply. The figure is nothing more than a straight tube of fabric with a ball on top. Yet it has all the necessary elements for any decorative doll: the proportions are right, making it ideal for dressing and characterisation; it is quick and easy to make, allowing one to start the next stage – developing the character – as soon as possible; and it stands independently, the flat base keeping it firm and steady.

Obviously it is essential to try to incorporate all these important features when developing a more sophisticated figure for a more elaborate decoration. Whether you want to make a romantic wedding centrepiece or are planning a collection of dolls in historical costume or national dress, you will need a quick-to-make basic doll with a 'model' figure.

Although this elegant 'fashion doll' is larger, more shapely and has adjustable arms, it still retains the basic advantages of the simple lavender lady. Subtle differences can be conveyed in shape and form by clever stuffing and emphasis. Height can be altered, and of course you can widen the pattern for a more generously proportioned character. There is also a child-size version made in exactly the same way.

The success of a figure on this scale relies on good quality felt: it must be firm and even, neither too thick nor too thin, without undue stretch. Cream is the best choice for a pale-skinned character; so-called 'flesh colour' gives a more ruddy complexion, if that is what you want; whilst a deep 'coffee-with-cream' tone is best for a dark-skinned figure, as it contrasts strikingly with black eyes and hair.

SEAMS: *Oversew (overcast) edges of felt to join; approximately 1.5mm (¹/₁₆in) is allowed for seams.*

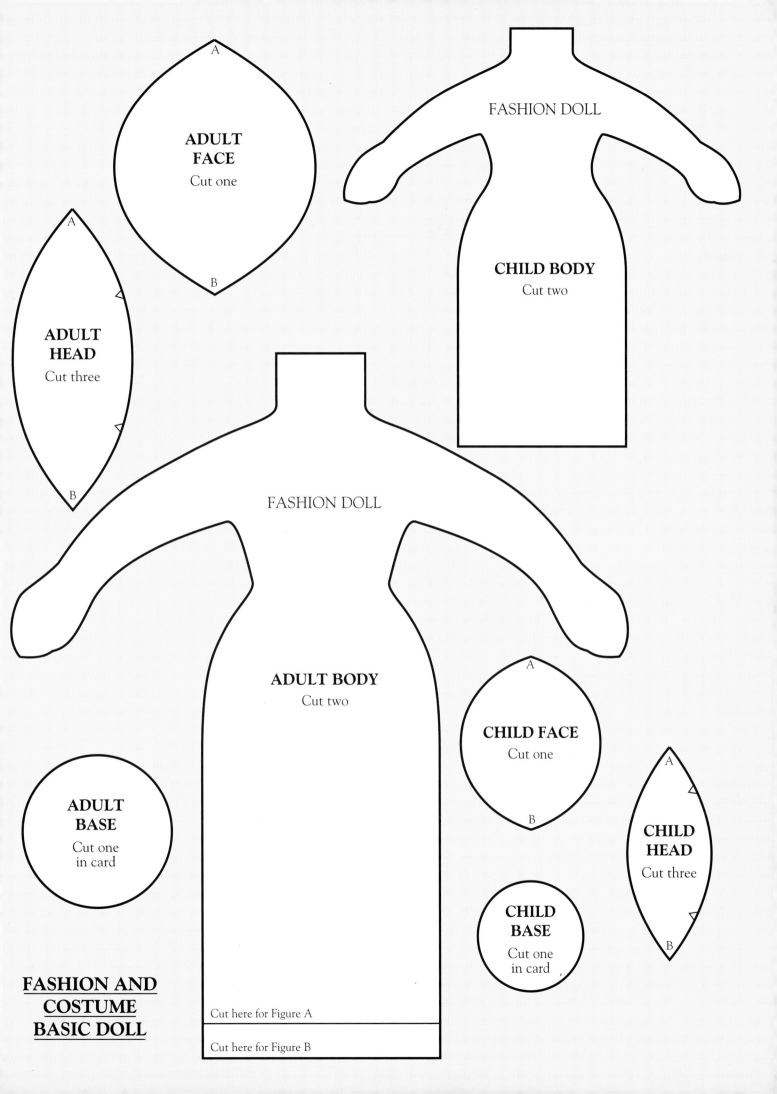

ADULT
FACE
Cut one

FASHION DOLL

ADULT
HEAD
Cut three

CHILD BODY
Cut two

A

B

A

B

FASHION DOLL

ADULT BODY
Cut two

CHILD FACE
Cut one

A

B

ADULT
BASE
Cut one
in card

CHILD
HEAD
Cut three

A

B

CHILD
BASE
Cut one
in card

Cut here for Figure A

Cut here for Figure B

**FASHION AND
COSTUME
BASIC DOLL**

MATERIALS (for any figure)

One 30cm (12in) square (*or* two 20cm/8in squares) of
    flesh-coloured felt, for the ADULT figure (A or B)
Or one 20cm (8in) square of flesh-coloured felt for the
    CHILD
Polyester stuffing
2 pipe cleaners (chenille stems), 16.5cm (6½in) long
Medium-weight paper
Scrap of stiff card
2oz modelling clay for the ADULT figure
Or 1oz modelling clay for the CHILD
Kitchen foil
Matching sewing thread
Clear adhesive

1. Trace off the appropriate patterns for the doll that
you are making. Cut the body twice, the face once and
the head section three times, in flesh felt.

    Cut the base in card, then glue it lightly to felt and
cut the felt about 2mm (a good ¹/₁₆in) from the edge of
the card.

    Cut a strip of paper 8cm (3in) deep × 30cm (12in)
wide for the ADULT figure A, or 9 × 30cm (3½ ×
12in) for figure B; or 4cm (1½in) deep × 20cm (8in)
wide for the CHILD.

2. Join two head pieces between A-B. Join on the
other piece, but leave open between the notches. Then
join the sides of the head to each side of the face, again
matching points A and B.

3. Turn to the right side and stuff *very* firmly indeed,
pushing the filling well up into the top and bottom
(points A and B), and moulding to shape with the
hands. Slip-stitch the opening neatly.

4. Join the two body pieces at each side, between the
neck and base, leaving the top and bottom edges open:
stitch closely and neatly, especially around the neck
and hands. Turn to the right side.

5. Roll up the paper to form a tube, then push it up
into the lower part of the figure, the bottom of the
paper about 1cm (³/₈in) above the base of the felt.
Allow the paper to open out inside, pulling it tight
against the felt; then tack the paper to the felt, near the
bottom, to hold it in position.

6. Stuff the lower part of the figure firmly, almost to
the bottom, pushing the filling up into the hips and
waist.

7. Roll up a strip of modelling clay, flattening and
shaping it to fit inside the bottom of the figure, making
it slightly smaller than the diameter. Wrap the clay
very carefully in foil, then fit it inside.

8. Fit the base over the bottom of the figure (card
inside) and oversew all round the edge.

9. For the ADULT figure, bend back one end of a pipe
cleaner or chenille stem 1cm (³/₈in), then bend it over
again; this forms the hand. Insert the bent end through
the neck and slide it down the arm into a hand,

temporarily hooking the other end over the edge of the
neck to prevent it slipping inside.

    Push tiny bits of stuffing down into the hand and
arm, shaping them carefully, followed by larger
amounts to fill the shoulder.

    For the CHILD, bend the pipe cleaner in *half*, push
the bent end down into the hand, then continue as for
the adult.

10. Repeat for the other arm, then complete stuffing
the top of the body to the base of the neck, pushing the
top ends of the pipe cleaners down into the body.

11. For the ADULT, cut a piece of paper 1.5cm (⁵/₈in)
deep × 10cm (4in) wide and roll it up as before; insert
it into the neck, allowing it to open out before tacking
it into position, just below the top edge.

    Do the same for the CHILD, but cut the paper 1 ×
6cm (³/₈ × 2½in).

12. Complete stuffing the figure; push two pins parallel
across the top of the neck to hold the filling down while
you stitch the head on.

13. Push a darning needle through the head between
A-B, then insert the point down into the centre of the
neck to hold the head in position while you ladder-
stitch it firmly and neatly into place.

CHAPTER 15

The Valentine Miss

You will have noticed how closely the basic costume doll resembles an old-fashioned dressmaker's dummy. This is no accident. The figure is specifically designed in this way so that the clothes can actually be made onto it. This ensures a perfect fit, smooth curves and contours – and also means a great deal less work. On the other hand, neatness, care and accuracy are vital when you are working on such a small scale. But if you follow the directions and patterns carefully, you can't go wrong.

The Valentine Miss is an elegant example. Even though the wide variety of dolls may differ considerably in the details of characterisation, the basic principle is the same. This method of dollmaking is a complete contrast to the dolls in the first two sections; compared to the realistically-made garments of the play dolls, it feels like cheating! But once you have tried it, you may be surprised how simple, quick and effective it is. And the more experience you gain, the more you will be tempted to experiment with your own designs for characters and occasions.

First make the basic figure, as described in Chapter 14, following figure A.

MATERIALS
(Patterns on pages 135/139)

20cm (8in) medium-weight cotton-type fabric, 90cm (36in) wide, for the dress, hat and parasol

14 × 25cm (5½ × 10in) medium-weight cotton-type fabric, for the petticoat

2 × 4cm (¾ × 1½in) red felt for her purse

Scrap of black or very dark brown felt, for her eyes

14 × 25cm (5½ × 10in) heavyweight Vilene or Pellon interlining

1.8m (2yd) lace, 10mm (⅜in) deep

Heavy lace motif, about 2.5cm (1in) diameter, for the purse

25cm (10in) broderie anglaise (eyelet embroidery), 10mm (⅜in) deep

35cm (14in) very narrow white braid

40cm (16in) double-face red satin ribbon, 9mm (⅜in) wide

10cm (4in) red satin ribbon, 1.5mm (¹⁄₁₆in) wide

15cm (6in) single-face white satin ribbon, 9mm (⅜in) wide

30cm (12in) white satin ribbon, 3mm (⅛in) wide

Assorted tiny red and white artificial flowers

Knitting yarn for hair

Thin bamboo meat skewer

Red bead, about 10mm (⅜in) diameter, for parasol

Matching and black sewing threads

Pinky-red stranded embroidery cotton (floss) or sewing thread

Stiff card

Clear adhesive

1. Join the side edges of the petticoat fabric to form the centre back seam. Press open and turn to the right side.
2. Turn the top edge under and gather close to the folded edge. Fit on the figure and pin the marked points at centre front and sides, 1cm (⅜in) below the natural waistline. Draw up the gathers and stitch to the figure, distributing them evenly.

3. Turn up a hem and herringbone-stitch over the raw edge, so that the bottom of the petticoat is exactly 1cm (³⁄₈in) above the ground when the figure is standing on a flat surface. Then stitch the broderie anglaise (eyelet embroidery) so that it just touches the ground.

4. Cut the skirt, the bodice front, and the parasol once each, and the back and sleeve twice each, in the dress fabric; leave sufficient to cut the hat twice, allowing extra fabric all round (as broken line surrounding pattern).

5. To make each sleeve, join the side seam, then turn to the right side. Gather round the top, as indicated. Turn the wrist edge narrowly under and gather close to the fold. Fit the sleeve over the arm and draw up the wrist gathers tightly. Take the top of the sleeve over the doll's shoulder and pin it to the body, drawing up the gathers to fit and distributing them evenly as you stitch the raw edge of the fabric neatly to the figure.

6. Join the bodice front to the back pieces at each shoulder, ending the seam 3mm (¹⁄₈in) from the

armhole edge.

Join the side seams, beginning 3mm (1/8in) below the armhole edge, and ending 5mm (1/4in) above the waist edge. Clip the curve.

7. Turn the raw edge around the armholes narrowly under and tack. Turn to the right side.

8. Fit the bodice on the doll, adjusting to fit if necessary. Overlap the centre back edges, turning the upper one under and slip-stitching to the other. Draw the lower edge smoothly down and stitch it to the body. Catch the armhole edges neatly to the figure, over the sleeve gathers.

9. Stitch lace around the neck to form a stand-up collar.

10. Gather 10cm (4in) lace for each cuff and draw up evenly over the wrist edge of the sleeve.

11. Gather 25cm (10in) lace for the yoke frill; pin equally round the shoulders, as illustrated, draw up to fit and stitch neatly to the figure, distributing the gathers evenly between the pins.

12. Join the centre back seam of the skirt, as the petticoat. Gather the top edge as indicated, then fold the raw edge under along the gathering line and tack. Turn to the right side.

Fit the skirt on the figure and pin the marked points at centre front and sides of the waist, over the lower edge of the bodice. Draw up the gathers to fit and stitch neatly to the figure, distributing them evenly.

13. Turn up a hem and herringbone-stitch over the raw edge, so that the bottom of the skirt is about 5mm (1/4in) above the ground.

Stitch two rows of lace around the skirt, as illustrated; the lower one is 3mm (1/8in) above the edge of the skirt, and the other 3mm (1/8in) above the previous one.

14. Circle the waist with narrow white ribbon and stitch the join at the back.

Make the wider white ribbon into a butterfly bow, points b 3.5cm (1 1/2in) from a; stitch at back of waist, over narrow ribbon.

15. Wind the yarn 25-40 times (according to thickness) around a 20cm (8in) deep card; tie tightly at each edge with a single strand, then slide off the card and tie the centre loosely with another strand.

Glue the centre to the top of the head, then take the skein down at each side of the face, as illustrated, gluing it into place and knotting the ties at the nape of the neck; catch to the back of the head with matching thread.

Make a similar skein, but tie the centre *tightly*. Stitch this centre to the back of the head, over the tied ends of the previous skein. Take both sides of the skein up, spreading them out to cover the back of the head and gluing into place. Stitch to the top of the head, behind the centre of the first skein, turning the excess neatly over to form a flat bun on the crown; stitch securely and finish off the ends tidily.

16. Cut the hat twice in Vilene or Pellon. Tack each piece to the wrong side of your fabric and cut it as the broken line around the pattern. Turn the surplus neatly over to the wrong side and press.

Pin the two pieces together, wrong sides facing, and oversew (overcast) neatly together all round the edge. Press again.

17. Stitch the straight edge of the lace around the edge of the hat so that it overlaps downwards as illustrated. Glue narrow braid over your stitches.

Make a butterfly bow at the centre of the wider red ribbon, points b 5cm (2in) from A. Stitch at X, so that the streamers will fall down behind the head.

18. Stitch the hat securely to the top of the head, using the bun to angle it forward over the face, as illustrated.

Bunch tiny red and white flowers together and glue to the top of the hat, in front of the bow.

19. Cut the eyes in black or brown felt and pin them to the face. Make a tiny straight stitch in black between them, level with the bottom of the circles, for the nose.

Embroider a fly-stitch for the mouth, using two strands of embroidery cotton (floss) or double sewing thread.

Adjust the eyes if necessary and, when you are satisfied with the expression, glue them into place.

20. To make her parasol, cut the sharp tip off the point of the skewer. Then cut the other end to make it 12.5cm (5in) long.

Fold the fabric in half as indicated, right side inside, then glue the raw straight edges A-B to the skewer, point B 1.5cm (5/8in) from the pointed tip. Wrap the fabric neatly round the skewer, keeping the curved edges at top and bottom level, so that it forms a cone; glue the folded edge lightly to hold in shape.

Gather close to the top edge and draw up tightly round the skewer. Gather 10cm (4in) lace and draw up over the gathered fabric, with the frill downwards. Gather another 10cm (4in) and draw up above the first piece, frill up. Gather a final 10cm (4in), but this time along the *centre* of the lace, and draw up round the lower edge of the fabric.

21. Fix the bead to the top of the stick.

Make a butterfly bow from 15cm (6in) narrow white ribbon, points b 1.5cm (5/8in) from a. Fix about 2cm (3/4in) down the stick, then glue red and white flowers on top.

Glue the bead underneath the hand, then position the parasol and catch the bottom frill to the hem of her skirt to hold it in place.

22. Cut the purse twice in red felt.

Glue one end of the narrow red ribbon to the centre of the lace motif; loop it round and glue the other end to the other side, to form the handle of her purse. Glue a felt heart to each side of the lace, adding a tiny flower in the centre of each heart.

Stitch the top of the loop to her other hand.

Just Arrived!

I magine the delight of a new mother, receiving this lovingly made keepsake of her baby's birth. If you are making it beforehand, an all-white outfit is the safest choice for the infant; but after the event, you might wish to add a coloured trim – in the appropriate pink or blue.

Make the basic figure, as described in Chapter 14, following figure A. There is a special pattern for the baby's head, but it is made in the same way as the basic figure. Alternatively, you could use a craft ball, marking the features in sepia.

If you have already made the Valentine Doll, you will note that the skirt is stitched over the bodice for that doll, but the bodice of the Nursemaid's dress is sewn over the skirt. You can use either method; this one helps the skirt to fall smoothly over the hips, whereas the other version emphasises the gathers around the waist.

MATERIALS
(Patterns on pages 135/139)

Blue/white-striped medium-weight cotton-type fabric, 20cm (8in) deep × 50cm (20in) wide, for the dress

14 × 25cm (5½ × 10in) medium-weight cotton-type fabric, for the petticoat

10 × 20cm (4 × 8in) light- or medium-weight white cotton-type fabric for her apron and cap

15 × 20cm (6 × 8in) white spotted voile (dotted Swiss) for the baby

5 × 10cm (2 × 4in) cream felt (or a 2.5cm/1in diameter flesh-coloured craft ball), for the baby's head

1.5m (1⅝yd) white lace, 10mm (⅜in) deep, for the nursemaid

13cm (5in) white lace, 10mm (⅜in) deep, for the baby's bonnet

70cm (¾yd) white lace, 10mm (⅜in) deep, for the baby's shawl

White guipure lace motif, 2.5cm (1in) diameter, for the nurse's cap

1m (1⅛yd) white ribbon, 6mm (¼in) wide, for apron and cap

Brown double-knit yarn for the nursemaid's hair

One 76cm (30in) strand Twilley's stranded embroidery wool, shade 81 (or fine knitting yarn), for the baby's hair

Polyester stuffing

2 brown domed sequins, 5mm (³⁄₁₆in) diameter

Matching, black and pinky-red sewing threads

Stiff card

1. Join the side edges of the petticoat fabric to form the centre back seam. Press open and turn to the right side.
2. Turn the top edge under and gather close to the folded edge. Fit on the figure and pin the marked points at centre front and sides, 1cm (⅜in) below the natural waistline. Draw up the gathers and stitch to the figure, distributing them evenly.
3. Turn up a hem and herringbone-stitch over the raw edge, so that the bottom of the petticoat is exactly 5mm (¼in) above the ground when the figure is standing on a flat surface. Then trim the hem with lace so that it just touches the ground.
4. Cut the skirt and bodice front once each, and the bodice back and sleeve twice each, in the dress fabric.
5. Join the centre back seam of the skirt, as the petticoat, and turn to the right side. Gather the top edge.

Fit the skirt on the figure and pin the marked points at centre front and sides of the waist, above the petticoat. Draw up the gathers to fit and stitch neatly to the figure, distributing them evenly.

Turn up a hem and herringbone-stitch over the raw edge, so that the bottom of the skirt just touches the ground.
6. To make the sleeves and bodice, follow the directions for the Valentine Doll (Chapter 15), steps 5-7 inclusive.
7. Turn up the lower edge of the bodice and tack. Then fit on the doll, adjusting the seams if necessary.

Overlap the centre back edges, turning the upper one under and slip-stitching to the other.

Catch the armhole and waist edges neatly to the figure, over the sleeve and skirt gathers.

8. Stitch a double layer of lace around the neck to form a stand-up collar.

9. Stitch lace neatly over the wrist edge of each sleeve.

10. Cut out the apron, but *not* the cap.

11. Stitch lace over the raw edges of the sides and bottom of the apron. Gather top.

Place the apron over the skirt front and pin the top corners over the bottom of the bodice side seams. Pin the centre front, then draw up the gathers, distributing them evenly between the pins. Stitch the gathers neatly across the bottom of the bodice.

12. Circle the waist with ribbon, to cover the raw top edge of the apron, joining at the back. Catch into place.

Gather a 35cm (14in) length of lace; pin the centre over the centre front of the waistband, then take the sides over the shoulders to form straps, pinning the ends against the back of the waistband.

Draw up and stitch the gathers, distributing them evenly at back and front, but allowing more over the shoulders. Then overlap the gathered edge with ribbon to form straps, as illustrated, folding it in a V-shape at the centre front, with the ends at the back; catch at centre front and back.

Make a butterfly bow at the centre of a 30cm (12in) length of ribbon (points b 4cm/1½in from a); stitch at centre back of waistband and trim the cut ends neatly.

13. Double-knit yarn was used for the doll in the photograph; if you are using a thinner or thicker alternative, adjust the following directions accordingly.

Wind double-knit yarn twenty-five times around a 20cm (8in) deep card; tie tightly at each edge with a single strand, then slip the skein off the card and tie the centre loosely.

Stitch the tied centre of the skein to the top of the head, then take each side down over the face, as illustrated, and knot the ties at the nape of the neck; stitch securely, drawing up any loose strands neatly.

Wind the yarn fifteen times around the same card. Tie the edges as before and slip off the card; but then make a *knot* at the centre of the skein, pulling it very tight. Bind the two sides of the skein tightly with thread close to the knot, then stitch to the back of the head so that the bun falls over the previous tied ends.

Take the ends of the skein smoothly up to cover the back of the head and stitch to the crown immediately behind the centre of the first skein.

14. To make her cap, lightly mark the edge of the pattern on the fabric in pencil.

Gather the remaining lace, then join the cut ends and pin evenly over the marked circle. Draw up the gathers and stitch to the fabric, distributing them evenly. Then cut the surplus fabric away underneath the gathered lace, about 3mm (⅛in) from the stitching.

Stitch the lace motif in the centre of the cap.

Fold a 25cm (10in) length of ribbon slightly off-centre and stitch the fold underneath the back of the cap to form streamers; trim the cut ends neatly.

Stitch the cap to the top of her head, as illustrated.

15. Position the sequins for the eyes and mark the other features; when you are satisfied, sew on the eyes with single black thread, make straight stitches for the nose and eyebrows in double thread, and work the mouth in stem (outline) stitch, using double thread (or three strands of embroidery cotton/floss).

16. Cut the baby's face once and the head three times in felt. Follow the directions in Chapter 14, steps 2-3.

17. Cut the baby's body, shawl and bonnet in voile.

18. Fold the body in half and join the side seams to form a 'bag'. Turn to the right side and gather across the fold; draw up tightly.

Gather round the top edge, then stuff lightly and draw up the gathers.

19. Turn under the front edge of the bonnet and tack. Pin lace on the right side, overlapping the front edge; stitch it on with a gathering thread.

Gather the back edge on the wrong side; draw up tightly. Turn to the right side.

Fit the bonnet on the head, drawing up the front gathers around the face.

20. Using a darning needle, position the head on top of the body, then ladder-stitch it into place.

21. Cut 10cm (4in) off the strand of embroidery wool, then wind the remainder around the tip of your forefinger. Slip the loops off your finger onto the short piece and tie them tightly. Then fold the loops at the tied point and cut them opposite the fold.

Tuck the tied area inside the top of the bonnet, then trim the cut ends neatly to form a fringe across the forehead.

22. Make straight stitches in double black thread for the eyes, with a tiny stitch between in single thread, for the nose.

23. Stitch lace all round the shawl, overlapping the raw edge.

24. Fold one corner over to the centre of the shawl, on the wrong side. Then wrap the shawl around the baby, catching the centre of the fold to the back of the bonnet. Arrange the shawl attractively and hold it in place with a few stitches.

25. Place the baby in the Nursemaid's arms as illustrated, and catch it securely into position.

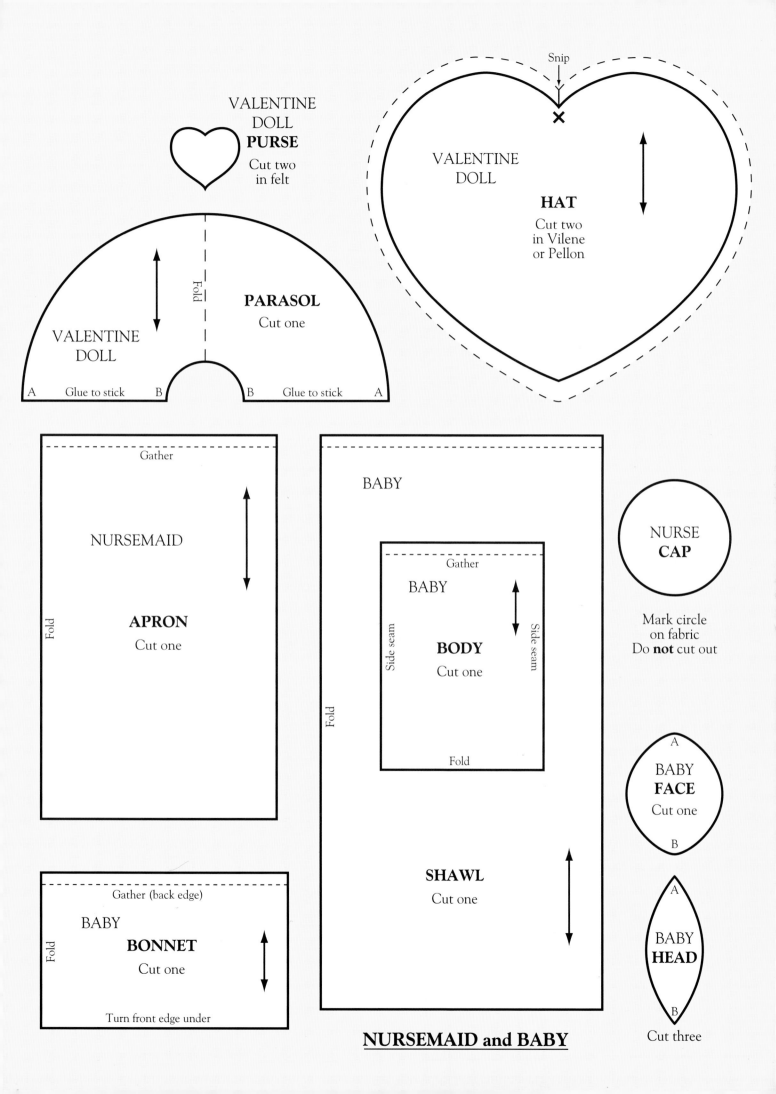

VALENTINE DOLL **PURSE** Cut two in felt

VALENTINE DOLL **PARASOL** Cut one

Fold

A Glue to stick B B Glue to stick A

VALENTINE DOLL **HAT** Cut two in Vilene or Pellon

Snip

✕

Gather

NURSEMAID **APRON** Cut one

Fold

BABY

Fold

BABY **BODY** Cut one

Gather

Side seam Side seam

Fold

SHAWL Cut one

NURSE **CAP**

Mark circle on fabric Do **not** cut out

BABY **FACE** Cut one

A

B

BABY **HEAD**

A

B

Cut three

Gather (back edge)

BABY **BONNET** Cut one

Fold

Turn front edge under

NURSEMAID and BABY

CHAPTER 17

Country Girl Going to Church

T̲he check cloth in her basket hides pots of honey and home-made jam, butter from the churn and freshly-baked bread; the flowers are from her own cottage garden. It isn't difficult to weave a story around this pretty lass with the country air. First make the basic doll in Chapter 14, using figure A.

MATERIALS

20cm (8in) flower-printed medium-weight cotton-type fabric, 90cm (36in) wide, for the dress and headscarf

14 × 25cm (5½ × 10in) medium-weight cotton-type fabric, for the petticoat

11cm (4⅜in) square of plain medium-weight cotton-type fabric, for her apron

10cm (4in) square of check cotton-type fabric, for the basket cover

25cm (10in) white lace, 10mm (⅜in) deep, for the petticoat

5cm (2in) white lace, 25mm (1in) deep, for the bodice insertion

40cm (½yd) black lace, 10mm (⅜in) deep, to edge apron

11cm (4⅜in) black lace, 5mm (¼in) deep, to trim apron

1.2m (1¼yd) deep rose satin ribbon, 1.5mm (¹⁄₁₆in) wide, to edge neckline etc

15cm (6in) black satin ribbon, 1.5mm (¹⁄₁₆in) wide

Honey-coloured double-knit yarn (or alternative) for her hair

Polyester stuffing or cotton wool (absorbent cotton)

Garden raffia (and matching thread)

2 blue domed sequins, 5mm (³⁄₁₆in) diameter

Pink diamanté for necklace

Small dried (or artificial) flowers

Matching and pinky-red sewing threads

Stiff card

Clear adhesive

1. To make the petticoat, follow the directions for the Nursemaid in Chapter 16, steps 1-3 inclusive.

2 Cut the skirt, bodice front and headscarf once each, and the bodice back and sleeve twice each, in the dress fabric. Cut the apron in plain fabric.

3. To make each sleeve, join the side seam, then turn to the right side. Gather round the top, as indicated.

Gather the lower edge also, but then fold the raw edge under along the gathering line, and tack. Fit the sleeve over the arm, taking the top edge over the doll's shoulder and pinning it to the body; draw up the gathers to fit, distributing them evenly as you stitch the raw edge of the fabric to the figure. Then draw up the lower gathers evenly round the arm.

4. Pin the wide lace over the chest, as illustrated, the top edge about 2cm (¾in) below the shoulder seams.

5. Follow the directions for the Valentine Doll's bodice (Chapter 15), steps 6-8 inclusive, but check the position of the lace insertion as you fit the bodice; when it is satisfactory, catch it into place. Then continue to stitch the bodice to the figure.

6. Plait the rose ribbon to make braid, and glue it over the edge of the neckline and also close against the lower sleeve gathers, as illustrated.

7. Follow the directions for the Valentine doll's skirt, steps 12 and 13, omitting the lace.

8. Stitch the wider black lace over the raw side and bottom edges of the apron, with a narrow decorative band as indicated by the broken line. Gather the top, then turn the raw edge under and tack, as for the skirt.

Pin the top corners at each side of the waist, over the bodice seams, and pin the centre front. Then draw up the gathers, distributing them evenly and stitch into place.

9. Make a tiny butterfly bow from 5cm (2in) black ribbon, points b 1.5cm (⅝in) from a. Stitch at centre front of lace insertion, as illustrated.

10. Circle the neck with a band of ribbon, joining at the back, and stitch diamanté at centre front.

11. Double-knit yarn was used for the hair of the doll in the photograph. If you are using a thinner or thicker alternative, adjust the directions accordingly.

Wind the yarn fifteen times around a 30cm (12in)

deep card: cut the loops at each edge, then tie them loosely together at the centre with a single strand, keeping the cut ends level.

Stitch the tied centre to the top of the head, then bring the sides smoothly down over the face, as illustrated, and catch securely to the side of the head, level with the jawline. Divide the strands equally into three, then plait them neatly, binding the ends with thread and trimming level.

Wind yarn fifteen times around an 8cm (3in) deep card: tie tightly at one edge and loosely at the other. Make another skein in the same way. Then stitch the tightly tied ends to the crown of the head, behind the centre of the first piece. Take the two skeins down, spreading them out to cover the back of the head, then stitch the other ends down across the base of the head.

12. Draw threads along the edges of the headscarf to prevent fraying, then fold it in half diagonally and drape over the head as shown. Stitch the front corners securely under the chin, and catch the scarf invisibly to the sides and back of the head.

13. Add the features as described for the Nursemaid, step 15.

14. To make her basket, take two thick strands of raffia (more if thinner) and make a knot at one end. Wind the raffia smoothly and closely round the knot, oversewing (overcasting) it neatly into place. Continue in this way until you have worked a flat 'mat' 3cm (1¼in) in diameter. Then turn the raffia and stitch it at a right angle to the previous round, to begin the sides of the basket. Continue stitching, adding more strands of raffia as necessary, and shaping the basket so that it widens as illustrated. Finish off neatly when it is 4cm (1½in) high.

Bind several strands of raffia tightly with thread to form a 10cm (4in) long handle, then stitch the ends inside the basket.

15. Wrap a small amount of stuffing or cotton wool in the check fabric, then fit it inside the basket and catch into place.

Stitch the handle securely to the doll's bent arm.

16. Make a neat bunch of dried flowers, as shown, and bind the stems tightly together. Then stitch to her right hand.

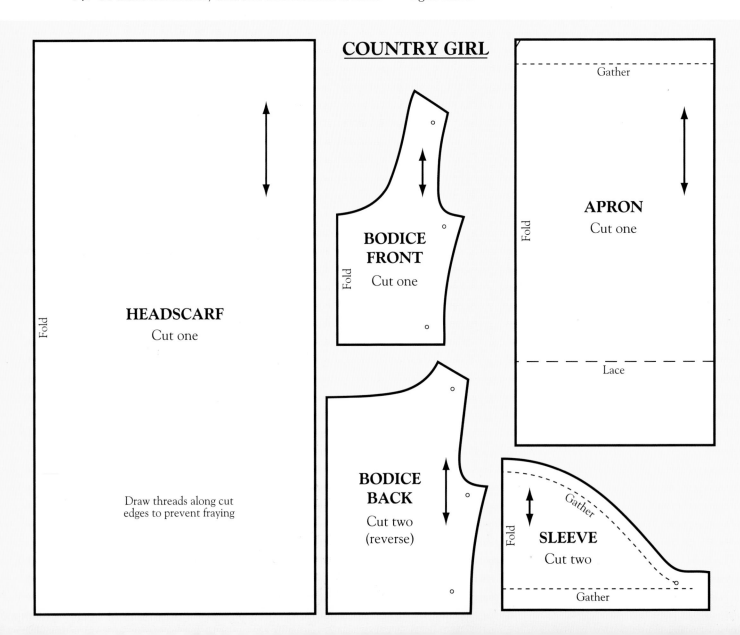

COUNTRY GIRL

HEADSCARF
Cut one

Fold

Draw threads along cut edges to prevent fraying

BODICE
FRONT
Cut one

Fold

BODICE
BACK
Cut two
(reverse)

APRON
Cut one

Fold

Gather

Lace

SLEEVE
Cut two

Fold

Gather

Gather

Cutting line for Skirt

Cutting line for Petticoat

VALENTINE
NURSEMAID
COUNTRY GIRL

Centre front   Fold

**SKIRT
AND
PETTICOAT**

Cutting line for Petticoat: centre back seam

Cutting line for Skirt: centre back seam

Cutting line for Skirt and Petticoat

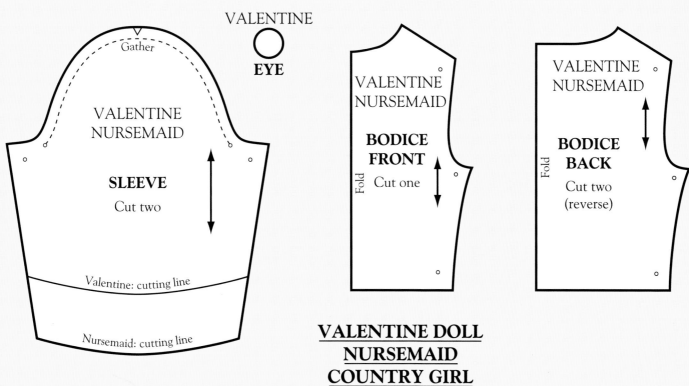

VALENTINE

EYE

Gather

VALENTINE
NURSEMAID

SLEEVE

Cut two

Valentine: cutting line

Nursemaid: cutting line

VALENTINE
NURSEMAID

**BODICE
FRONT**

Fold

Cut one

VALENTINE
NURSEMAID

**BODICE
BACK**

Fold

Cut two
(reverse)

**VALENTINE DOLL
NURSEMAID
COUNTRY GIRL**

CHAPTER 18

Bride and Bridesmaid

This elegant conversation piece embodies all the romance and magic of a traditional white wedding, and would provide a wonderful memento of the Great Day. Make the basic doll in Chapter 14, using figure B for the bride.

THE BRIDE

MATERIALS

20cm (8in) white medium-weight cotton-type fabric, 90cm (36in) wide, for the dress and petticoat
15 × 35cm (6 × 14in) white spotted voile (dotted Swiss), or alternative fabric, for the underskirt
20cm (¼yd) white tulle or fine net, 90cm (36in) wide, for the veil
Scrap of brown felt for eyes
30cm (12in) lace, 15mm (⅝in) deep, to edge petticoat
2m (2¼yd) lace, 10mm (⅜in) deep, for underskirt, neck and sleeves
60cm (¾yd) very narrow lace to trim the overskirt
1.7m (2yd) single-face white satin ribbon, 6mm (¼in) wide
3.3m (3¾yd) white satin ribbon, 1.5mm (¹⁄₁₆in) wide
Tiny pearl beads for necklace
2 small pearl beads for earrings
1m (1yd) string tiny pearl beads
Knitting yarn for hair (see step 9)
Bunch of tiny artificial flowers for her bouquet
Mother-of-pearl flower sequins
2 brown domed sequins, 5mm (³⁄₁₆in) diameter
Pins
Matching, black and pinky-red sewing threads
Stiff card
Clear adhesive

1. Cut the bodice front, overskirt and petticoat once each, and the bodice back and sleeve twice each, in the main dress fabric. Cut the underskirt once in voile or alternative.
2. Follow the directions for making the Nursemaid's petticoat in Chapter 16, steps 1-3 inclusive.
3. To make each sleeve, join the side seam, then turn to the right side. Gather round the top, as indicated.
Gather the lower edge also, but then fold the raw edge under along the gathering line, and tack. Fit the sleeve over the arm, taking the top edge over the doll's shoulder and pinning it to the body: draw up the gathers to fit, distributing them evenly as you stitch the raw edge of the fabric to the figure. Then draw up the lower gathers evenly around the arm.
4. Join the bodice front to the back pieces at each side, beginning 3mm (⅛in) below the armhole edge, and ending 5mm (¼in) above the waist edge. Clip the curve.
5. Turn the raw edge around the armholes narrowly under and tack. Turn to the right side.
6. Fit the bodice on the doll, adjusting to fit if necessary; pin the top corners so that they meet on the shoulder, over the top edge of the sleeve. Overlap the centre back edges, turning the upper one under and slip-stitching to the other.
Catch the raw neck edge smoothly to the figure and stitch the armhole edges neatly over the sleeve gathers. Draw lower edge smoothly down and stitch to body.
7. Gather 30cm (12in) of the wider lace and pin the top edge evenly round the neckline of the dress, 3mm (⅛in) below the raw edge (join at back). Draw up to fit and stitch neatly into place.
Gather another 30cm (12in) length of lace and pin it 5mm (¼in) above the previous row; draw up and stitch as before.
8. Gather 10cm (4in) of the same lace and draw up close against the lower edge of each sleeve; join the cut ends and stitch into place.
9. The same textured yarn was used for the hair as for

the Valentine Doll, but an ordinary double-knit yarn would be quite satisfactory. Just calculate the number of strands accordingly.

Wind the yarn 25-40 times (according to thickness) around a 20cm (8in) deep card. Tie tightly at both edges, then slide the skein off the card and tie it more loosely a little off-centre. Glue or stitch this piece across the top of the head as illustrated, taking the ends round to the back and stitching them neatly together at the nape of the neck.

Make another skein in the same way, but don't tie the centre. Knot the ties together and then stitch them to the top of the head, behind the tied section of the first skein, so that the looped centre hangs down over the back of the head. Glue and stitch it neatly to cover the head.

10. Cut the eyes in brown felt and pin to the face. Mark the position of the nose and mouth with pins, then embroider the mouth in stem (outline) stitch, using double sewing thread (or three strands of embroidery cotton/floss). Make a tiny straight stitch for the nose, and longer ones for the eyebrows, in double black thread. Use single thread to stitch the eyes to the face, sewing a sequin in the centre of each felt circle.

11. Make up the voile underskirt as the petticoat, fitting it over the petticoat, but drawing up the gathers just below the natural waistline.

Turn up a narrow hem, then stitch a row of lace so that it just touches the ground. Stitch two more rows of lace above, each slightly overlapping the piece below.

12. Make a very narrow hem around the lower edge of the overskirt, then stitch narrow lace so that it overlaps the edge.

Plait the narrow ribbon to make braid, then glue it over the top edge of the lace. Stitch the remaining braid over the top edge of the lace bordering the underskirt.

Make a butterfly bow from 14cm (5½in) of the wider ribbon (points b 3cm/1¼in from a) and stitch it at the centre front as illustrated. Then make a rose from 15cm (6in) of the same ribbon, and stitch it on top.

Gather and turn over the top edge as before, then fit it on the doll and draw up the gathers evenly around the natural waistline.

13. Make two more butterfly bows, each from 8cm (3in) ribbon, points b 2.5cm (1in) from a. Stitch one to each sleeve, above the lace frill. Make another rose, from 12.5cm (5½in) ribbon, and stitch at centre front of neckline.

14. Fix a necklace of tiny pearls around her neck.

Stitch a larger pearl at each side of the face for her earrings.

15. Cut the pearl trimming into three equal lengths and tie them together at the centre with thread, then fold in half. Divide the strings into three and plait them neatly; bind the ends with thread, snipping off any odd pearls.

Pin over the head, as illustrated.

16. Gather one long edge of the tulle and draw it up to equal the length of the pearl plait; stitch the gathers underneath the plait, distributing them evenly. Then stitch the plait over the head, as illustrated.

Hold the veil in place with flower sequins pinned into the back of the head.

17. Make four more roses from 15cm (6in) lengths of ribbon and stitch or glue two at each end of the plait, as illustrated.

18. Arrange the flowers to make an attractive bouquet, then stitch it to her hand, adding 25cm (10in) looped ribbon, as illustrated.

THE BRIDESMAID

First make the child-size version of the basic doll in Chapter 14, using figure C.

MATERIALS

12 × 45cm (5 × 18in) blue spotted voile (dotted Swiss) for the dress
9 × 20cm (3½ × 8in) white spotted voile (dotted Swiss), or alternative, for the petticoat
20cm (8in) white lace, 10mm (⅜in) deep, to trim petticoat
65cm (¾yd) white lace, 10mm (⅜in) deep, for the dress, etc
12cm (5in) blue satin ribbon, 3mm (⅛in) wide, for her belt
25cm (10in) blue satin ribbon, 9mm (⅜in) wide, for back bow
Tiny blue forget-me-nots, or alternative artificial flowers

Garden raffia (and matching sewing thread)
Twenty-three 76cm (30in) strands Twilley's stranded embroidery wool, shade 81, or fine knitting yarn, for hair
2 blue domed sequins, 5mm (³⁄₁₆in) diameter
Matching, black and pinky-red sewing threads
Clear adhesive

1. Cut the skirt and bodice front once each, and the bodice back and sleeve twice each, in the dress fabric.
2. To make each sleeve, follow the directions for the Country Girl (Chapter 17), step 3.
3. Follow the directions for the Valentine Doll's bodice (Chapter 15) steps 6-8 inclusive.
4. To make the petticoat, follow the directions for the Nursemaid in Chapter 16, steps 1-3 inclusive, *but*

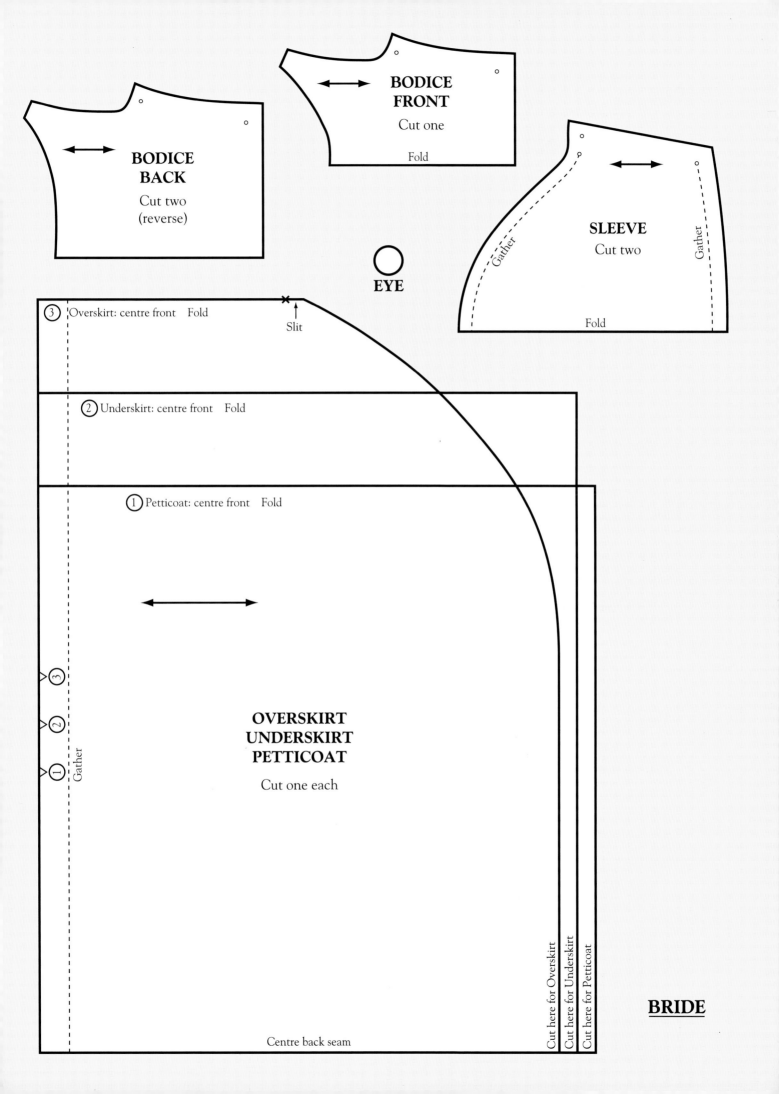

BODICE BACK
Cut two
(reverse)

BODICE FRONT
Cut one

Fold

EYE

SLEEVE
Cut two

Gather

Gather

Fold

③ Overskirt: centre front   Fold

Slit

② Underskirt: centre front   Fold

① Petticoat: centre front   Fold

③

②

①

Gather

**OVERSKIRT
UNDERSKIRT
PETTICOAT**

Cut one each

Cut here for Overskirt

Cut here for Underskirt

Cut here for Petticoat

Centre back seam

BRIDE

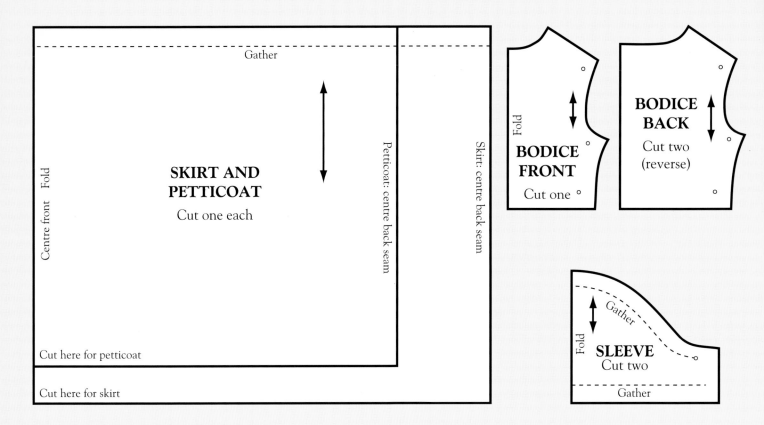

BRIDESMAID

stitch the gathered top edge to the figure at waist level, over the bodice.

5. Gather 15cm (6in) lace and draw up round the neck, join at back, distributing the gathers evenly to form a collar.

6. Follow the directions for the Valentine Doll's skirt, steps 12 and 13, *but* stitch the gathered top edge *above* the natural waistline, just below the sleeves, and trim the hem with only one row of lace, over the stitching line.

7. Fit narrow ribbon around lower edge of bodice, join at back.

8. Make a butterfly bow from the wider ribbon, points b 4.5cm (1¾in) from a, and stitch over centre back of waistband.

9. Cut ten strands of embroidery wool into 12.5cm (5in) lengths; tie loosely with a single strand, 3cm (1¼in) from one end. Stitch the tied section to the top of the head, so that the cut ends fall down at the back, and over the forehead to form a fringe.

Cut twelve strands of wool into 19cm (7½in) lengths and tie the centre loosely. Stitch neatly across the top of the head, over the previous strands, so that it hangs at each side.

Spread glue underneath to hold the hair smoothly in place, then trim all the cut ends neatly to length.

10. Position the sequins for the eyes and mark the nose and mouth: when you are satisfied, sew on the eyes with single black thread, making a tiny straight stitch between for the nose.

Embroider the mouth with a fly-stitch or two straight stitches, using double thread (or three strands of embroidery cotton/floss).

11. Gather 20cm (8in) lace and draw up to measure 8cm (3½in). Join the cut ends to form a circle, then pin to the top of the head, distributing the gathers evenly: stitch into place.

Glue flower-heads in a circle, over the gathered lace, as illustrated.

12. Follow the general directions for the Country Girl's basket (Chapter 17; step 14), but stitch the raffia to form a gently rounded shape, as illustrated, to make a basket 2.5cm (1in) diameter and 1.5cm (⅝in) high. The handle is 6cm (2½in) long, and the ends are stitched *outside* the basket.

Fill with flower-heads and stitch the handle to the hand.

CHAPTER 19

Easter Bonnet Eggs

An Easter Parade of fashionable chapeaux illustrates a charming way to say Happy Easter to anyone who likes pretty things. Instructions are for the basic idea, but this can be your big chance to try your hand at millinery design, once you have made the simple figure and set it in an empty eggshell.

Begin by serving boiled eggs for breakfast – pointed end up – with instructions to eat from that end!

MATERIALS

15cm (6in) single-face satin ribbon, 39mm (1½in) wide
OR 30cm (12in) single-face satin ribbon, 23mm (1in) wide
Scraps of light- or medium-weight toning fabric for hat
Flesh-tinted turned paper craft ball, 3cm (1¼in) diameter,
    for the head
Pipe cleaner (chenille stem), 8cm (3in) long
Polyester stuffing
Empty eggshell (as illustrated)
Lace, ribbon, braid, etc
4cm (1½in) ribbon, 6mm (¼in) wide, for collar
10cm (4in) ribbon, 3mm (⅛in) wide, for belt
Seven 76cm (30in) strands Twilley's stranded embroidery
    wool, for hair, or fine knitting yarn
Tiny beads for earrings
Matching sewing threads
Medium-weight paper
Pins
Flesh-coloured poster paint (if the ball is not coloured)
Sepia (or black) watercolour pencil or ball-point pen or
    ink, to draw the features
Glue stick
Clear adhesive

1. Cut the ribbon into two (or four) 7cm (2¾in) lengths and oversew the woven edges together to form a tube. Turn the raw edges at the top and bottom over to the wrong side and tack. Turn to the right side.
2. Gather very close to the top edge, then bend the pipe cleaner in half and push it down through the top, drawing up the gathers tightly round it so that the cut ends protrude 1cm (⅜in).
3. Gather the lower edge in the same way, but stuff the tube firmly, keeping the pipe cleaner in the centre, before drawing up the gathers to leave a small hole in the centre.
4. For the collar, overlap and glue the cut ends of a 4cm (1½in) length of 6mm (¼in) wide ribbon to form a circle, then slip it over the protruding pipe cleaner.
5. Fix the head onto the pipe cleaner.
6. Circle the body with 3mm (⅛in) wide ribbon at waist level, joining the cut ends at the back.
7. Use six 76cm (30in) strands of embroidery wool for the hair, folding them in half twice to make a 19cm (7½in) skein. Tie the centre loosely with a single strand, and glue it to the top of the head. Then take each end smoothly down over the side of the head and round to the back, gluing to hold in position; cross the ends and take them up to cover the back of the head.
8. Cut the hat shape of your choice in paper and cover one side with fabric; trim the fabric level with the edge of the paper. Repeat for the other side.
    If wished, glue very narrow braid around the edge.
    Trim the hat with gathered lace, either underneath or on top; then prepare ribbon roses and butterfly bows and artificial flowers. Pin the hat securely to the head, then pin or glue the trimmings into position.
9. Mark the eyes and nose.
    Glue earrings to sides of head.
10. Wash and dry the eggshell, then carefully break bits off until you have just the bottom half of the egg. Make a tiny hole in the base.
    Line the shell with a little polyester filling, then sit the doll inside and push a pin up through the hole to hold it in position. Push the stuffing down a little to keep it steady. Then set the shell in a basket of straw, as illustrated, or a pretty egg cup.

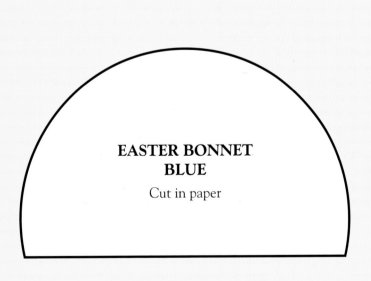

**EASTER BONNET
BLUE**

Cut in paper

**EASTER HAT
GREEN: PINK**

Cut in paper

**EASTER
HAT
LILAC**

Cut in paper

EASTER PARADE

CHAPTER 20

Ha✦a✦appy Hallowe'en!

Y et another very simple basic figure – but again with great potential. The stylised shape is merely a slim cone with a ball on top, but it can be used to convey an aura of sophistication, drama, elegance, mystery or regal dignity.

Imagine it robed in vivid purple, emerald or azure, trimmed with shimmering gold and silver braids and crowned with sparkling jewels – for a breathtaking representation of the Three Wise Men. Or draped in pastel shades of softest floating chiffon to create a scene from the ballet. Whilst lace, pearls and sequins would suggest an ethereal Christmas angel.

In this chapter the basic figure celebrates Hallowe'en with a creepy couple to send shivers up and down your spine. Choose between an extremely forbidding witch, and a spooky ghost.

NOTE: Where a fold is indicated, trace the pattern onto folded tracing paper, then open out to cut each piece in single thickness felt of paper.

BASIC FIGURE

MATERIALS

15 × 12cm (6 × 5in) felt to cover
Turned paper ball, 3.5cm (1³/₈in) diameter, flesh-tinted
   if possible, for the head
Polyester stuffing
Pipe cleaner (chenille stem), 16.5cm (6¹/₂in) long
Medium-weight paper
Stiff card
1oz modelling clay
Kitchen foil
Flesh poster colour (if ball is not coloured)
Matching sewing thread
Clear adhesive

1. Cut the body in felt and join the two straight edges to form the centre back seam, then turn to the right side.

2. Cut the inner body in paper and roll into a tight cone; place inside the body and allow the paper to open out until it fits snugly against the sides, the lower edge of the paper just above the felt. Tack to hold.

3. Bend the pipe cleaner in half and push the two ends up through the top of the cone so that they extend about 1-1.5cm (¹/₂in).

4. Fill the cone with stuffing.

5. Roll the clay into a ball, then flatten it to fit inside the bottom of the cone, wrapping it first in foil.

6. Cut the base in card and glue it to felt. Cut the felt as the broken line, then place over the bottom of the cone (card inside), and oversew (overcast) neatly together all round.

7. Paint the head, if necessary, then fit it onto the pipe cleaner, gluing to hold (see individual directions before fixing permanently).

THE HALLOWE'EN WITCH

Now see how easy it is to turn the basic shape into a traditional character. Cover the basic cone shape with mid-grey felt.

ADDITIONAL MATERIALS

20cm (8in) square of black felt
15cm (6in) black ribbon, braid or lace, to trim hem
Twelve 76cm (30in) strands Twilley's stranded embroidery wool, shade 3, or fine knitting yarn, for hair
6cm (2½in) circle of stiff black paper (or thin card)
Small natural wood bead (about 5mm/¼in diameter), for nose
Black ball-point pen, pencil or ink
Matching black sewing thread

1. Make the basic figure as directed, in grey felt. Glue trimming around the lower edge.
2. Cut the cloak, cape and hat in black felt.
3. Fit the cloak round the cone, 5mm (¼in) below the top. Catch into place.
4. Gather the neck edge of the cape, then fit it round the top of the cone, *upside-down*, so that it meets the top edge of the cloak; draw up and catch into place. Then turn the cape down over the cloak.
5. Cut the embroidery wool into forty-eight 19cm (7½in) lengths. Tie the centre loosely with one strand, then glue the centre to the top of the head. Spread glue over the sides and back of the head and draw the strands smoothly down all round, so that it is evenly covered. Trim the ends neatly.
6. Cut the hat brim in black paper.
   Run a little glue underneath the inner edge, then press it down on top of the head.
7. Join the centre back seam of the hat, then turn to the right side.
8. Cut the inner hat in paper, then fit inside as for the body cone.
9. Run glue round the inside edge of the hat, then press it down firmly over the brim.
10. Glue the bead to the centre of the face, for her nose.
11. Mark the features, as illustrated.

THE HALLOWE'EN GHOST

Another traditional characterisation – this one even more scary on a dark night than the witch!
   Cover the cone with white felt, and use an un-coloured ball for the head.

ADDITIONAL MATERIALS

20 × 45cm (8 × 18in) white muslin
Twelve 76cm (30in) strands Twilley's stranded embroidery wool, shade 4, or fine knitting yarn, for hair
White pipe cleaner (chenille stem), 16.5cm (6½in) long

1. Make the basic figure, as directed, in white felt; don't fix the head.
2. Cut the robe and shroud in muslin.
3. Join the centre back seam of the robe. Turn it to the right side and fit over the body cone.
4. Stitch the centre of the horizontal pipe cleaner securely over the centre back seams of the robe and body, 1.5cm (⅝in) below the top.
5. Fix the head in place, then follow the directions for the witch's hair (step 5), but don't trim the ends quite so neatly!
6. Draw threads all round to fray the edge of the shroud, then drape it over the head as illustrated. Take the upper corners under the pipe cleaner 'arms' and round to the back; overlap and catch them over the back seams of the body and robe. Catch the centre of the lower edge to the bottom of the centre back seam of the robe.
   Drape the front of the shroud round as shown, using the pipe cleaner; catch at each side, to hold in position.
7. Pull the hair forward and bend the head down, as illustrated.

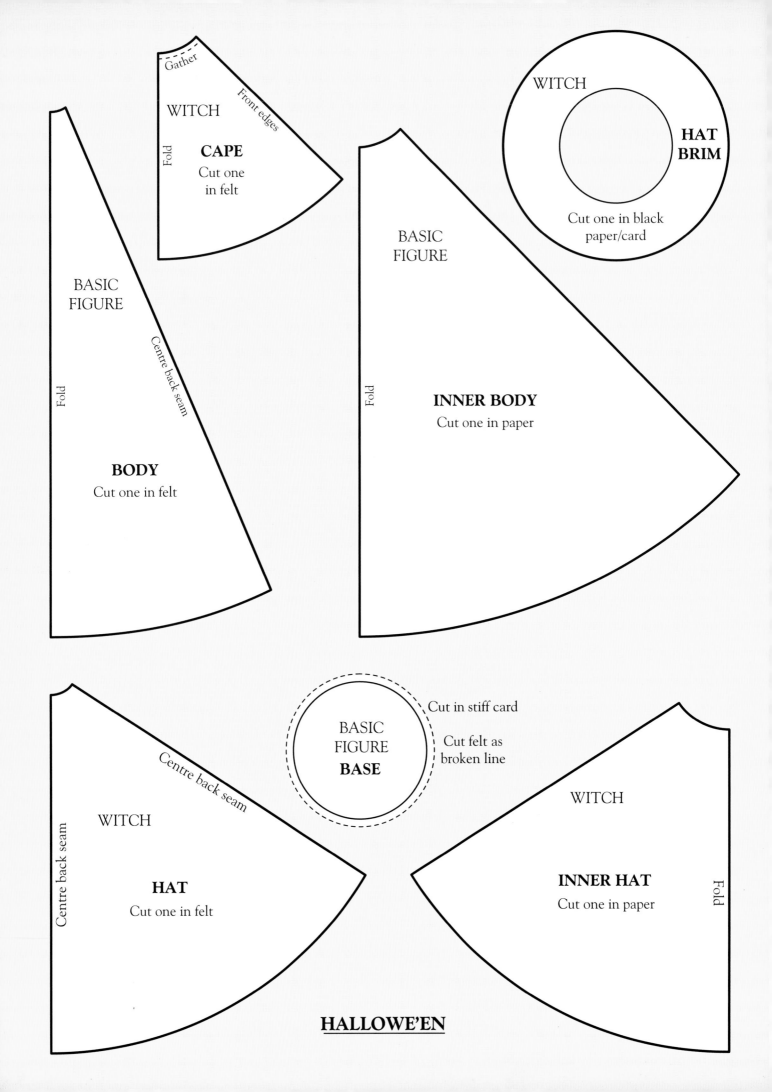

WITCH

CAPE

Cut one in felt

Gather

Front edges

Fold

BASIC
FIGURE

Fold

Centre back seam

BODY

Cut one in felt

BASIC
FIGURE

Fold

INNER BODY

Cut one in paper

WITCH

**HAT
BRIM**

Cut one in black
paper/card

Centre back seam

BASIC
FIGURE

BASE

Cut in stiff card

Cut felt as
broken line

Centre back seam

WITCH

HAT

Cut one in felt

WITCH

INNER HAT

Cut one in paper

Fold

HALLOWE'EN

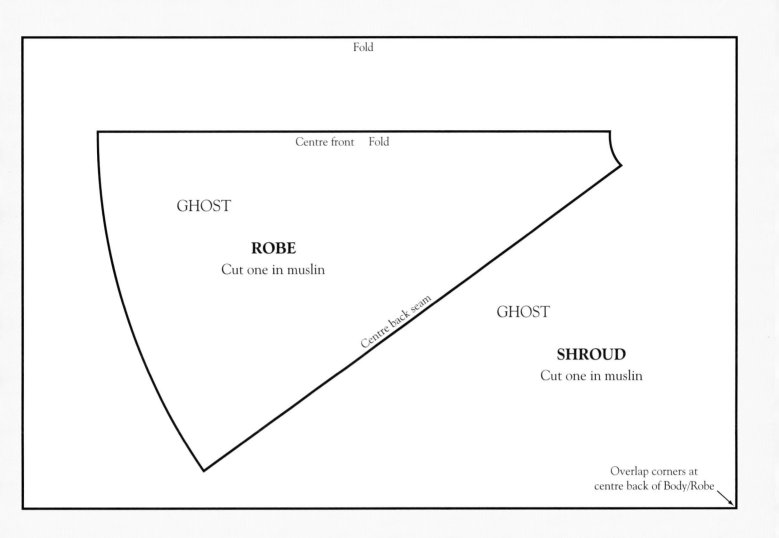

Fold

Centre front　Fold

GHOST

ROBE

Cut one in muslin

Centre back seam

GHOST

SHROUD

Cut one in muslin

Overlap corners at
centre back of Body/Robe

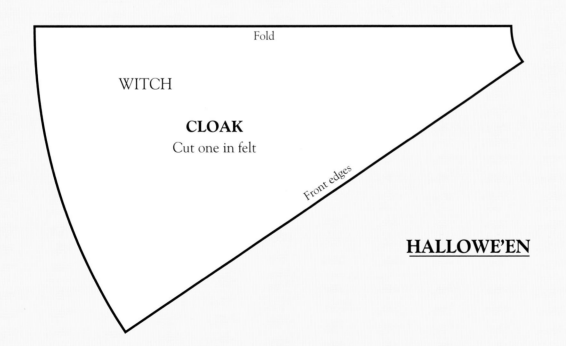

Fold

WITCH

CLOAK

Cut one in felt

Front edges

HALLOWE'EN

CHAPTER 21

Victorian Figures for the Christmas Tree

Give your tree a Victorian air with these enchanting little figures. And straight from the tree, they would make a charming take-home gift for modern little girls – of any age – to hang on their dressing-table mirror.

Once again this is the simple basic figure used for the Mobile Mascots. Now see how quick and easy it is to turn it into these small characters, each of which evokes the nostalgia of a traditionally frosty Victorian Christmas.

CHARLOTTE
Velvet-trimmed hooded purple cloak and muff

Make the basic figure, as directed in Chapter 11, using black velvet tubing.

ADDITIONAL MATERIALS

15cm (6in) square of purple felt
40cm (1/2yd) white velvet tubing
60cm (3/4yd) white satin ribbon, 1.5mm (1/16in) wide
Four 76cm (30in) strands Twilley's stranded embroidery
  wool, shade 53, or fine knitting yarn, for hair
Matching purple sewing thread
20cm (1/4yd) satin ribbon, 1.5mm (1/16in) wide, and a pin,
  to hang

1. Cut the cloak (making slits for the armholes, as indicated), hood and muff once each in purple felt.
2. Join the front edges of the cloak, then turn to the right side.
3. Glue velvet tubing down the centre front, over the seam. Then glue it all round the hem.
4. Gather the top edge, then slip the cloak over the figure and draw up round the neck, catching it securely into position.
5. Glue the head into place.
6. Fold three strands of wool in half three times; tie the centre loosely with a single strand.
  Glue to the top of the head, then bring each side smoothly down over the face and round to the side of the head, as illustrated, gluing to hold in position.
7. Gather both the front and back edges of the hood with separate threads, but do not draw up. Fit on the doll and draw up the back gathers round the neck. Then draw up the front gathers.
  Glue velvet tubing all round the face, over the front edge of the hood.
8. Join the short edges of the muff, and turn to the right side.
9. Plait the white ribbon to make braid, then glue around edges of muff.
10. Bend the arms and fit the hands inside the muff.
11. Make the narrow ribbon into a loop and fix the cut ends to the top of the head, so that the figure hangs correctly.

LUCY
Brown dress, cape and bonnet

Make the basic figure, as directed in Chapter 11, using white velvet tubing for the arms and body, and black for the legs.

ADDITIONAL MATERIALS

15cm (6in) square of brown felt
3m (3 1/2yd) brown satin ribbon, 1.5mm (1/16in) wide
25cm (10in) white lace, 10mm (3/8in) deep
Four 76cm (30in) strands Twilley's stranded embroidery
  wool, shade 81, or fine knitting yarn, for hair
Matching brown sewing thread
20cm (1/4yd) satin ribbon, 1.5mm (1/16in) wide, and a pin,
  to hang

1. Cut the dress, cape and bonnet once each in brown felt.
2. Join the straight edges of the dress to form the centre back seam, and turn to the right side.
3. Plait the brown ribbon to make braid, then glue two rows around the hem, as illustrated.
4. Glue lace inside the dress, so that the edge shows just below the hem.
5. Slip the dress onto the doll and join the top corners over the shoulders, catching it to the figure.
6. Glue braid around the front and lower edges of the cape.
  Gather the top edge and draw it up around the neck, over the dress.
7. Glue the head into place. Glue braid around the top edge of the neck.
8. Follow the directions for Charlotte's hair (step 6).
9. Glue braid round the outside edge of the bonnet front. Gather the back edge and draw it up around the doll's neck.
10. Gather 10cm (4in) lace and draw it up to measure about 6cm (2 1/2in). Insert a little glue between the bonnet brim and the hair, then poke the gathered lace in so that it surrounds the face as illustrated.
11. Make the narrow ribbon into a loop and fix the cut ends to the top of the head, so that the figure hangs correctly.

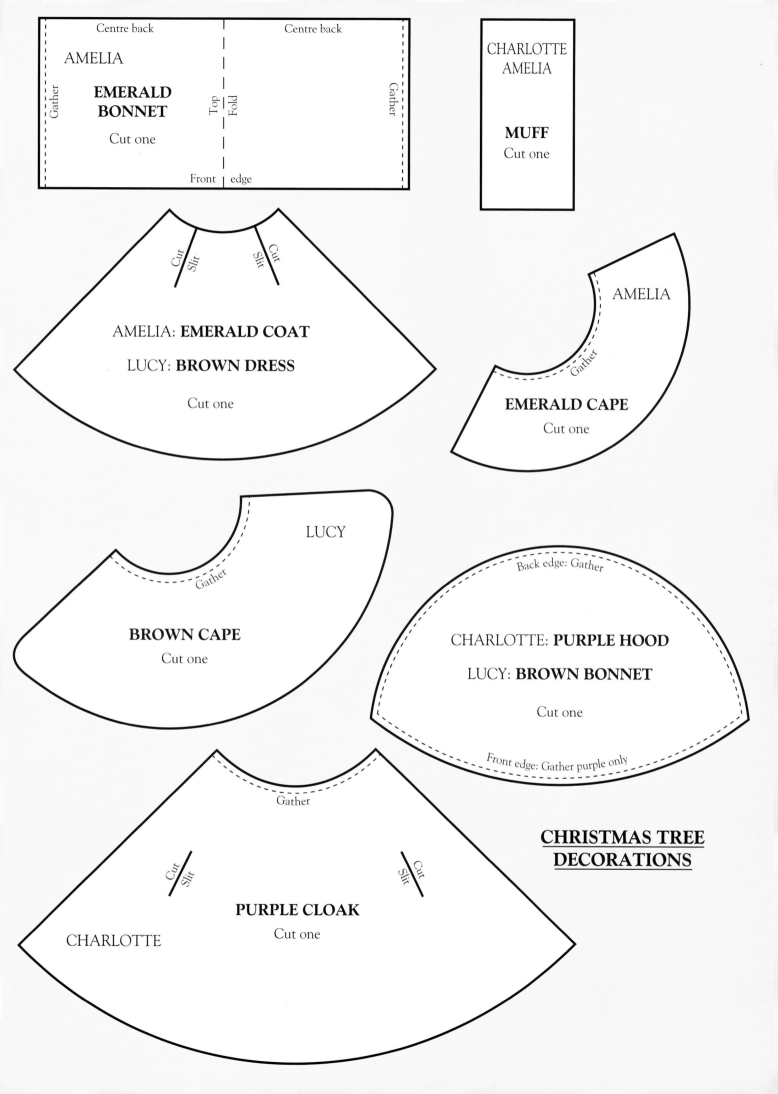

Centre back   Centre back

AMELIA

EMERALD BONNET

Top   Fold   Gather

Gather

Cut one

Front | edge

CHARLOTTE AMELIA

MUFF
Cut one

Cut Slit   Cut Slit

AMELIA: **EMERALD COAT**

LUCY: **BROWN DRESS**

Cut one

AMELIA

Gather

EMERALD CAPE

Cut one

LUCY

Gather

BROWN CAPE
Cut one

Back edge: Gather

CHARLOTTE: **PURPLE HOOD**

LUCY: **BROWN BONNET**

Cut one

Front edge: Gather purple only

Gather

Cut Slit   Cut Slit

PURPLE CLOAK
Cut one

CHARLOTTE

CHRISTMAS TREE DECORATIONS

AMELIA
Green caped coat, bonnet and muff

Make the basic figure, as directed in Chapter 11, using emerald velvet tubing.

ADDITIONAL MATERIALS

15cm (6in) square of emerald felt
90cm (1yd) very narrow black braid (or 45cm/¹/₂yd
    8-10mm/¹/₄-³/₈in wide braid, cut in half)
Four 76cm (30in) strands Twilley's stranded embroidery
    wool, shade 97, or fine knitting yarn, for hair
Matching emerald sewing thread
20cm (¹/₄yd) satin ribbon, 1.5mm (¹/₁₆in) wide, and a pin,
    to hang

1. Cut the coat, cape, bonnet and muff once each in emerald felt.
2. Join the straight edges of the coat to form the centre front, and turn to the right side.
3. Glue a double width of braid (or a single width of un-cut wider braid) over the seam. Then glue narrow braid all round the hem, as illustrated.
4. Slip the coat onto the doll and join the top corners over the shoulders, catching it to the figure.
5. Glue braid around the front and lower edges of the cape.
    Gather the top edge and draw it up around the neck, over the coat.
6. Glue the head into place.
7. Fold three strands of wool in half four times; tie with a single strand, 1cm (³/₈in) from one end. Cut the loops at the other end, then glue the tied end to the top of the head so that the cut wool hangs over the face.
8. Fold the bonnet in half, as indicated, and join the centre back seam. Turn to the right side and glue braid around the front edge.
    Gather the lower edge, fit the bonnet on the doll and draw up securely round the neck.
9. Join the short edges of the muff and turn to the right side.
    Glue braid around edges.
10. Bend the arms and fit the hands inside the muff.
11. Make the narrow ribbon into a loop and fix the cut ends to the top of the head, so that the figure hangs correctly.

ROSE
Red dress, white pinafore and mob cap

Make the basic figure, as directed in Chapter 11, using scarlet velvet tubing for the body and arms, and white for the legs.

ADDITIONAL MATERIALS

10cm (4in) square of scarlet felt
9cm (3¹/₂in) square of white felt
10cm (4in) diameter circle of light/medium-weight white
    cotton-type fabric
70cm (³/₄yd) white lace, 10mm (³/₈in) deep
6cm (2¹/₄in) scarlet satin ribbon, 1.5mm (¹/₁₆in) wide
Six 76cm (30in) strands Twilley's embroidery wool,
    shade 49, or fine knitting yarn, for hair
Matching sewing threads
20cm (¹/₄yd) satin ribbon, 1.5mm (¹/₁₆in) wide, and a pin,
    to hang

1. Cut the dress once in scarlet felt, and the pinafore in white. Cut the mob cap in fabric.
2. Join the straight edges of the dress to form the centre back seam, and turn to the right side.
    Slip the dress onto the doll and join the top corners over the shoulders, catching it to the figure.
3. Join the straight edges of the pinafore to form the centre back seam, and turn to the right side.
    Stitch or glue lace under the lower edge, to extend below as illustrated.
    Slip the pinafore over the dress and join over the shoulders as before.
    Gather 15cm (6in) lace and draw up around the top edge of the pinafore, distributing the gathers evenly before catching it into place.
4. Make her fringe as directed for Amelia, step 7.
    To make each plait, cut a single strand into six equal lengths; tie the centre and fold in half. Divide the strands into three and plait them evenly, binding the ends with matching thread and trimming neatly.
    Remove the tie at the top and pin or glue at each side of the head, as illustrated.
5. To make the mob cap, stitch lace round the fabric as figure 1. Then turn the raw edge under and gather close to the edge of the cap as figure 2. (*Note:* lace will not lie flat as in the diagram!)
    Draw up round the doll's head, distributing the gathers so that they are mainly around the top and sides; stitch to the head.
    Make the scarlet ribbon into a butterfly bow, points b 1.5cm (⁵/₈in) from a; stitch to front of cap, as illustrated.
6. Make the narrow ribbon into a loop and fix the cut ends to the top of the head, so that the figure hangs correctly.

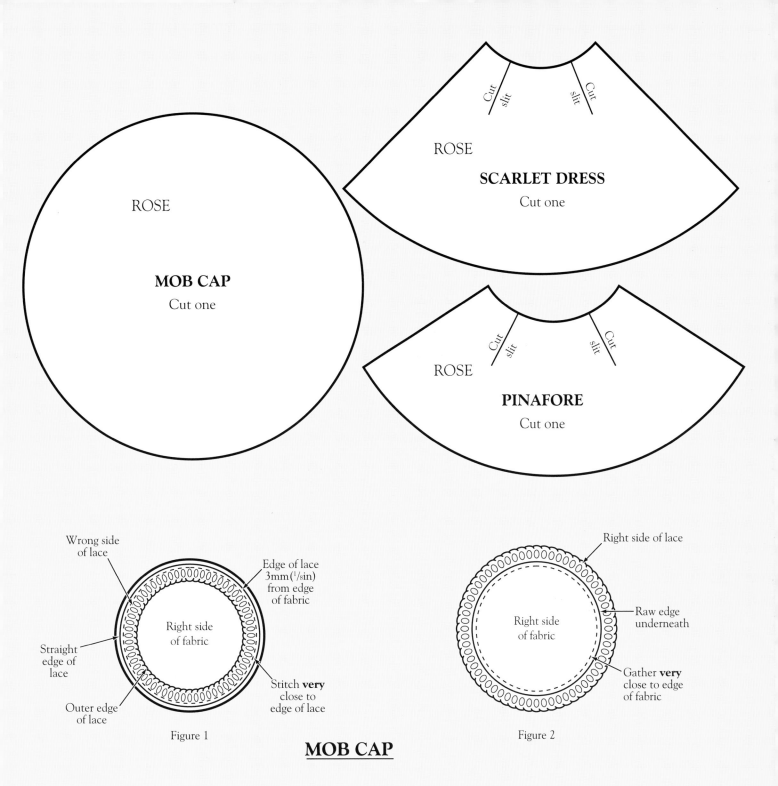

ROSE

MOB CAP
Cut one

ROSE

SCARLET DRESS
Cut one

Cut slit   Cut slit

ROSE

PINAFORE
Cut one

Cut slit   Cut slit

Wrong side of lace

Edge of lace 3mm (1/8in) from edge of fabric

Right side of fabric

Straight edge of lace

Outer edge of lace

Stitch **very** close to edge of lace

Figure 1

Right side of lace

Right side of fabric

Raw edge underneath

Gather **very** close to edge of fabric

Figure 2

MOB CAP

CHRISTMAS TREE DECORATIONS

Join ends

FAIRY WING

THE FAIRY ON TOP OF THE TREE

CHAPTER 22

The Christmas Fairy

No Christmas tree is complete without the traditional fairy on top – a star is a very poor substitute! Layers and layers of snowy white lace, frills and shimmering pearls combine to make this one everything that the perfect tree-top fairy should be: ethereal, romantic and glamorous.

Make the basic figure, as directed in Chapter 11, using white velvet tubing.

ADDITIONAL MATERIALS

A piece 10 × 20cm (4 × 8in), and a 15cm (6in) square,
   of fine white net or tulle
2.8m (3¼yd) white lace, 10mm (⅜in) deep
1.2m (1½yd) white satin ribbon, 1.5mm (1/16in) wide
Eleven 76cm (30in) strands Twilley's stranded embroidery
   wool, shade 81, or fine knitting yarn, for hair
65cm (¾yd) string of tiny pearl bead trimming
Tiny pearl beads to match above trimming
2 small pearl beads for earrings
Tiny silver star sequins
2 pipe cleaners (chenille stems), 16.5cm (6½in) long
Tiny pin (optional)
Matching white sewing thread

1. Pin a 20cm (8in) length of lace along the bottom of
the net or tulle, slightly overlapping the edge. Stitch
the straight edge to the net.

   Pin another piece of lace above, slightly overlapping
the stitched top edge of the previous piece, and stitch
again. Repeat until the net is completely covered, leaving about 5mm (¼in) free at the top.
2. Join the side edges of the net to form the centre back
seam. Then turn to the right side after flattening the
seam.

   Turn the surplus net at the top inside and gather the
top edge of the top layer of lace.

   Fit the skirt on the doll and draw up the gathers
evenly around the waist, securing at the back.
3. Glue the head into place.
4. Cut a 30cm (12in) length of lace in half; gather one
half and draw it up round the neck as illustrated, join at
back.
5. Cut the remaining 15cm (6in) lace in half and
gather each piece *along the centre*, then draw up around
the wrists, to form cuffs.

6. Fold four strands of embroidery wool in half twice
for the hair, to make a 19cm (7½in) skein. Tie the
centre loosely with a single strand, and glue it to the
top of the head. Then take each end smoothly down
over the side of the head and round to the back, gluing
to hold in position: cross the ends and take them up
over the back of the head.

   Fold six strands of wool in half; tie the centre tightly
with a single strand and fold in half again. Divide the
strands into three and plait loosely. Glue the end of the
plait to the back of the head, then twist it up and glue it
round in a circle over the crown, tucking the top end
into the centre of the circle.
7. Fold a 30cm (12in) length of pearls in half and
catch the loop at the back of the coiled plait; then twist
the pearls and surround the coil as illustrated, finishing
the ends at the back by passing them through the loop.
8. Glue tiny pearl beads and a few sequins all over the
hair.
9. Glue small pearl beads at the sides of the face, for
earrings.
10. To make each wing, bend a pipe cleaner into
shape, following the pattern; join by bending the two
ends so that they are interlinked.
11. Place the shape flat on the table and run glue along
the pipe cleaner; lay net smoothly on top, pressing
it down into the glue. Cut the net 5-10mm (¼-⅜in)
outside the cleaner.

   Cover the other side of the wing in the same way, but
turn the net in the other direction, so that it is running
crosswise to the first side. Trim off the surplus close to
the pipe cleaner. Make braid and glue over the pipe
cleaner. Then glue pearls around the outer edge of the
wing. Finally, glue a few stars to the net.
12. Stitch the top corners of the wings together, then
glue to the back of the fairy, anchoring with a tiny pin,
if necessary.

Index

Figures in *italic* refer to illustrations